Russia's Capitalist Realism

SRLT

NORTHWESTERN UNIVERSITY PRESS
Studies in Russian Literature and Theory

SERIES EDITORS
Caryl Emerson
Gary Saul Morson
William Mills Todd III
Andrew Wachtel
Justin Weir

Russia's Capitalist Realism

Tolstoy, Dostoevsky, and Chekhov

Vadim Shneyder

NORTHWESTERN UNIVERSITY PRESS / EVANSTON, ILLINOIS

Northwestern University Press
www.nupress.northwestern.edu

Publication of this book was made possible, in part, by a grant from the First Book
Subvention Program of the Association for Slavic, East European, and Eurasian
Studies.

Printed in the United States of America

10   9   8   7   6   5   4   3   2   1

ISBN 978-0-8101-4249-7 (cloth)
ISBN 978-0-8101-4248-0 (paper)
ISBN 978-0-8101-4250-3 (ebook)

Cataloging-in-Publication data are available from the Library of Congress.

Contents

Contents

Acknowledgments

PROBABLY LIKE ANY work of scholarship, this one is in small part an unintentional autobiography. Let me bring out a little of what is hidden between the lines. This project is, in its way, a product of history: I set out on a scholarly career during the financial crisis of 2008–9, when the world economy's seams started to show. That experience left me wondering how we, collectively, have managed to create a state of affairs that now confronts us as if it were fate.

Before I could even contemplate becoming a scholar, history made a (very young) refugee of me. Growing up knowing that you are from somewhere else that no longer exists is an exceptional lesson in *ostranenie*. My university education was bought with many years of labor by my parents, Aleksandr and Yevgeniya. That labor, through the uncertainties and indignities of the immigrant experience, is the sine qua non of everything I have done. I work in the hope that someday, what I have produced will have been worth it.

My professors at the College of William and Mary taught me that scholars are not deposited, ready made, into their offices, but trained in graduate school. They also gave me the courage to take the leap into the humanities, and so I did. For that, and much more, I thank Elena and Alexander Prokhorov, Frederick Corney, Viktoria Ivleva, Jennifer Jenkins, Robert Leventhal, and Ronald Schechter.

I came to Yale wondering if I had made a terrible mistake, but the solidarity of my fellow students and the intellectual vitality of the faculty soon assuaged my doubts. To the friends and current and future colleagues I met in seminar rooms, libraries, and—in the spirit of candor—drinking establishments: thank you for your insight and your conversation, Ainur Begim, Carlotta Chenoweth, Rossen Djagalov, Daria Ezerova, Maria Hristova, Bryant Kirkland, Yasha Klots, Nicholas Kupensky, Mina Magda, Mihaela Mihailova, Tara Menon, Ansgar Monkern, Ingrid Nordgaard, Cassio de Oliveira, Chloe Papadopolous, Viktoria Paranyuk, Marc Petersdorff, Megan Race, Richard Riddick, Raisa Sidenova, Ksenia Sidorenko, David Willey, and

Aura Young. To my dear friends Fabrizio Fenghi and Roman Utkin—I don't know whether we're more like Hölderlin, Hegel, and Schelling or Alyosha, Ivan, and Mitia, but I do know that I am a better scholar and human being thanks to our camaraderie.

As for the faculty of the Yale Slavic Department: an offhand remark by Tomas Venclova about Boborykin informed the book before I had begun the dissertation. Molly Brunson's seminar on Russian realism inspired my conversion to the nineteenth century. Her subsequent uncompromising comments on innumerable drafts taught me never to let laziness write my paragraph transitions, and much more besides. She also suggested the title of what would become this book before I even understood that I was writing about capitalism. My classes and conversations with Vladimir Alexandrov, Marijeta Bozovic, Katerina Clark, Irina Dolgova, and Harvey Goldblatt shaped my thinking in ways that I continue to discover.

This project took initial shape as a dissertation under the direction of Bella Grigoryan and John MacKay. Their polymathic range, readerly sharpness, creativity, and intellectual generosity have given me two models of scholarship and mentorship to aspire to. If I had learned more from them, this book would have been better. Without them, it would be no book at all.

The dissertation assumed the form of a book after I came to UCLA, where I have been fortunate to find a supportive intellectual home. I extend my gratitude to my colleagues Roman Koropeckyj, Susan Kresin, Anna Kudyma, Gail Lenhoff, Igor Pilschikov, and Ronald Vroon for the many times they have read or listened to portions of this project. I wish I could show these acknowledgments to the late Olga Kagan, who extended a warm welcome to me in Los Angeles.

Among the current and former UCLA graduate students, I thank Yana Demeshko, Nicholas Fedosenko, Natalia Kuvelas, Michael Lavery, Cooper Lynn, Elena Makarova, Sasha Razor, Lydia Roberts, Elena Skudskaia, Inna Wendell, and Peter Winsky for their insights in class and far beyond it. I am particularly grateful to Dane Reighard, whose keen-eyed editorial assistance was invaluable, even if I regularly failed to send him chapters on time and rewrote them again after he saw them.

I thank many colleagues, both in and outside the Slavic field, for their encouragement, advice, and generous engagement with my work at various stages. Among Slavicists, I extend my gratitude especially to Carol Apollonio, Brian Armstrong, Anna Berman, Katherine Bowers, Boris Dralyuk, Melissa Frazier, Sean Griffin, Kate Holland, Chloë Kitzinger, Konstantine Klioutchkine, Allison Leigh, Sarah Ruth Lorenz, Anne Lounsbery, Deborah Martinsen, Greta Matzner-Gore, Robin Feuer Miller, Eric Naiman, Jonathan Paine, Jillian Porter, Tom Roberts, Robert Romanchuk, Sven Spieker, William Mills Todd III, and Alexei Vdovin. I was very lucky with the two anonymous reviewers who read my manuscript for Northwestern University Press and responded to it with kind but rigorous attention. I found a generous collocutor, wise mentor, and valued friend in Eliyahu Stern. A fortuitous meeting at the conference of the American Comparative Literature Association introduced me to Ericka Beckman and Oded Nir. I thank them both for helping me think about my project beyond the confines of Slavic studies. I am grateful to the staff at Northwestern University Press, especially Trevor Perri and Maia Rigas, who have both been professional, efficient, and patient with this first-time author's nervousness.

I reserve a note of special thanks to Cklara, who has lightened and lighted the last steps on this long path. Having finally written a book of my own, I understand why acknowledgments sections are so long.

The vast majority of the research for this book was carried out at four research centers: Sterling Memorial Library at Yale, the Slavic Research Laboratory at the University of Illinois at Urbana-Champaign, the Slavonic Library of the National Library of Finland, and the Young Research Library at UCLA. I am grateful to the staff members for their advice and aid.

The material support of several foundations was indispensable for funding my research and securing time to write. A Whiting Dissertation Fellowship supported this project at an early stage. A UCLA Hellman Fellowship allowed me to complete it.

An earlier version of chapter 3 appeared as "Myshkin's Million: Merchants, Capitalists, and the Economic Imaginary in *The Idiot*," *Russian Review* 77, no. 2 (April 2018): 241–58.

The most precious books in my library—volumes of Pushkin, Chekhov, Tolstoy, Sholem Aleichem, Tsvetaeva, Pasternak—are those that my family collected in the Soviet Union and carried with them to the United States. I dedicate this book to my grandparents—Yefim and Yevgeniya Shneyder and Gerard and Larissa Levitskiy—who taught me the importance of books.

Note on the Text

WHEN TRANSLITERATING FROM Russian to English in the main text of the book, I have used a simplified version of the Library of Congress system, omitting diacritical marks. I have made occasional modifications when dealing with names likely familiar to Anglophone readers: for example, *Fyodor Dostoevsky* rather than *Fedor Dostoevskii*. In notes and bibliography, I adhere strictly to the simplified Library of Congress system (without diacritical marks). When quoting from Russian texts published before 1918, I have modernized spelling in accordance with modern orthography before transliterating.

Where possible, I have cited published translations of foreign-language texts so that the interested reader might locate the passage in question within the larger work. However, I have often modified these for emphasis or accuracy. All uncredited translations are my own. Frequently referenced sources are cited in the text using the following abbreviations:

Ch   A. P. Chekhov, *Polnoe sobranie sochinenii i pisem v tridtsati tomakh*, 30 vols. (Moscow: Nauka, 1974–83)

ChN   Anton Chekhov, *Anton Chekhov's Selected Short Stories*, edited by Cathy Popkin (New York: Norton, 2014)

ChV   Anton Chekhov, *The Complete Short Novels*, translated by Richard Pevear and Larissa Volokhonsky (New York: Vintage, 2004)

D   F. M. Dostoevskii, *Polnoe sobranie sochinenii v tridtsati tomakh*, 30 vols. (Leningrad: Nauka, 1972–90)

BKF   Fyodor Dostoevsky, *The Brothers Karamazov*, translated by Richard Pevear and Larissa Volokhonsky (New York: Farrar, Straus and Giroux, 1990)

IPV   Fyodor Dostoevsky, *The Idiot*, translated by Richard Pevear and Larissa Volokhonsky (New York: Vintage, 2001)

AKN   L. N. Tolstoi, *Anna Karenina*, edited by V. A. Zhdanov and E. E. Zaidenshnur (Moscow: Nauka, 1970)

LNT   L. N. Tolstoi, *Polnoe sobranie sochinenii*, 90 vols. (Moscow: Khudo-zhestvennaia literatura, 1928–58)

AKP   L. N. Tolstoy, *Anna Karenina*, translated by Richard Pevear and Larissa Volokhonsky (London: Penguin, 2000)

T   I. S. Turgenev, *Polnoe sobranie sochinenii i pisem*, 30 vols., 2nd ed. (Moscow: Nauka, 1978–)

VA   Ivan Turgenev, *Virgin Soil*, translated by Michael Pursglove (Richmond, Eng.: Alma Classics, 2015)

Other references to individual authors' collected works are cited with the author's last name followed by either *PSS* (for *Polnoe sobranie sochinenii*) or *SS* (for *Sobranie sochinenii*).

Introduction

> One point I made was that it is literature,
> not history, which has created a map of this
> or that society. . . . We all know about pre-
> revolutionary Russia because of Tolstoy,
> Dostoevsky, Turgenev, Chekhov and the rest.
> Up got a businessman, a prominent one, it
> seems, to make the point that before the
> Revolution in Russia an industrial revolution
> was well under way, but it nowhere appears in
> literature.
> —Doris Lessing, "Unwritten Novels"

> The economy of intellectual powers is nothing
> other than rigorous and consistent realism.
> —Dmitry Pisarev, "Realisty"

RASKOLNIKOV'S DEBT AND EPANCHIN'S FACTORY

Every reader of nineteenth-century Russian literature knows that the titular crime in Fyodor Dostoevsky's *Crime and Punishment* is murder. Raskolnikov, overcome by ideas circulating "in the air" and in the media, decides
to kill the old moneylender Alyona Ivanovna, whether to prove that he is
a human being and not a "trembling creature," or to save his family from
penury, or perhaps because of an overheard conversation in a tavern.[1] In any
event, by the end of part 1 the deed has been done, and when Raskolnikov
wakes up in part 2 to a summons from the police, he—and, likely, the reader,
too—is certain that it has something to do with the brutal killing of Alyona
Ivanovna and her half-sister Lizaveta. But that is not so. When Raskolnikov
arrives at the police station, a clerk shows him the paper on account of which
he has been ordered to present himself: he owes money. As it turns out,
Raskolnikov has not paid his rent for four months, instead giving his landlady
a promissory note for 115 rubles. The landlady, in turn, has sold his debt as
payment to a certain Chebarov, who has evidently filed a request with the
police for the recovery of this money.[2]

1

While Raskolnikov's claim that "I . . . don't owe anyone anything!" seems to express the isolation encoded in his very name (the root of his surname, *raskol*, suggests schism), he quite obviously *does* owe people something, that is, money, and the police, carrying out one of their standard duties in Imperial Russia, have called on him to enforce the collection of this debt.[3] Scholars have observed the corrosive effects of money on social bonds in Dostoevsky, often in opposition to other kinds of nonmonetary indebtedness that hold people together.[4] However, in *Crime and Punishment*, a network of economic relations stretches between the characters, motivating their actions and thus doing much of the work of driving the plot forward.[5] On this occasion, Raskolnikov is relieved that the police are interested in money: "'Money, what money?' Raskolnikov thought. 'But . . . then it surely can't be *that*!' And he gave a joyful start. He suddenly felt terribly, inexpressibly light. Everything fell from his shoulders."[6] Raskolnikov's debt restores him to society. For a moment, he is not an outcast or a murderer, but merely a poor person who cannot afford to pay the rent, just another out-of-work ex-student among former civil servants like Marmeladov, déclassé nobles like Katerina Ivanovna, and impoverished women faced with the prospect of sex work like Sonia Marmeladova and his own sister, Dunia. Later Raskolnikov will find himself alone even among the prisoners in Siberia. There the peasants will critique his choice of murder weapon: noblemen shouldn't kill people with axes.[7] But here, in the police station, Raskolnikov is a debtor, just like everyone else.

Crime and Punishment is a novel mostly about poor people, and so characters like Razumikhin, Lizaveta, and Raskolnikov (at least, before he becomes obsessed with his Napoleonic plan) spend their time performing odd jobs in the gig economy of postreform Russia. Commercial ties bring the old friends Raskolnikov and Razumikhin back together, since the former is desperate for work and the latter is scheming to earn a few rubles from shoddy translations. Lizaveta is supposed to be out of the house on the day of the planned murder because she ordinarily goes to the marketplace to arrange private sales between impoverished residents of Saint Petersburg. When Raskolnikov overhears about her planned absence, he thinks that this is the action of fate.[8] In reality, the narrator explains, it is an altogether different force, and one that is much more widespread in *Crime and Punishment*: financial need. This connection between mysterious fate and economic law—the latter figured as an "invisible hand," in Adam Smith's immortal image—is far from arbitrary in nineteenth-century European culture, and scholars have examined how British literature in particular grappled with the eerie operations of economic forces.[9] But Raskolnikov, this intelligent young man formed by a steady diet of Western ideas, does not understand what powers he is actually dealing with.[10] He does not understand that what made it possible for him to find Alyona Ivanovna alone in her apartment was, ultimately, the migration of people into the capital in search of better economic opportunities, which—ordinarily, as the narrator calmly observes—results only in their further impoverishment.

The power of economic forces makes itself felt just as much among the rich in Dostoevsky's other works. In his next novel, *The Idiot* (1868–69), it is inheritance, deployed on a scale that baffled critics, that facilitates Myshkin's entry into the novel's competition over Nastasia Filippovna. While Myshkin can enter into the major events of the novel thanks to the traditional melodramatic device of the unexpected inheritance, other characters gain more lasting power by means of more modern and less spectacular kinds of wealth. The successful businessman General Epanchin collects money from a variety of sources, including rental properties and "some sort of factory"—note the typical vagueness of its description—on the outskirts of Saint Petersburg. Like much of the economic activity in *Crime and Punishment*, this factory in *The Idiot* is *somewhere else*, on the margins of the novel's diegesis. The narrative function of this factory is limited but nonetheless important. In this case, Epanchin's sources of wealth explain how a low-born man has come to be so respected. Unlike a nobleman, whose status would depend on that of his ancestors, Epanchin is consummately a product of his historical moment. He owes his success to the possibilities for social mobility opened up by the emergence of new opportunities for making money. Indeed, neither Myshkin's inheritance nor Epanchin's factory is an incidental detail. These businesses and bags of (what we later learn is merchants') money, as well as the financial and legal relationships that radiate out from them, fix the events of *The Idiot* in historical time and assign some characters to the future while consigning others, irrevocably, to obsolescence.

Raskolnikov's debt and Epanchin's factory illustrate two of the major themes of this book: literature's contribution to the imagination of a Russian society increasingly shaped by economic relationships and the representational challenges posed for Russian literature by the new spaces and temporalities of incipient capitalism. These themes crystallize in several key objects of representation, including the accumulative activity of capitalists, circulating capital, industrial labor, and the factory interior. My choice of texts has been conditioned by several considerations. Two canonical novels by Dostoevsky—*The Idiot* and *The Brothers Karamazov*—and one by Leo Tolstoy—*Anna Karenina*—provide vivid examples of the formal and thematic diversity of the Russian realist tradition's responses to capitalism. Chekhov's late works offer a contrastive sample of texts in which representations of economic forces and historical change are conditioned by the different formal constraints of the short story and novella as well as Chekhov's epistemological reticence. Around and between extended readings of these major authors, I examine the work of a number of others, some well-known like Ivan Turgenev and Nikolai Leskov, some less often examined, such as Dmitry Grigorovich,

Fyodor Reshetnikov, Pyotr Boborykin, Dmitry Mamin-Sibiriak, and Aleksandr Kuprin. These works provide evidence for a wide-ranging engagement with economic change in Russian literature in the age of realism. As the following pages demonstrate, capitalism entered Russian literature as much more than a set of themes that could be integrated unproblematically with the existing conventions of the tradition. Rather, in the second half of the nineteenth century, a distinct kind of capitalist realism registered a profound transformation in temporal, spatial, and causal relationships that organized the experience of everyday life and its discursive representation.

The primary textual objects examined in these chapters are some of the best-studied classics of Russian realist literature, but this book modifies the interpretive frame through which scholars have tended to read them. At times, the book pays greater attention to marginal characters and episodes. At others, it returns to some of the most famous scenes in Russian literature but brings these together in a constellation whose contours trace an emergent conception of a historically dynamic economic whole. One of the arguments of this book is that, by examining factories, capitalists, and piles of cash, we can gain new insights into Russian literature's multifaceted response to a whole complex of changes—cultural and social, economic and ethical, observed and anticipated—that characterized the years between the Great Reforms of Alexander II (1861–74) and the cycles of industrial boom and recession at the end of the century. While neither personal debts nor industrial manufacturing were innovations of those years, these and other signs of economic modernity became increasingly important objects of literary representation in this period. The growing prominence of these signs came to shape the response of Russian realist literature, on the levels of description and narration, to an expanding range of historical prospects. In the public discourse of the time, it seemed that a fan of possibilities had opened for the future of Russian society, and the novel was one of the key sites for imagining, testing, and debating the consequences and meanings of these possible futures.[11] As Ilya Kliger puts it, "By the late 1850s and after a period of prolonged 'stagnation,' we find the conditions for what might be called a metahistorical stance, one that surveys all historically unfolding ideological positions simultaneously as competing trajectories for future development."[12] Some of the changes that appeared on the horizon did not yet have adequate concepts. Here, too, literature would play an important role. Russian realism would help imagine what it meant to live in an economy before the word "economy" was itself in circulation. Russian novels would likewise give narrative form to the tremendous transformation that would eventually be encompassed by the word "capitalism."

I have titled this book *Russia's Capitalist Realism* because I believe that the tradition of Russian realism developed in the midst of, and largely in response to, a sense of turbulent change that was as much economic as it was social and political. In the decades following the emancipation of the serfs in 1861, millions of peasants found seasonal work in factories, which expanded rapidly with the influx of newly available labor. Railroads, financed by foreign capital, began to crisscross European Russia and stretched across the Eurasian landmass. With its increased reliance on European investment and trade, Russia's economy was swept up in international financial crises. The major cities, especially Saint Petersburg and Moscow, quickly became some of the largest metropolises in Europe, their populations swelled by economic migrants from the countryside, and, together with the growing population, a self-consciously modern urban retail environment began to develop.[13] It is, of course, important not to lose sight of the fact that these changes took place later and took effect less fully in Russia than in the West. The literary response to these changes was also different. It is in light of these differences that the unnamed businessman in the first epigraph to this introduction observes that there are no novels that capture the tremendous social displacements that came with Russia's rapid economic transformation in the second half of the nineteenth century.

Unlike Lessing's businessman, this book argues that many—indeed, in some sense most—realist writers were acutely concerned with Russia's tumultuous and uneven movement into modernity; their novels registered the effects of uneven historical change on every level, from individual words to narrative form as a whole. While readers have often regarded Russian realism as a literature of ideas from the periphery of European modernity, this book recovers another side—both materialist and materialistic—of this tradition and shows that these works raise fundamental questions about what it means to live in an age of global capitalism—questions that remain crucial in our own times of economic crisis and uneven modernity. Once we begin to notice the signs of incipient economic modernity in these works, we can begin to see how nineteenth-century Russian realism concerned itself with how to make literary sense of economic change. Literature responded both to changes that were taking place in the socioeconomic order of Imperial Russia and to those possibilities that still lay on the horizon, and for which Western Europe offered illustrations and warnings. Russia was changing, too slowly for some and too rapidly for others, but the many responses to these changes examined in the following pages demonstrate their unquestionable impact on contemporary literature. When we add an additional layer of context, reading these works of literature alongside contemporary journalism, studies by economists, and reports by travelers and ethnographers, we see how fiction added its distinct ways of representing a complex and changing social reality to a multigeneric discourse that was, in the years and decades after the Great Reforms, busy trying to describe and comprehend what it meant to live in a capitalist economy.

FROM *DEAD SOULS* TO THE RHETORIC OF SOUL

Already in the nineteenth century, Western readers encountered Russian literature outside that discursive context in which literature was both a participant and an object of discussion. To take an early and foundational example, in Nikolai Gogol's *Dead Souls* (1842), Chichikov's scheme involves buying up the titular souls in order to establish himself as a paper nobleman and make use of the resultant financial advantages. To several generations of Russian readers, Gogol's book spoke out against the horrors of serfdom, the institution, in Aleksandr Herzen's phrase, of "baptized property."[14] Yet when this book appeared in English translation in 1854, the publisher changed its title to *Home Life in Russia* and offered it to readers as a documentary record of the "innate propensity" of Russians—Great Britain's enemy in the Crimean War—to fraud, rather than as a work situated in a changing historical context.[15]

The early reception of Russian realist literature in the West generally disregarded the context of lively economic debate in which it was written, published, read, and reviewed. This reception, in turn, contributed to the impression that Russian realism was peculiarly uninterested in material questions. There is, indeed, a tendency in early Western writings to take Russian writers out of space and time. One gets a sense of this in a key text in the early history of this reception, Eugène-Melchior de Vogüé's *The Russian Novel* (1886), a work that did much to introduce some of the major nineteenth-century Russian writers to the Western reading public. Proclaiming Tolstoy one of the greatest masters "who bear witness to this century," de Vogüé immediately asks: "Is it possible to speak thus grandiosely of a contemporary, who is not even dead, who can be seen every day in his long overcoat, with his long beard, eating, reading the newspapers, receiving cash for his writings and investing the money, who in a word performs all the ordinary commonplace things of daily life?"[16] Making money from one's writings and investing those profits seem like utterly ordinary activities to de Vogüé and therefore somehow incompatible with Tolstoy's magnitude. De Vogüé then wonders whether it is not too soon to pass such judgment, but nevertheless reports how Flaubert, when shown Tolstoy's work by Turgenev, could only proclaim, "This is Shakespeare!" Even while their author was still living, Tolstoy's works seemed to refuse to remain in their own time. In their transcendental greatness, they seemed totally separate from their author's economic life, not to mention their own embeddedness in such timeliness.

We can see another response to the apparent universality and untimeliness of the Russians in Virginia Woolf's famous essay "The Russian Point of View," where she remarks that the works of Dostoevsky are "composed purely and wholly of the stuff of the soul."[17] What Woolf finds striking about the Russian writers is the way they lay bare the fundamental problems that subtend the ephemera of history. The consequence of this focus on first and last things is a neglect of the everyday middle:

> We open the door and find ourselves in a room full of Russian generals, the tutors of Russian generals, their step-daughters and cousins, and crowds of miscellaneous people who are all talking at the tops of their voices about their most private affairs. But where are we? Surely it is the part of a novelist to inform us whether we are in an hotel, a flat, or hired lodging. Nobody thinks of explaining. We are souls, tortured, unhappy souls, whose only business it is to talk, to reveal, to confess, to draw up at whatever rending of flesh and nerve those crabbed sins which crawl on the sand at the bottom of us.[18]

Woolf is commenting here on her experience of reading Dostoevsky's 1866 novella *The Gambler*. It is one of Dostoevsky's most pointedly polemical works, as well as one where his national particularism comes most clearly to the fore. The opposition of calculated accumulation and uncalculating passion defines the coordinates of a national typology. Germans are cold accumulators, while Russians are passionate gamblers; that is to say, for Dostoevsky unhappy souls are not equally distributed among the nations of the world. It is crucial for the articulation of this work's nationalist ideology that the bulk of the narrative takes place in the German town of Roulettenburg, where the Russians are beleaguered by the rigid Germans and the perfidious French, just as it is crucial that the narrator Aleksei Ivanovich chooses to squander his miraculous winnings in Paris, the capital of Dostoevsky's grotesquely commercial Europe. In other words, the question of *where* these events take place (admittedly in regard to national territory, rather than vividly rendered interior spaces) is absolutely central to the ideological organization of *The Gambler*.

Those aspects of the *Gambler* that Woolf neglects are precisely the ones that illustrate the connections between economic behavior and the potential of this behavior to generate absorbing stories. Below, I will modify the terms of Dostoevsky's opposition slightly, so as to fold his passionate gamblers into a slightly more capacious category of characters who are interesting for their capacity to accumulate descriptive detail and hold narrative attention. A second reorientation of Dostoevsky's oppositions will sketch out the temporal trajectories of the chapters to follow. What Dostoevsky treats as national difference will be discussed in this book, borrowing the terminology of Raymond Williams, as emergent and residual tendencies coexisting within Russian society.[19] The following chapters will turn to those marginal capitalists who, like the hyperrational Germans in *The Gambler*, may be hard to notice and even harder to remember, but whose steady, long-term accumulation comes to exert a powerful force on the narrative form of the Russian novel. Before that, however, it will be necessary to sketch out the discursive and conceptual context in which Russia's capitalist realism took shape.

ECONOMY AND HISTORY

Those seeking to make sense of Russia's economic life in the postreform period, whether economists or novelists, confronted a multitude of changes in an emerging world of stock market speculation, expanding railroad infrastructure, and industrialization. However, the key words that we use in the twenty-first century to make sense of our collective life in the wake of this transformation—terms such as "capitalism" and "the economy"—were not readily available, either in Russia or the West. Usually taken for granted in our everyday life, the concepts of capitalism and the economy have a history. As Adam Tooze explains, "'The economy' is not preexisting reality, an object which we simply observe and theorize about. Our understanding of 'the economy' as a distinct entity, a distinct social 'sphere' or social 'system,' is the product of a dramatic process of imaginative abstraction and representational labor."[20] Karl Polanyi, in his pathbreaking *The Great Transformation*, argued that, contrary to the axiom of nineteenth-century liberal economic theory, an economy based on self-regulating market prices was not the natural and inevitable form of economic life, but only came into existence as a result of particular state policies and technological developments during the Industrial Revolution. "Laissez faire," he famously argued, "was planned."[21] The process of describing and defining the economy helped bring it into being. According to Susan Buck-Morss, data visualizations created by late eighteenth-century political economists played a crucial role in making the economy legible: "Because the economy is not found as an empirical object among worldly things," she argues, "in order for it to be 'seen' by the human perceptual apparatus it has to undergo a process, crucial for science, of representational mapping."[22] It took generations for these ideas to percolate through even the most advanced capitalist societies. Mary Poovey argues that, even in Great Britain in the mid-1860s, the idea that local communities constituted a national or even global economy traversed by real but invisible relationships "had yet to become the culture's commonsense understanding of events that could still seem unrelated to each other."[23] A number of scholars have reached the conclusion that, in the West, the notion that there exists such a thing as an economy and that it operates in accordance with its own laws became widespread only in the twentieth century alongisde increasingly sophisticated kinds of economic knowledge for use by modern states.[24] According to most accounts, the notion of the economy as a concrete thing emerged in the West in an age when such an object, its operations ostensibly governed by objective laws, needed to be analyzed and understood by government planners and businesses. In other words, people began to think in terms of the economy in the age of capitalism, and the histories of these two concepts are closely connected.

In nineteenth-century Russia, writers, journalists, economists, and ethnographers all contributed to a multigeneric public discourse in which concepts like "the economy" and "capitalism" were gradually elaborated. For some, Russia, like any other place, was governed by universal laws. For example, the scholar Ivan Gorlov argued in his *Foundations of Political Economy* (1859–62) that if "artificial" conditions—in other words, historical contingencies such as the institution of serfdom—were done away with, Russia would join the economically developed societies of Western Europe.[25] Once this happened, Gorlov paraphrased Adam Smith, Russian society would become one in which "each person is more or less a buyer and seller, while the whole of society constitutes a multifaceted and boundless [*neobozrimuiu*] system of exchanges."[26] The two volumes of Gorlov's book were published on either side of 1861, the year when the Russian state embarked on the liberation of the serfs. As a result, millions of peasants and countless agricultural estates would gradually enter Russia's expanding money economy. Still, at the time that Gorlov was writing, it would be hard to describe Russia as a country in which each person was more or less a buyer and a seller linked together in a boundless system of exchanges. Yet what was theory in Gorlov becomes narrative in Dostoevsky, as flows of money trace elaborate connections between characters, such as when Raskolnikov's mother, Pulkheria Aleksandrovna, borrows money from a merchant (who has no other function in the plot) and forwards it to Razumikhin, who uses it to buy clothes for Raskolnikov.

While Gorlov's and other visions of Russia's economic development perceived all of society as part of a national and even global economic system, public discourse still lacked a word for the "economy" in its modern sense, by which to describe this system as a whole. *Khoziaistvo*, frequently used in the mid-nineteenth century, overlaps only partially with the word "economy" or its modern Russian equivalent *ekonomika* and in most reference works refers primarily to the activity of management, rather than an intangible thing that exists whether one manages it or not. Vladimir Dal' only includes entries for *ekonomiia* and *khoziaistvo* in his dictionary, neither of which means anything like the modern concept of the totality of simultaneous transactions linking together flows of people, goods, and capital on a national scale.[27] A. D. Mikhel'son's 1883 dictionary of foreign words that have entered Russian includes *ekonomika* as a synonym for "political economy," that is, an intellectual discipline that concerns itself with "state *khoziaistvo"* rather than an object that is presumed to exist independently of its representations.[28] Looking ahead several decades to the beginning of the twentieth century, we can find something comparable to the modern concept of the economy in Russian public discourse: by then, the term *narodnoe khoziaistvo*, modeled on *Volkswirtschaft* and *économie nationale*, had come to refer to "the totality of social relations, since production, trade, and the distribution of material goods constitutes the content of these relations," as the political economist Pyotr Struve defined it in his 1897 article on "narodnoe khoziaistvo" in the *Brockhaus-Efron Encyclopedic Dictionary*.[29]

In Russia, as elsewhere, the activity of the state helped gradually define an independent sphere of economic activity. Here is how Yanni Kotsonis describes the effect of a new regime of taxation, which required the state to accumulate an unprecedented amount of knowledge about the people and property under its jurisdiction, on the notion of the national economy:

> For the first time the state was creating a neat separation between itself and a private sector and in the process outlined the features of both the state sector and the private economy. . . . Uniform tax codes were applied to whole sectors of trade and production in order to view them as a single and coherent market. The multiplicity of local agricultural practices and rural pursuits was rendered uniform in a system that measured only land; diverse businesses looked comparable when expressed in money.[30]

The very idea of laissez-faire—the notion that the state should not interfere in the natural operations of a self-regulating market economy—was predicated on the existence of such an independent sphere of private economic activity. However, Kotsonis, continues, "the private sphere of production, trade, and wealth was a state undertaking from the outset, a public view of the private. . . . Liberalism in the nineteenth century served to bring into being a conception of the economy that was discrete and observable; the state was active in creating that economic space."[31] As the state separated itself from the private economic sphere in order to understand it (and therefore tax it) better, it also played a major part in generating the kinds of knowledge necessary to imagine this sphere as an interconnected, dynamic whole.

By the end of the century, the concept of the economy became central to state planning. In 1899, Finance Minister Sergei Witte wrote a secret memorandum to Nicholas II about the need for a unified industrial policy for the empire. As a result of profound social and economic changes, the whole Russian Empire, Witte argued, had become a vast economic whole:

> The entire economic structure of the empire has been transformed in the course of the second half of the current century, so that now the market and

10

its price structure represent the collective interest of all private enterprises which constitute our national economy. Buying and selling and wage labor penetrate now into much deeper layers of our national existence than was the case at the time of the serf economy, when the landlord in his village constituted a self-sufficient economic little world, leading an independent life, almost without relation to the market. The division of labor; the specialization of skills; the increased exchange of goods among a population increasingly divided among towns, villages, factories, and mines; the greater complexity of the demands of the population—all these processes rapidly developed in our fatherland under the influence of the emancipation of the serfs, the construction of a railroad network, the development of credit, and the extraordinary growth of foreign trade. Now all organs and branches of our national economy [*narodnogo khoziaistva*] are drawn into a common economic life.[32]

The idea that the economy changed and grew over time, as new technologies and new commercial practices generated and redistributed new wealth and transformed social relations, was crucial. The concept of national and global economies emerged together with a sense of the enormous dynamism of modernity. Marx and Engels recognized the world-shaping accomplishments of capitalism, "wonders far surpassing Egyptian pyramids, Roman aqueducts, and Gothic cathedrals."[33] Although there are few Russian novels in which the achievements of the bourgeoisie can be compared favorably to the pyramids (Boborykin is a notable outlier in this regard), a concern with this new class's ceaseless transformative energy nevertheless pervaded Russian realism. However, as with "the economy," another of the key words that we use to conceptualize this transformation was largely absent from both the work of the founders of Marxism and from the Russian novel.

The word "capitalism" is considerably younger than the phenomenon it names.[34] As Fernand Braudel observed, "capital" and "capitalist," as terms of art in the discourse of commerce, emerged centuries before "capitalism."[35] According to Eric Hobsbawm, the latter word first entered wide circulation in the 1860s, and then only in France.[36] By the early 1870s, German readers could encounter *Kapitalismus* in the work of the scholar Albert Schäffle, whose lectures, published in 1870, were translated into Russian the following year as *Kapitalizm i sotsializm*.[37] The term evidently entered English even later, in the early years of the twentieth century.[38] Although Marx's analysis of capitalism is foundational, he rarely used that word, preferring the phrase "capitalist mode of production" (*kapitalistische Produktsionsweise*, translated as *kapitaliticheskii sposob proizvodstva* in the 1872 Russian translation of *Capital*, volume 1).[39] One of the earliest instances of "capitalism" in Russian appeared in a study by the economist Nikolai Ziber, *Marx's Economic Theory*, which was serialized in the journal *Knowledge* (Znanie) in 1876–77 and then continued in *The Word* (Slovo) over the course of 1878. Ziber's study features discussions of the relationship between "capitalism" (*kapitalizmom*) and "the industrial organization of labor" (*manufakturnoe slozhenie truda*).[40] Elsewhere, Ziber discusses Marx's theory in terms of "capitalist society" (*kapitalisticheskogo obshchestva*).[41] The word "capitalism" became more prominent in Russian economic discourse in the 1880s, when it appeared in such important works as Vasilii Vorontsov's *The Fate of Capitalism in Russia* (1882). The word had therefore been circulating in Russian public discourse for several decades when it appeared in the title of Vladimir Lenin's *The Development of Capitalism in Russia* in 1899. The word "capitalism" was thus in its initial formative stages in both Western Europe and Russia at the time that Tolstoy and Dostoevsky were writing their most famous works, and although this word does not appear in the works of Dostoevsky or in *Anna Karenina*, the writers and social theorists of the time all responded to—and hoped to shape—the same complex arrangement of changes for which this new word was emerging.

THE BENEFITS OF BACKWARDNESS

There remained, however, a gap between theory and economic reality. Throughout the nineteenth century, Russia lagged far behind the other Great Powers in economic development. Even after the industrial surge of the 1890s, Russia retained a predominantly agricultural economy, with a lower level of urbanization and a smaller percentage of industrial workers than the advanced states of the West.[42] Even in terms of railroad construction, one of the most notable achievements of Russian economic modernization, it could not compare with the United States.[43] While Russian writers at the end of the nineteenth century wrote extensively about the rise of a Russian bourgeoisie, modern scholarship has tended to emphasize the absence of anything like a Western middle class in Russia, together with weak traditions of private property and a lack of private credit institutions.[44]

Why, then, speak about capitalism and the nineteenth-century realist novel in Russia? One answer is that a growing number of historians have started to qualify the long-standing tendency to emphasize Russia's difference, or, indeed, deviation, from the Western historical norm. For example, Sergei Antonov has written an important corrective to the notion that institutions, legislation, and cultural attitudes related to credit and debt in Imperial Russia were qualitatively different (and implicitly lacking) compared to those of the West.[45] Ekaterina Pravilova's work on the development of the notion of the public domain in Russia has helped to shift the focus away from what she calls the "obsession" with Russia's inadequate private property rights.[46] While many historical accounts have emphasized the poor performance of the Russian economy and the low productivity of its labor force, Paul Gregory has argued instead that "Russian industrial and agricultural productivity does not appear to be much different from that of other countries" in the late Imperial period.[47] Among earlier scholarship, Peter Gatrell concludes his history of the Russian economy from 1850 to 1917 by arguing that "the temptation to describe pre-revolutionary Russia as a backward economy is powerful, but it is a temptation that should be resisted."[48]

The notion of Russian backwardness that Gatrell evokes serves as a handy illustration of the major spatiotemporal vector of much Russian writing about economic questions in the nineteenth century.[49] The metaphor of backwardness implies that Europe and Russia occupy the same continuum of development. Even if Russia was lagging behind, the very possibility of ascertaining the right direction by reference to Europe indicated that there existed a common space-time in which both Europe and Russia had the potential to make progress. In other words, the West showed the future—as promise or as nightmare—and the relatively small changes already taking place in Russia took on a huge anticipatory significance in its light. This kind of backwardness could offer a significant epistemic advantage. As the economic historian Alexander Gerschenkron argued in his classic essay "Economic Backwardness in Historical Perspective," backward countries could adjust their own plans and policies in accordance with changes that more advanced economies had already undergone. They could, for instance, import the most advanced technologies available and rapidly develop their own manufacturing techniques using the latest machinery. As a result, the backward country could gain a (temporary) advantage by leapfrogging over the more advanced country, whose industry had developed over time and still possessed all the older, less productive machines and plants that the newly and rapidly industrialized newcomer could skip.[50]

Alternatively, a backward country might choose to avoid the mistakes made by its more advanced but also more path-dependent neighbors. The philosopher of history Pyotr Chaadaev, in his "Apology of a Madman," maintained that Peter the Great's transformative reforms were possible "only in a nation whose past did not mandate the path it must follow."[51] Numerous nineteenth-century opponents of capitalism and industrialization would develop Chaadaev's argument to maintain that Russia could, or must, create a future for itself that would not resemble Europe's recent past.[52] As an enlightened bureaucrat commented on the emancipation legislation in 1860, "Our country has been given the opportunity of utilizing the experiences of other lands . . . to comprehend all at once the path that lies ahead."[53] A decade later, some of the first Russian readers of Marx's *Capital* interpreted his discussion of British industrialization as a warning about how *not* to modernize.[54]

Russia's material poverty and historical belatedness gave it more room to maneuver than the built-up Western countries that were plunging ahead into the uncharted future.

There were some observers who nevertheless thought that Russia was rapidly converging with the West. Its cities were being transformed into major industrial and commercial centers, and its old social hierarchy appeared to be dissolving as merchant entrepreneurs emerged as the motive force of progress. Such a view is clearly expressed in the voluminous writings of Pyotr Boborykin, a novelist, journalist, theater critic, and literary historian who is now mostly known for his novels about Moscow life and for popularizing the term "intelligentsia."[55] In the March 1881 issue of the *Herald of Europe*, Boborykin published the first of his "Letters about Moscow," in which he declared that a new kind of educated, worldly Russian merchant was transforming the city's economic and cultural life. "Towards the end of the nineteenth century," he wrote, "commercial and industrial Moscow became, at one and the same time, Manchester, London, and New York."[56] What higher praise for *Moskva kupecheskaia*—merchant Moscow—could one offer than to compare it to these world capitals of industry and finance?

Of course, far from all observers were this sanguine about the possibility or, indeed, about the desirability of economic modernization. Debates raged in the Russian periodical press, with different factions forming around such journals as the liberal-leaning *Herald of Europe* or *Notes of the Fatherland*, which became the major organ for the populists (*narodniki*) after Nikolai Nekrasov took over as editor in 1868.[57] Advocates of classical political economy, like Gorlov, supported free trade and government policies encouraging industrialization and insisted that Russia should develop along Western lines. On the other hand, a range of thinkers opposed to the very idea of universal economic laws, including slavophiles, populists, and certain liberals, insisted that Russia's economic and social development would have to take a different form from that of the West.[58] What united them was the widespread anticipatory character of these reflections on capitalism. Those who did not welcome factories and joint-stock companies but, rather, dreaded their destructive effects also focused extensively on what was coming in the future. Richard Wortman has characterized the attitudes of the Russian intelligentsia in the following terms:

> Most of all, the members of the intelligentsia dreaded the prospect of uncontrolled economic change and the behemoth of modern industrialism, which, being unknown and distant, assumed terrible proportions in their imaginations. They feared the chaotic development that they envisioned blighting the West and threatening to engulf Russia. Capitalism embodied for them the

callousness and egoism that had appalled them in Russian life, and its spread promised to destroy everything they held dear.[59]

The very distance of British-style industrialization from late nineteenth-century Russian life only increased the scale of the threat. The Ukrainian economic historian Mykhailo Tuhan-Baranovsky observed that many influential writers of the postreform period, including the radicals organized around *The Contemporary* in the early 1860s and, in the following decade, the populists associated with *Notes of the Fatherland*, were desperate to deny the very possibility of Russian industrialization.[60] In their eagerness to defend traditional forms of property ownership, such as the peasant commune (*mir*), and production, such as small-scale handicrafts (*kustar'*), they made the same arguments against industrialization as their political enemies, the serf-owning advocates of protectionism a generation earlier. Populist thinkers like Vorontsov and Nikolai Mikhailovsky insisted that Western-style capitalism was impossible in Russia and that industrialization would inevitably bring destitution and destruction to the peasantry.[61]

The fundamental terms of these debates—whether or not a common set of universal laws governed the economic development of all societies; whether industrialization inevitably brought destitution and the dissolution of social bonds—raised their imaginative stakes in ways that sometimes blurred the boundaries between scholarship and imaginative literature. In 1882, Boris Chicherin, one of Russia's preeminent legal scholars, published a formidable two-volume study titled *Property and the State*. In this work, Chicherin set out to lay the philosophical and legal foundations for Russian liberalism. His argument for the central importance of the individual as the possessor of rights, against all kinds of collectivist abstractions, bears directly on his economic views as well. In a chapter titled "Economic Society," Chicherin attacks those theories that assign ontological priority to the social whole over the individual. In developing his argument, he frequently turns to an analysis of his opponents' language. A century before the pioneering work of Deirdre McCloskey, Chicherin argues that it is crucial to understand the rhetoric of economics, and especially its capacity to mislead.[62] In order to defend his vision of the free market, which places the autonomous individual at the center, Chicherin engages with leading economic thinkers of his time, including Schäffle, a member of the historical school of German economists, and Herbert Spencer, one of the most wide-ranging and influential thinkers of the nineteenth century.[63] At the heart of Chicherin's polemic against these and other thinkers is their irresponsible use of metaphor, which causes notions such as the organic structure of society—notions that are indefensible, according to Chicherin—to spring into existence.

Attacking Spencer's *Principles of Sociology* (1876), he focuses on the English philosopher's misuse of rhetorical figures: "Thus, regarding growth, he says that societies, just like living bodies, begin as embryos and then, by way of the gradual multiplication of their constituent parts or the external conjoining of groups, achieve considerable size. . . . To compare small migratory bands [*ordy*] to physical embryos, as Spencer does, means to play around with metaphors."[64] Even though Schäffle and Spencer argue from opposing standpoints, they draw on the same metaphors and thus allow various impossible social organisms to creep into their theories. By contrast, Chicherin's expressed aim is to set "economic science" on a rigorous foundation, free of such rhetorical excesses. For the time being, however, it appears that even the most serious scholars, when attempting to represent verbally the totality of economic and legal relationships, are hampered by the literary blurriness of the available language.

Further narrowing the gap between the work of political economists trying to figure out how to represent Russia under changing economic conditions and realist writers attempting to give aesthetic form to a complex and differentially changing society were those critics who wrote about both literary and social topics. Already in 1846, Vissarion Belinsky posited an analogy between industrialization and literature. Both, he argued, were essential to the process of transforming a hierarchy of rigidly segregated estates into a dynamic and internally communicative society. On one side, "railroads will run their tunnels and bridges through and beneath the walls; through the development of industry and commerce they will interweave the interests of people of all estates and classes [*vsekh soslovii i klassov*]." On the other, "our literature has created the morals of our society, has already educated several generations of widely divergent character, has paved the way for an inner *rapprochement* of the estates."[65] At the time that Belinsky wrote these words, rail transport in Russia was primarily a matter of future prospects. Indeed, even in the West the railroad was a younger technology in 1846 than the internet is in 2020. The world's first public railway using steam locomotives, the Darlington and Stockton Railway in England, began operations in 1825. The Tsarskoe Selo Railway, opened in 1837, was the first in Russia. By the time that Belinsky's article appeared, work had started on two commercially important Russian railways: the Warsaw-Vienna Railway, which would be completed in 1848, and the Saint Petersburg–Moscow Railway.[66] Whereas the railroad would increasingly assume a threatening, invasive presence in numerous works of literature, where it would come to be linked to irrevocable change and to the speculative excesses of the "railway mania" of the late 1860s and '70s, in Belinsky's view the railway was capable of bridging both spatial and social divides, which linked it to literature's capacity to do the same by constructing a socially diverse reading public.[67]

16

Among the next generation of critics, Dmitry Pisarev would argue for an even more direct connection between economic development and literature as an instrument for social progress.[68] For Pisarev, the word "realist" both referred to questions of artistic method and described a mode of social action. Thus, in his essay "The Realists," he wove together these two different meanings of the word "realism"—the proscientific and iconoclastic stance that he praises in the character of Bazarov, the hero of Ivan Turgenev's 1862 novel *Fathers and Children*, and the much-debated term of nineteenth-century aesthetic theory—into an argument which located the value of literature in an economic system that encompassed both material and intellectual production. Pisarev argues that literature, like all intellectual labor, must be managed as a scarce economic resource:

> The economy of intellectual powers will increase our intellectual capital, and this increased capital, applied to beneficial production, will increase the amount of bread, meat, clothing, footwear, tools, and all the other material products of labor. The duty to develop this tendency lies wholly on our literature, because in this sphere literature can act independently. . . . The economy of intellectual powers is nothing other than rigorous and consistent realism.[69]

In this essay, Pisarev borrows economic terminology and employs it metaphorically ("intellectual capital should bring good returns [*khoroshie protsenty*] to society") in order to inscribe cultural artifacts into an all-encompassing system of production whose goal is the material enrichment of the country.[70] As we will see in chapters 3 and 4, Dostoevsky's novels represent the disaster of runaway economic dilation by ensnaring their characters in all-encompassing monetary relationships that extend far beyond the world of stock markets and business. Pisarev, for his part, constructs a similarly hypertrophied rhetorical economy, not as a critique of emerging capitalism but to assert the role of all human activity in promoting or obstructing progress. With very different aims, both Dostoevsky's fictions and Pisarev's criticism offer models of society in which economic considerations determine the meaning and value of apparently all human activity.

HOW TO WRITE A CAPITALIST

To be sure, neither characters engaged in commerce nor the institutions and relationships they create make their first appearance in the Russian realist novel after the Great Reforms. Nor does literature discover money or economic concepts in the second half of the nineteenth century. Connections between literature and economics are much older, and the relationship between the two has taken many different forms. Marc Shell has traced a link between the origins of literature and the invention of coinage in classical antiquity.[71] The New Economic Criticism, which has been prominently represented among economically oriented literary scholarship of the past two decades, had its origins in the study of early modern British literature.[72] In Russia, too, fictional representations of economic life emerged long before the realist period. Merchant tales, like the "Tale of Karp Sutulov" and the "Tale of Savva Grutsyn," appeared in the seventeenth century.[73] In the following century, Russian classicism was rich in didactic representations of misers, such as in the works of Aleksandr Sumarokov and Mikhail Kheraskov.[74] A few decades later, Nikolai Karamzin's *Letters of a Russian Traveler* (1791–1801) would articulate a theory of moral development that, as Konstanine Klioutchkine has shown, corresponded to the contemporary economic theory of mercantilism.[75] In the Romantic era, among numerous works concerned with the poetics of money, Evgeny Baratynsky envisioned a dystopian postscarcity society in his poem "The Last Death" (1827).[76] And in the 1830s and '40s, the changing social structure, reforms of the monetary system, and the burgeoning periodical press would all contribute to the proliferation of economic themes and economically inflected narrative forms in Russian literature, as Jillian Porter has recently examined in detail.[77]

Of all the literary precursors to Russia's capitalist realism, the most important is Nikolai Gogol's *Dead Souls* (1842). Scholars have repeatedly drawn attention to the ways Chichikov's scheme—and the very fact of its centrality to the plot of the novel—signals the growing importance of economic calculation as an object of representation in Russian literature. Seamas O'Driscoll sees Gogol's work as the first major attempt to "turn *homo oeconomicus* into the hero of a Russian novel."[78] Gerschenkron observes that Chichikov is the first Russian literary protagonist who acts in accordance with a long-term "entrepreneurial time horizon"—that is, his scheme requires extensive planning, rational calculation, and self-denial in the short term.[79] In Russell Valentino's view, Gogol draws on the eighteenth-century discourse of passions and interests to define Chichikov as a person driven by the "calm passion" of modern self-interest rather than, like Pliushkin, by an atavistic avarice.[80] The preoccupation of *Dead Souls* with the transformation of human beings into units of economic abstraction represented by documents allows this novel to speak simultaneously to the dehumanization of "souls" under serfdom, the hypertrophy of the Russian bureaucracy, and the principle of universal calculability that underlay emerging capitalism. In outline, its narrative form looks back to the picaresque novel, but *Dead Souls* also brims with innovations that shaped successive generations of Russian literature and introduced techniques that would contribute to key developments in later works, such as the poetics of the factory, examined in the next chapter.

In some important respects, particularly in the way it imagines the relationship of its plot to the movement of history, *Dead Souls* differs from the works that are the main focus of this book. Chichikov's adventures in the provincial town of NN do not seem to leave a lasting mark on its inhabitants or on the larger world. After scandal erupts, he flees with his dead souls amid an explosion of rumors to the effect that he is actually Napoleon in disguise or even the impossible Captain Kopeikin. These rumors fix Chichikov in a frame of reference that links him to the past, rather than the future, as does his vision of success—a serf-owning landlord's prosperity. In a broader sense, the Russian expanses he traverses do not seem to be infused by the felt omnipresence of history, as virtually every space in the later literature will be. Even Levin's estate in *Anna Karenina*, where preindustrial rhythms define the lives of landowner and peasants alike, is perpetually under threat of the ever-approaching railroad, which invariably brings the dissolution of this kind of isolated local community.

Gogol's novel is nonetheless a crucial part of the long literary tradition that shaped Russia's capitalist realism. To get at the specificity of the later, properly realist response to economic change, it will be useful to look at another earlier work that was deeply enmeshed in the economic conditions of the 1820s and '30s: Aleksandr Pushkin's "The Queen of Spades." In the view of several Soviet scholars, an emerging concern with the new "age of money" subtended the story's fantastic plot. Grigory Gukovsky considers the 1830s a period of social instability, characterized by weakening class structures and the emergence of new social elites whose power lay in their control of capital:

> Fantastic occurrences and strong passions; unnatural events and the wild play of chance, which elevated one person in the blink of an eye and cast down another; the delirium and hysterical madness of the game: these become, as it were, images of ultra-modernity in the 1830s, of the soulless and meaningless power of money of this period. This was an attempt to find the artistic incarnation of those laws of the new society, which appeared to be lawless in the highest degree, like the incomprehensible (fantastical) arbitrariness of chance, as it triumphed on the card table.[81]

In Gukovsky's reading, literature of this period turns to the fantastic as a response to the inscrutability of economic conditions, for which the game of chance becomes an apt metaphor. Furthermore, what is particularly important in this argument is that Pushkin's story does more than merely reflect real economic conditions: it also provides cognitive tools for their analysis. Accordingly, its protagonist, Germann, exhibits signs of what Ilya Kliger has termed the "veredictory mutation" in modern literature, as a result of which truth ceases to be temporally transcendent, instead becoming immanent to time and therefore historical.[82] Thus, according to Gukovsky, Pushkin marks Germann as a symptomatic social type, rather than the embodiment of a universal moral quality, by identifying him as an engineer, a modern technical professional. Germann's ambition, as much as his downfall, are likewise conditioned by the particular social and economic conditions in which he lives, and his story helps to make those conditions legible.

Yuri Lotman developed this argument by examining card games in the literature of the 1820s and '30s as allegories for the changing logic of Russian economic life. Accordingly, as a result of the nonsynchronous development of the economic base and the social superstructure, changes in the wealth of nobles came to seem unpredictable—appearing as strokes of fortune—and the game of chance became a popular expression of this apparent arbitrariness of success. Meanwhile, the bidding game, linked to "the action of economic laws, planning and productive efforts in the acquisition of wealth," seemed to contradict "the nobility's interpretation of the very concept of wealth" and became unpopular.[83] When Germann decides, against his better judgment, to find out the old countess's winning combination of cards, he gives himself over to this world of sudden and seemingly unmotivated fluctuations of wealth, which defined the experiences of the nobility.

These interpretations of "The Queen of Spades," together with Porter's examination of several other important works of the period, amply demonstrate the new significance of economic ambition in the context of literary Romanticism, government reform of the monetary system, and the proliferation of news about promotions at home and revolutions abroad by means of the growing periodical press. However, despite the increasing literary prominence of ambitious characters and moneymaking schemes, the results of this ambition tended to be rather unprepossessing. The typical path of the man of ambition, as Porter traces, was from humble beginnings to the madhouse—by way of an absorbing story, which is, in the final analysis, the only real payoff of his ambitions. Germann is no exception to this tendency. When the rational half-German gives in to his own passionate, half-Russian nature and decides to seek the old countess's secret combination of cards, he sets himself on a course to catastrophe, but he also sets the narrative of "The Queen of Spades" in motion. In the path that Germann follows in this story, two crucial features emerge that will distinguish "The Queen of Spades" from the fictional treatments of businessmen and capitalists in the postreform years and will thereby illuminate the broader differences between these two literary-historical periods.

The first important difference is that, in the struggle between the new tendency represented by Germann and the old ways of the nobility, it is the latter that triumphs. Germann employs all the cold, calculating rationality at his disposal to gain access to the countess and her eighteenth-century secrets in an effort to employ them against the ruling powers of the nineteenth. Nevertheless, fate defeats him. After winning twice against his aristocratic opponents, he plays a third time. Although Germann has seemingly staked everything on the ace, it turns out, bafflingly, that he has actually chosen the queen of spades, so he loses all his winnings, perhaps having failed all the while to get any closer to attaining the real object of his ambition: social parity with the aristocrats.[84] After his attempt to rise above his station ends in disaster, Germann is sent off to the madhouse. The rigid social system, for its part, snaps back into place as if the perturbation caused by the would-be parvenu had never disturbed it. The brevity of the epilogue to "The Queen of Spades" is an eloquent testament to the ultimate lack of consequences of Germann's ambition for anyone but himself. The motive force of the first sentence is a single perfective-past-tense verb, which consigns the events of Germann's life to the absolute past: "Germann lost his mind." The second sentence, describing Germann in the epilogue's *now*, contains a series of three imperfective verbs in the present tense: sitting in the asylum, refusing to answer questions, and muttering incessantly about the "three, seven, and ace," Germann now inhabits the eternal present of madness. Narrative events are no longer possible for him. The next paragraph then shifts to the story of Lizaveta Ivanovna, the young orphan whom he had tried to seduce to gain access to the countess. Lizaveta has gotten married and is now living with her prosperous husband. A final clause informs us that he is the son of the countess's former household manager. We had learned earlier that the countess's staff stole from her constantly, but this enrichment of others at her own expense did not seem to affect the countess very much. Now her former charge and the son of her former manager will live off her wealth, their lives also extending indefinitely into a future that seemingly no longer bears any traces of the historical specificity that scholars have located in the character of Germann and his ambition. Germann arrived on the historical stage, played his part, and departed, and nothing, ultimately, seems to have changed.

In the literature of the later period, representatives of the old world will be haunted constantly by the expectation of decline. In the works of Goncharov, Turgenev, Dostoevsky, and even Tolstoy, the future will appear to belong not to the noble landowners but to all manner of merchants, capitalists, and entrepreneurs. Even if their advance can be temporarily arrested, as in *Anna Karenina*, their factories and railroads cannot simply be consigned to oblivion like Germann's ambition in "The Queen of Spades." The novels of the postreform period are almost all suffused with a sense of ineluctable historical change. This would sometimes be cause for quiet melancholy at the prospect of losing something beautiful but outmoded, as in Turgenev and Goncharov. On the other hand, especially with the growing influence of naturalist aesthetics toward the end of the century, the old world of the nobility would at times be marked not just by decline but by physical and mental degeneration, as abundantly demonstrated in works by such writers as Mikhail Saltykov-Shchedrin and Boborykin.[85]

The second crucial difference between the representation of historical change in "The Queen of Spades" and the literature that follows concerns what is and what is not adequate material for literary narrative. In Pushkin's story, as long as Germann insists that he will not "sacrifice what is necessary in hopes of acquiring what is excessive," there is no story; rather, there is only the expectation that he will not remain faithful to his principle.[86] There could be no "Queen of Spades" if Germann had continued to go to work every day, living on his modest salary and letting his inheritance accumulate interest. This would, indeed, amount to the very absence of narrative, constituting instead an endless succession of the same unremarkable and uninteresting activity.[87] It is only by giving in to the desire for the very thing he had earlier repudiated—"the superfluous"—that Germann steps out of an endless succession of workdays and into the plot of a Romantic short story. It is remarkable, then, that one of Germann's literary descendants, the half-German, half-Russian Andrei Stolz in Goncharov's 1859 novel *Oblomov*, takes the very path that Germann had to abandon. Stolz may have to forfeit protagonicity to do so, but he nonetheless enters the plot of *Oblomov* not as a miser or a gambler but as a capitalist who keeps careful watch over his finances and goes on boring business trips. The business—the *delo*—that will occupy men like Stolz or the businessmen in *The Idiot* is fundamentally different from the *delo* in which the card players are engaged in the epigraph to chapter 1 of "The Queen of Spades."[88] The crucial distinction here is not simply between gambling and calculation—contrasting evaluations, particularly moral, of these different strategies have been a fixture of literature for centuries—so much as the changing narrative potential of the latter.

Compared to the ambitious seekers of fortune in the 1830s, the later capitalists have a much longer time horizon.[89] That is, they accumulate wealth and power with an eye toward the distant future. Correspondingly, their narrative trajectories tend to differ from those of their earlier economically active counterparts. In Porter's reading of the literature of the Nicholaevian period, ambition expresses a contradiction between the felt possibility of change (encapsulated by Napoleon's phrase about the new "career open to all talents" and his own meteoric rise) and the reality of an unyielding social system.[90] As a result, characters attempting to achieve a degree of social mobility are generally thwarted, with their quests typically ending in the madhouse or the grave. After the character attempting to rise above his station in life through the accumulation of money is defeated, the social system returns to its status quo. By contrast, the later capitalists tend to carry on their patient accumulation, growing ever richer, while their more interesting—and more extensively elaborated—noble counterparts face deterioration and defeat. The future appears to belong to the Epanchins and Stolzes, even if this means, as chapter 3 will consider, that the realist novel might reach its representational limits in the moment of their triumph.

Just as they avoid the fate of the men of ambition, the capitalists of the later period do not fall into the closed loop of greed that traditionally defines the miser, whether on a minor scale, like Dostoevsky's Mr. Prokharchin, who hides his coins in his mattress, or far more magnificently, as in the case of Balzac's titanic Gobseck, who rules Paris as an "unknown king," but dies among a vast trove of rotting goods, which his greed has prevented him from turning into capital.[91] A certain kind of economic irrationality allows the misers to rise to great heights of dramatic intensity. The capitalists are considerably more prosaic: their stories just keep going. As Kliger puts it, the bourgeois is "so thoroughly knowable and predictable as to be nearly unrepresentable in narrative."[92] The near-unrepresentability of the bourgeois or the capitalist proved both a challenge and an opportunity for the Russian realist novel as it responded to historically unprecedented changes to established spatial, temporal, and causal relationships.

What Germann must cease doing in order for his story to begin is what Stolz, Epanchin, Totsky, Stiva Oblonsky's colleagues at the United Agency for the Credit-Mutual [kreditno-vzaimnogo] Balance of the Southerly Rail [iuzhno-zheleznykh] Roads and Banking Institutions, and many others do continuously in the novels of the 1860s, '70s, and beyond. Often this meant that Germann's successors became more forgettable, even for real-life businessmen who read Russian literature. Pavel Buryshkin, émigré heir to a commercial fortune, begins his memoirs of prerevolutionary Moscow business life with a literary anecdote from *Anna Karenina*. It concerns the meeting of Stiva and a merchant who has come to buy his forest. There is only one problem: Buryshkin confuses this merchant's name—Riabinin—with the scheming seminarian Rakitin from *The Brothers Karamazov*.[93] Indeed, the literary capitalists generally do not become major characters without deviating in some way from their day-to-day activity. In the literature of the 1880s and '90s, capitalists generally attain protagonicity by turning to crime (as in the case of Paltusov from Boborykin's *Kitai-Gorod*) or by agonizing over their reluctance to run the family business (as in Mamin-Sibiriak's *Privalov's Millions* or some of the late works of Chekhov). However, even while the sheer repetitiveness of their work remains a problem for literary narration, business-minded characters and the temporality of business activity come to exert a determinate influence on the works of Russia's capitalist realism. At the end of the century, Chekhov's stories and novellas are filled with reluctant capitalists who hate their jobs and fear their own factories. Unlike Germann, however, they usually keep going to work, and the narrative relates the consequences of their doing so.

"SOME SORT OF COMPANY"

Oblomov, one of the first works in this new tradition, is structured by the opposition between two childhood friends—the nobleman Ilya Oblomov and Stolz, who is the son of an estate manager. The contrast between the lazy Russian nobleman and the hardworking German commoner has profound structural consequences. As Anne Lounsbery has shown, Oblomov and Stolz are linked to two different conceptions of space. While Oblomov dwells in perpetual torpor, refusing to move, and regards his childhood home and his current apartment as precious for incalculable personal reasons, Stolz is always in motion through "a landscape thoroughly knowable, mappable, and traversable, aimed at facilitating the circulation of people, goods, and money."[94]

Since Oblomov tends to remain at rest while Stolz tends to remain in motion, the two characters come to be associated in this novel with, respectively, description and narration. The first part of the novel, where Oblomov famously fails to get out of bed for a hundred pages, affords ample opportunity for the narrator to dwell on the details of his apartment, from the dusty books that Oblomov never reads to the voluminous *khalat* that he never removes. Stolz, on the other hand, travels around the Russian Empire and abroad in pursuit of his business activity. The narrator is not particularly informative regarding the exact nature of this work:

> Stolz . . . served, went into retirement, busied himself with his own affairs and in fact managed to accumulate a house and money. He participated in some sort of company [*v kakoi-to kompanii*], which sent goods abroad. He is constantly in motion: if the society should need to send an agent to Belgium or England, they would send him; if some project should need to be written or a new idea applied, they would choose him.[95]

The narrative makes short work of Stolz's career: a series of verbs, separated by commas, account for years of striving and presumably hard-earned success. Although Stolz's character is defined by his labor, the narrative is evasive to the point of dismissiveness about the nature of his work. Concerning the identity of Stolz's employer, the reader only learns that he works for *some sort* of company, exporting undetermined goods. Whatever this work is, it keeps Stolz sufficiently busy that he never seems to pause long enough for the narrator to describe much of anything in his life.

The novel thus seems to have solved one problem and run into another. On the one hand, in Pushkin's story, Germann's refusal to devote his life to work was the very condition of narrative. Now, twenty-five years later, Stolz, who does nothing but work, appears as a positive example, as a path toward progress for Russia. But his devotion to this ceaseless activity is precisely the reason that many readers have found him flat and unmemorable. Tellingly, Dostoevsky forgot Stolz's name in a letter to Apollon Maikov in which he formulated his plan for the largely unrealized *Life of a Great Sinner*.[96] Dostoevsky goes through the old list of mostly unsuccessful positive heroes before he offers his own proposal: "No sir, this won't be Kostanzhoglo, nor the German (I forget his surname) from *Oblomov*, nor a Lopukhov, nor a Rakhmetov."[97] Stolz's work, which results in the mostly uneventful accumulation of wealth, remains outside the narrative of Goncharov's novel, which offers only the briefest sketch of what his day-to-day life must be like. It seems that this life, like the "some sort of company" that Stolz is involved in, is simply not interesting enough—certainly not as interesting as Oblomov's intensively described inactivity. In his famous article "What is Oblomovshchina?," Nikolai Dobroliubov likens the privileged Oblomov, somewhat incongruously, to a person who has climbed high up in a tree while his comrades struggle to make progress through the swampy terrain below.[98] The man in the tree may see farther, but now, claims Dobroliubov, the time has come to get down from the tree and get to work. Even if this is the case, it appears that, for literary representation, the perceptive and sensitive tree-dweller would become far less interesting if he were to give up his perch and join in the labor of building up society.

Nevertheless, businessmen and entrepreneurs proliferate in the following years and decades, even if they usually appear as harmful symptoms of social decay rather than promises of future progress. In Dostoevsky's *The Idiot*, the self-made Epanchin will own "some sort of factory," the successor to Stolz's "some sort of company." For much of the coming period, it remained difficult for characters devoted single-mindedly to business to become protagonists. One reason for this may be that the temporality of capitalist accumulation is itself antithetical to the kind of narrative development that the protagonist of a typical nineteenth-century novel has to undergo. What Franco Moretti writes about the unsuitability of business as a career for the protagonist of the classical bildungsroman is generally true for the nineteenth-century novel: "Capital, due to its purely quantitative nature, and the competition it is subject to, can be a fortune only in so far as it *keeps growing*." As a result, "the merchant's journey can never come to a conclusion in those ideal places . . . where everything is 'well-being, transparency and concreteness.'"[99] As we will see, in some works of Russian realism, such as *The Idiot*, the merchants, when they are distinguished from capitalists, never start out on journeys at all. But Moretti is evidently right that the life of the literary capitalist seems to be locked into the perpetual motion of capital itself. Perhaps that is one reason that, in the novels of Boborykin, where the economic transformation of Russia is often a central preoccupation, protagonists tend to be less vibrant than the exactingly described marketplaces and banks they frequent. In the novel *Kitai-Gorod*, the erstwhile protagonist Paltusov vows to avenge the declining nobility by going to war "against the merchant money bag."[100] In the end, however, all his plans for reasserting the economic power of his estate end with him embezzling some merchant funds. The crime and subsequent trial receive minimal narrative attention—certainly far less than the lavish, perhaps excessive, descriptions of Moscow's commercial center, for which Boborykin earned comparisons with Émile Zola.[101] It seems that, where capitalists predominate, the balance of novelistic description and narration fails.

The tendency of a capitalist's life to collapse into his work reaches its absurd culmination in Mikhail Saltykov-Shchedrin's satirical novel *A Contemporary Idyll* (1877–83). There, in one of the book's many interpolated texts, we encounter the autobiography (*zhizneopisanie*) of a certain Onufry Paramonov, a merchant of the first guild (that is, one of the wealthiest merchants). This autobiography turns out to be nothing more than a balance sheet, which lists, in three columns, a brief description of each transaction (life event), the cost in rubles, and the remainder of the cost in kopeks, respectively. As we follow the entries, which amount primarily to a list of ever-larger bribes and self-serving charitable contributions, we "read" the major events of Paramonov's life and his participation in key events of Russian history, such as when he pays an enormous sum in the service of *potriatizm* (*sic*) in 1877 (the beginning of yet another Russo-Turkish War). In one series of transactions, we follow the merchant on a journey from Saint Petersburg to Moscow and back, during which he visits many of the same places as Aleksandr Radishchev had passed through in his *Journey from Saint Petersburg to Moscow* nearly one hundred years earlier.[102] However, while Radishchev's various stops had given occasion for him to reflect on the corruption of Russian society and the injustices perpetrated by the state and the system of serfdom, Paramonov's travels are motivated by a desire to outrun government officials pursuing him for embezzlement. Each location is marked by an expense, from a large sum paid in Moscow to avoid being sent to Siberia, to a much smaller amount paid to a coachman in Krestsy to take the back alleys. At the end of his life's story, Paramonov draws up the balance. His life has amounted to expenditures of 1,167,465.77 rubles in silver and 15,475.40 in paper. Paramonov's collocutor is impressed by both the neatness of the conclusion and the apparently low cost of doing business in Russia: "Not one kopek more or less—a whole life in the palm of your hand [*kak na ladoni*]! And truly, it didn't cost that much!"[103]

A whole life in the palm of your hand: a merchant's life is so thoroughly defined by his "work" that it ultimately amounts to a sum of expenses paid. But at least, in this case, Paramonov's ludicrous criminality makes him stand out. That is to say, in the course of his life he actually *did things*—at any rate, things that are distinctive enough to merit mention in a work of literature. On the other hand, Paramonov's more restrained colleagues, characters in less implacably oppositional novels, do not even have their outsized malfeasance as a claim to narrative attention. In the lives of these capitalists, nothing *interesting* happens, insofar as the interesting would constitute an interruption of the normal course of business. A biography of a successful businessman like Totsky in *The Idiot* could boil down to one activity, repeated ad infinitum: "made money." Indeed, what Totsky fears is the exposure of the one biographical event of which we are made aware: his rape of the adolescent Nastasia Filippovna. At the very moment when it seems like a scandal might erupt, he quietly makes his exit from the novel while spectacular money distracts everyone else present.[104] Yet the postreform novel can no longer leave these characters out of the story. On the contrary, as subsequent chapters will examine, both the capitalists and the often terrifying and inscrutable material world that they will create become increasingly important in shaping the narrative forms, epistemological boundaries, and metaphysical stakes of Russian realism.

THE STRUCTURE OF THE ARGUMENT

The argument of *Russia's Capitalist Realism* proceeds by way of several exemplary works of literature, each of which poses the problems of representing incipient and uneven Russian capitalism in ways that are particularly illuminating. The book's five chapters follow a loose chronological organization. However, in accordance with my claim that the economic imagination of Russian realism readily combined anticipations of the future, reflections on the present, and reconsiderations of the past, I have opted for a structure that sometimes privileges thematic coherence over chronology.

Chapter 1, "Industrial Labor and the Limits of Realism," sets the stage for the more localized analyses of subsequent chapters by ranging over the entire period under examination with one set of objects in focus: the mills and factories that appeared sporadically in Russian literature between the 1850s and the 1890s. These markers of a terrifying and disorienting modernity tend to strike characters encountering them as jarringly new and out of harmony with the social and physical landscapes around them. In order to represent the alienness of industry, fiction writers developed a remarkably consistent poetics of the factory, which adapted preexisting devices and developed these into a set of conventions for the literary representation of the factory's peculiar combination of terror and boredom.

The overwhelming sensory assault of the factory, before which realist description breaks down, provides comparative context for the utterly different representation of agricultural labor in chapter 2, "The Economies of *Anna Karenina*." This chapter examines the famously troublesome narrative form of *Anna Karenina*—a novel split into two stories, Anna's and Levin's, with almost no diegetic connections between them—with a focus on the novel's engagement with Russia's social and economic transformation. The narrative form of *Anna Karenina* models Levin's economic theory with its desynchronized double plots, one (Anna's) driven relentlessly forward by industrialization, the other (Levin's own) preserved by the rhythms of traditional agriculture. The irreconcilable divide between these two plotlines is most apparent in contrasting sets of peasants: on the one hand, the monstrous being, referred to as a little peasant (*muzhichok*) but coded as an embodiment of destructive industrialization, who haunts Anna's portion of the novel, and, on the other, the idealized peasants who labor in perfect sync on Levin's estate. The mowing scene that takes place there emerges as a focal point of the novel's resistance to modernity. This moment contains what is probably the most famous scene of labor in all of nineteenth-century Russian literature—one which is simultaneously capable of synchronizing description and narration and holding together the old social order of nobility and peasantry in the face of threatening socioeconomic change.

Whereas the first two chapters are concerned primarily with the descriptive and narrative means by which Russian realism accommodated new configurations of industrialized space and time, the following two chapters investigate the enormous significance of historically variable forms of money in two novels by Dostoevsky. In *The Idiot* and *The Brothers Karamazov*, money is not merely one theme among others but a decisive influence on narrative form. Chapter 3, "Myshkin among the Merchants: Forms of Money and Narrative Form in *The Idiot*," complicates the traditional view that Prince Myshkin is an isolated and otherworldly figure temporarily stranded in a corrupt and acquisitive Saint Petersburg. On the contrary, this chapter argues that Myshkin, like his fellow characters, is embedded in a novelized money economy undergoing an uneven transition to capitalism. Within this economic imaginary, two radically divergent conceptions of money are linked to two groups of rich characters, who in turn correspond to residual and emergent social groups: vivid merchants (whose primary representative is Rogozhin, but to whom Myshkin is also related through his mother) and faceless capitalists (Totsky and Epanchin). Whereas the merchants and their money are maximally dramatic and interesting, the capitalists are as indistinct as their money is invisible. When, at the end of the novel, the capitalists have vanquished the merchants, the novel enters a new age of invisibly circulating capital and a temporality of incremental accumulation, in which the kinds of events that could support novelistic narration have become impossible. The spread of capitalism thus appears to pose a fundamental problem for realist narrative.

Chapter 4, "Heterogeneous Money in *The Brothers Karamazov*," turns to Dostoevsky's final novel. This work may seem like a step into the past, with its small-town setting and the centrality of religious questions, but the spatial constraints of Skotoprigonevsk channel the money economy into the theological realm. Ubiquitous money threatens to put a price on everything the novel can put into words. The figure of 3,000 rubles introduces the possibility of equivalence among an extraordinarily diverse selection of people, relationships, and things. However, money turns out to be heterogeneous, unequal to itself, and thus incapable of quantifying value. Monetary rhetoric also threatens to engulf the novel's theological concerns, but in its very profusion, it generates an alternative vision of unpayable debts and incalculable values.

The different strategies for giving narrative form to capitalism in the works examined in the first four chapters find a kind of summation at the end of the century in the works of Anton Chekhov, the focus of chapter 5, "Chekhov and the Naturalization of Capitalism." Taking Chekhov's contemporary critics at their word, that is, that Chekhov's distinctive narrative forms and epistemic murkiness are indeed symptomatic of changes in the literature and culture of the end of the century, I examine how several of his works respond to the accelerating industrialization of the 1890s. This chapter's particular focus is how, within these short, seemingly fragmentary works, agency tends to shift away from characters and to the institutions and infrastructure of Russian industrial capitalism. On the levels of narrative and even grammar, things carry out their mysterious operations, while people, even nominal property owners, respond with confusion or dread to the factories and businesses that surround them. Chekhov is able to reincorporate capitalists into the narrative—but only by driving a wedge between them and their factories and businesses, which they no longer understand or control. Chekhov's stories remain reticent regarding a final evaluation of the economic transformation that is so central to many of them. This is, in part, a matter of genre: whereas the totalizing form of the novel enabled Tolstoy and Dostoevsky to either synthesize an economic whole or model the impossibility of such a synthesis, Chekhov's shorter narrative forms instantiate the perspective of people struggling to orient themselves in the modern world's complexity. Thus, precisely when it becomes possible to analyze economic change with the aid of concepts like "capitalism," Chekhov's works turn insistently to the subjective experience of an increasingly alienated world in which the capitalists have gone from being difficult objects of representation to subjects as lost in the modern world as the older social groups they have superseded.

As this overview of the book's structure and argument makes clear, this study does not aim at a comprehensive survey of Russian literary representations of economic life. The vastness of the topic necessitated reducing both the corpus of primary texts and the range of perspectives from which they could be examined productively. *Russia's Capitalist Realism* rests on an interdisciplinary foundation, and I have tried to adjust for the architectonic complications that such a structure entails. This book is closest thematically to economic criticism—a vast scholarly literature, particularly in British literary studies, but growing in Russian and Slavic studies as well. With respect to nineteenth-century Russian literature, economic criticism encompasses literary analysis; the study of Russian print culture, its audiences, and institutions; social and cultural history; cultural theory; and, sometimes turning the tables, the importance of literature for economics.[105] In terms of interpretive strategy, this book is broadly aligned with those studies that examine how literature registers and responds to historical change formally, whether on the level of the entire narrative or more localized textual operations.[106]

Considerations of space and coherence drove my decision not to include chapters on several important writers from this period. In particular, the works of Ivan Goncharov offer particularly vivid narrative responses to the collision of a gentry-focused realist aesthetic with a new, and only partially assimilated, world of capitalist relations. Since excellent recent studies have examined this aspect of Goncharov's work, I have chosen to devote more attention to other writers whose engagement with capitalism has not been treated as explicitly or extensively in the scholarship.[107] Likewise, Aleksandr Ostrovsky, the leading dramatist of Russia's commercial life, did not make it into this book. In this case, the deciding factor was genre. Given my interest in the effects of distinctly capitalist forms of space and time on the narrative form of Russian realist prose fiction, Ostrovsky's dramas, although eminently deserving of study, had to be left out for the sake of cohesion. Beyond these major figures, a multitude of lesser-known writers wrote a vast amount of fiction about Russia's economic and social transformation. I consider selected works of some of these writers, like Reshetnikov, Boborykin, and Mamin-Sibiriak, at various points in following chapters. However, a number of other works, such as Pavel Melnikov-Pechersky's colossal novels about the Volga merchants, *In the Forests* and *On the Hills* (1871–81), Vladimir Nemirovich-Danchenko's *Tsars of the Stock Exchange* (1884), a novel about the excesses of postreform Russian finance, and Aleksandr Ertel's *The Gardenin Family* (1889), which depicts economic change in the Russian countryside, had to be left out. My major aim has been to show, primarily on the basis of a small set of carefully chosen examples examined in detail, how we can gain new understanding of the classics of Russian realism by going beyond the recognition that they rejected capitalist modernity. A careful consideration of the particular details of that rejection, and the accommodations that it forced writers to make, can help us understand why readers continue to turn to these works, even—or perhaps especially—in our own age, when the only limit to capitalism appears to be the carrying capacity of the planet.

The following chapters will trace both the workings of narrative and the impasses that narrative encountered as it attempted to assimilate the often recalcitrant objects of industrial modernity and the abstractions of financial calculation into the form of the novel. In the process, *Russia's Capitalist Realism* aims to reveal the diverse ways in which Russian literature confronted capitalism as something far greater than a matter of economics in the narrow, modern sense. In this respect, Russia's relative underdevelopment may well have intensified the perceived stakes, as the wide gap between what Russia was in the mid-nineteenth century and what it might become revealed the potential impermanence of virtually every category of experience. Even the institutional basis of Russian literature may have contributed to this future-oriented perspective: as Jonathan Paine has observed, Russian publishers adopted French strategies of mass-market appeal without (yet) having the corresponding readership.[108] The experience of backwardness provided Russian thinkers with a vantage point into the future, which seemed already present in the countries to the West. Semi-European Russians, residing on the semiperiphery of industrial Europe, turned the representational resources of realism, a semidomesticated literary tradition, to the task of thinking through this ambiguous historical position—one fraught with uncertainty but also enormously rich in imaginative potential.

Industrial Labor and the Limits of Realism

> Before me, rolled out like some long Eastern
> manuscript, lay stretched one continuous
> length of iron frame-work—multitudinous and
> mystical, with all sorts of rollers, wheels, and
> cylinders, in slowly-measured and unceasing
> motion.
> —Herman Melville, "The Paradise of Bachelors
> and the Tartarus of Maids"

THE INSCRUTABLE FACTORY

A nineteenth-century iron foundry must have been an overwhelming sight. "It produces such a strong impression upon an inexperienced person that you truly marvel how working people could get used to such an environment," recounts the journalist and publisher N. A. Blagoveshchensky in an 1873 sketch.[1] He goes on to describe the foundry's cavernous interior, where a "chaos of movement" takes place in the gloom of a few gas lamps and the fiery glow of the furnaces (6). Against this dim light, silhouettes of workers rush about the narrow passageways, dodging carts carrying chunks of glowing-hot metal. In the center of the building stands a massive steam engine whose colossal fly-wheel sets all the other machines in motion. "All of this thunders, pounds, and sends sparks flying" (6). Somehow, the workers have managed to get used to this environment, with its deafening machines and infernally glowing furnaces. While Blagoveshchensky marvels at the work, he realizes that the workers themselves take it all for granted. For them, he observes, fire has become as commonplace an element as air and water. He notes how the kinds of feats that astound villagers when performed by a traveling strongman are here regarded as relatively easy work, which men perform for twelve hours a day (13). The aim of Blagoveshchensky's sketch, which was published in Nekrasov's *Notes of the Fatherland*, was to draw readers' attention to inhumane working conditions in Russian factories. In order to do so, he described the terrifying impression that the foundry produced on the uninitiated visitor while also pointing out that the workers had become habituated even to this extreme environment.

Blagoveshchensky's sketch constantly emphasizes the different experiences of the uninitiated foundry visitor and the worker who has long grown used to his labor. The visitor on a tour of the foundry is likely to be overwhelmed and frightened, while the worker has become adapted to darkness, heat, and unremitting noise. Most nineteenth-century Russian literary treatments of the factory would foreground the perspective of a newcomer in order to emphasize this difference of perspectives. Indeed, one could say that the primary content of such scenes in Russian realist fiction is the impression that the factory produces on an observer, who is, more often than not, unfamiliar and overwhelmed by what he or she sees, and this reaction tends to overshadow the factory itself. Again and again in fictional works from the 1850s to the 1890s, a character will walk into a factory and witness a chaos of events so overwhelming that this observer, irrespective of his or her social status, political views, or relationship to Russian capitalism and industry, will experience a kind of sensory disintegration. Furthermore, the reader's access to the factory interior will be mediated by this overwhelmed observer's subjective experience, for which the complex operations of the factory will dissolve into incomprehensible noises, frightening flashes of movement, and fragments of rushing human bodies.

This chapter examines how realist fiction responded to both the observable facts and the anticipation of Russian industrial development by turning the factory into an object of literary representation. This process was conditioned by both politics and poetics. Perhaps no other site of labor was so rich in ideological ramifications in the late nineteenth century, given the decades of debates about the possibility or desirability of industrialization in Russia. At the same time, the factory presented special problems for realist narration and description, which are apparent in the various fleeting glimpses of the factory interior scattered throughout the literature of the period. Over the course of half a century, a relatively stable set of representational conventions developed around the factory. These tended to emphasize the alienness of the factory and the inscrutability of what went on within its walls, as well as the difficulty of capturing its meaning in the individual experience of any perceiving subject.

The typical factory scene is not, primarily, a scene of factory labor (although, as I discuss below, the factory's connection to manual labor contributes to its representational complexity). The rigorous narrative focalization through the consciousness of a single character that distinguishes nearly all these scenes means that the workers in the factory are either swallowed up, from the observer's standpoint, by the multitude of overwhelming details or, more rarely, simply overlooked by the experienced eye of the technician.[2] What generally comes into focus in these scenes is, rather, the complex process of mediation by which the factory makes its way into the realist narrative.

The different approaches to the problem of representing the factory examined in this chapter range from techniques approaching Shklovskian defamiliarization, where an observer's untrained eye and ear perceive a chaos of incoherent mechanical operations, to departures from a neutral narrative style in favor of retellings in nonnormative peasant speech. What we do not find is anything like the cohesive, encompassing descriptions that are so typical of the realist representation of all manner of other things, such as faces, rooms, meals, high society balls, and agricultural labor. Indeed, the impression that emerges from Russian literature's factory scenes is that the delicate machinery of realist representation starts to break down when confronted by these looms and furnaces, which dimly outline an economic system that is increasingly difficult to register empirically, whether in its local intricacy or on its global scale.

In other words, the factory scenes of Russian realism demonstrate one facet of a larger problem facing realist writers trying to represent different parts of a system that combined, to borrow Elaine Scarry's formulation, "the problematically abstract and the problematically concrete."[3] The excessive concreteness of the factory's sheer terrifying massiveness, together with the inscrutability of its technical details and the larger networks of production, exchange, and consumption of which it was necessarily a part, made for an awkward mismatch between the factory and available conventions of narration and description. Factories fit poorly into the experiences of the characters who encounter them for the first time and into the larger narrative forms in which they appear.

This and the following chapter will situate the factory in relation to several related types of scenes: on the one hand, predecessors to the factory scene, notably the government office, and, on the other, scenes of nonindustrial labor. There is a discernible line of development from Gogol's presentation of the inner workings of a provincial government chancellery to several of the key conventions of future factory scenes. As for the relationship between factory and manual labor, key scenes in Reshetnikov's *Where Is it Better?* (in this chapter) and Tolstoy's *Anna Karenina* (in the next) will clarify what the factory descriptions do not do. In both these novels, the description of manual labor achieves multiple balances—between movement and observation, the human body and its environment, narration and description—that are noticeably absent in Russian literature's factory scenes. In Tolstoy's novel in particular, agricultural manual labor manages to synchronize the movement of Russian history, the rhythms of labor, and the capacities of the human perceptual apparatus in such a way as to allow workers (and Levin in particular) to pause, take in their surroundings, appreciate the sensations of the natural world, and make visible progress in their work. In sum, Levin's mowing scene makes noncapitalist agricultural labor beautiful. On the other hand, the experience of the factory, whether focalized through the terrified newcomer or unremarked by the jaded technician, reveal the twin poles toward which representations of capitalism in Russian realism tended: either capitalism was monotonous and therefore difficult to narrate, or it was frightening and therefore difficult to describe.

THE PROBLEM OF LABOR IN THE NOVEL

Factory scenes are not primarily concerned with the representation of workers or their labor, but as a necessary condition for the factory's operation, labor is nevertheless always present in these scenes. The importance of labor in these places poses a problem because, as numerous scholars have pointed out, works of narrative fiction, including realist novels, tend not to afford the same kind of attention to labor as to other kinds of human activity. It is hard to disagree with Michael Denning's assessment that "it is a commonplace to note our reluctance to represent work in our popular stories. A Martian who hijacked the stock of the average video store would reasonably conclude that humans spent far more of their time engaged in sex than in work."[4] Admittedly, it would be uncharitable to fault realism for not modeling its distribution of fictional time on the proportions of typical human lives. Indeed, much of the work that characters implicitly carry out in realist fictions disappears below the "threshold of the functionally relevant," as Stephen Heath terms the boundary that "divides the narratable from the non-narratable, sequences below which are taken-for-granted."[5] However, even in the general context of nineteenth-century literature, Russian literature is particularly well-known for its nonworkers. Its most memorable protagonists include various categories of inactive men—both superfluous and underground— that overlap with groups of dreamers and sufferers of chronic Oblomovitis. These characters inhabit a world where, in Edward Wasiolek's evocative summation, "a veritable cauldron of speculation, dreams, and mental energy pours out of those lying in bed, guzzling champagne, slobbering at dinner parties, and vegetating in provincial towns, as if the Russians did not inhabit the world their feet were stuck in."[6] Turgenev's indecisive heroes and Dostoevsky's inveterate talkers have made the Russian realist novel famous for its intensity of thought and speech—an intensity often understood in relation to the proportionally attenuated capacity of Russian literary characters for social action, which is both a theme in many novels and often regarded as an element of the political life of the subjects of Russian autocracy.

To be sure, it is important not to exaggerate the extent to which such inactive characters define Russian realism. For every Oblomov there is a Zakhar who makes his idleness possible, as well as a host of more minor characters—whom Alex Woloch has called "the proletariat of the novel"—who do all sorts of work, both to drive the *siuzhet* forward and to produce the density of the *fabula*'s details.[7] As I noted in the introduction, Raskolnikov is surrounded by people who work, most of them women, and several working women make it possible for him to cogitate by sending him money, bringing him food, and allowing his unpaid rent to accumulate. Furthermore, many of Russian literature's plots do indeed focus on more active characters. In this respect, Jillian Porter's work offers an important corrective to the impression that Russian literature is filled with idlers by reminding us of the importance of the "ambition plot" from Pushkin to Dostoevsky. In the realist period, professionally and economically ambitious protagonists continue to appear, albeit not very often—for example, in Aleksei Pisemsky's *One Thousand Souls* (1859). However, the men of ambition whom Porter examines (or Pisemsky's Kalinovich, for that matter) rarely perform the kind of time-consuming, repetitive labor that I have in mind here. That kind of activity tends to be relegated to characters who are rarely the focus of a narrative.

Indeed, labor can be difficult to find even where we might most expect it. Take, for example, Nikolai Chernyshevsky's *What Is to Be Done?*: in one of the novel's main episodes, the female protagonist, Vera Pavlovna, decides to set up a sewing workshop in which workers will receive an equal share of the profits. As an illustration of how to reconcile rational egoism with economic justice, the workshop, voluntarily organized by Vera Pavlovna on account of her "passion" (*pristrastie*) to do so, was one of the most important ideas of the novel for contemporary readers.[8] Pisarev rated the workshop as "perhaps the most important section in the whole novel."[9] What is striking about Pisarev's assessment is that he writes that it is precisely the "description" (*opisanie*) of the workshop that is so important. Clearly, what Pisarev has in mind here is Chernyshevsky's description of the principles of the workshop's profit-sharing scheme. As for the material details of the workshop's day-to-day existence, the novel's narrator admits that he is only noting the most general features and that his main interest lies in the characterization of Vera Pavlovna. "I choose to omit many details here, because I'm not really describing [*opisyvaiu*] the workshop, merely mentioning it insofar as it's necessary to characterize Vera Pavlovna's activity."[10] Chernyshevsky is almost apologetic about his discussion of the workshop and repeatedly informs the reader of what it is *not* necessary to talk about, as if it would be unliterary to dwell on the workshop's actual work. "The basic principles were simple, in fact so simple in the beginning that there really isn't much to be said about them"; "Nor was there anything special"; "All of this can be portrayed in words very quickly; and even in reality it all seemed very easy, simple, and natural once it was established."[11] Even in this novel, where the practical elaboration of a materialist anthropology in the service of socialist ends is of central importance, the labor on which the exemplary workshop is based is omitted in favor of characterizing Vera Pavlovna and her ideas.

If we broaden the perspective in which we consider the Russian novel's reticence about labor, we can see that, in this regard, Russian literature is not anomalous. A number of readers of nineteenth-century British novels have noted that there, too, labor and laborers receive proportionally little attention. As much as readers associate Charles Dickens with the travails of the urban working poor, George Orwell complained that the working class was actually rather hard to find in his novels. "If you ask any ordinary reader which of Dickens's proletarian characters he can remember, the three he is almost certain to mention are Bill Sykes, Sam Weller, and Mrs. Gamp. A burglar, a valet, and a drunken midwife—not exactly a representative cross-section of the English working class."[12] Going beyond Dickens, Caroline Lesjak has encouraged us to "recognize that labor is *always hard to see* in the novel—even in the industrial novel."[13] In Lesjak's account, British industrial novelists like Elizabeth Gaskell turned away from the problems posed by the political and social condition of laborers, which could not be examined without confronting the possibility of revolutionary violence, and instead focused on domestic concerns, "which can be resolved in a way that the problems of labor cannot."[14] Raymond Williams concluded that the predominant attitude of the writers of British industrial novels combined sympathy for the working class with "fear of becoming involved."[15] Evidently, the political implications of representing labor presented a challenge to British literature in the context of a society that had largely managed to avoid violent continental upheavals like the revolutions of 1848.

Political considerations notwithstanding, even novelists who wanted to focus on labor faced the problem that, on the level of novelistic poetics, labor constitutes a particularly complex object of representation. Scarry observes that the repetitiousness of labor—"it is the essential nature of work to be perpetual, repetitive, habitual"—challenges the temporal boundaries of literary form: "To take one arbitrary segment of it, a 'typical eight-hour stretch' for example, is to falsify it precisely because it is in its repetitions that it is what it is—it can no more be represented by one segment of itself than the rhythm or rhyme of poetry can be indicated by the recitation of a single word."[16] Since an arbitrary segment of the work process would necessarily offer a false sense of the process as a whole, nineteenth-century writers arrived at two solutions: "subdivide the activity of work not into temporal units but into task-units," or focus on revealing ruptures in the work process, "moments when there is a tear or lapse in the activity that must be repaired, replaced, or rescued."[17] These reflections on the poetics of labor apply to the activity of a preindustrial weaver or farmer as well as to a factory worker or miner (it would thus appear that Russian writers discovered different representational affordances in manual labor than the French and British novelists Scarry examines). However, one of the writers she singles out for offering a solution to this problem is Zola, who turned his attention to the historically salient specifics of industrial labor in France during the Second Empire (1852–70).

Indeed, it is difficult to find another body of work in nineteenth-century literature that offers an analysis of labor in as much detail—and in as many settings—as Zola's twenty-volume *Rougon-Macquart* series.[18] In these books, complex industrial and social machines are not merely described; they become, for the typical Zola novel, "its dynamic principle, that force which motors the plot."[19] For example, *Germinal* (1885), Zola's great novel of coal mining in northern France in the 1860s, provides a revealing contrast to the factory scenes in Russian literature. The central location of the novel is the coal-mining pit of Le Voreux, and the narrator of *Germinal* describes the mine extensively, both from the point of view of an inexperienced worker, like Etienne at the beginning of the novel, and from the informed perspective of someone (like Zola himself) who studied the mines in detail. Thus, early in the novel, when Etienne enters the mine on his first day of work, the mysterious operations of the machinery overwhelm him in a way similar to what we find in numerous Russian novels. Machines move all around him, "without Etienne gaining any idea how these complex maneuvers were achieved."[20] However, over time he will learn much more about the workings of the mine, and the reader, after hundreds of pages, also gains a far more detailed sense of what is happening in this colossal machine. Descriptions of the hellish working conditions inside the mine, with its stifling heat and cramped passages, constitute significant portions of the novel, while the narrative covers both the operation of the mine under ordinary conditions and in an emergency, after the Russian anarchist Souvarine sabotages the mine shaft and causes a catastrophic collapse. By contrast, Russian realist fiction would only offer fleeting glimpses of the factory up until the late 1890s, when works such as Aleksandr Kuprin's *Molokh* would make the sites of industrial production the setting of an extended narrative. For decades before that, factories in Russian literature would interrupt narration and overwhelm description rather than constitute a setting in their own right.

FINDING THE FACTORY

The factories of Russian literature are not always easy to find, since they are often relegated to the margins of imaginary topographies.[21] As Julie Buckler has observed in the case of Saint Petersburg, the industrial infrastructure that encircled the wealthier parts of the city was peripheral in the Petersburg text as much as in the physical city.[22] The representational challenges presented by the industrial areas of the city seemed to expose the limits of the available narrative forms and perspectives of Russian literature, since the factory did not lend itself either to the physiological sketch, with its focus on the plight of the poor individual, or to forms celebrating the grandeur of the imperial capital. "Both pathos and patriotism prove inadequate tonalities for treating this unfamiliar subject, which seems similarly intractable within the available Russian literary forms of sketch, distended novel, and civic verse."[23] Even the investigations of the Russian Natural School of the mid-1840s, which purported to offer the reading public rigorously objective accounts of the squalid lives of the city's poor, did not venture into the factories. In numerous works of Russian realism, factories remain outside the narrative. They play a role in the plot, generating profits for their owners or providing necessary experiences for those who visit them, but they tend to remain *somewhere else*, like Epanchin's factory in *The Idiot*.

One reason for this reticence about the factory probably stems from the instability of certain key elements of the discourse about industrialization, such as the concept of a Russian industrial working class. Both in terms of their actual position in Russian society and in their treatment in literature, industrial workers were a mutable category. Throughout the late nineteenth century, the majority of Russian industrial laborers retained close personal ties to the villages from which they came. One of the major considerations that led to the Russian state's decision to emancipate the serfs with land was that failing to do so would lead to the creation of a politically volatile proletariat.[24] As the population of the Russian peasantry swelled in the later decades of the century and it became ever harder to earn enough from agriculture to pay burdensome taxes and redemption payments, large numbers of peasants began to practice what was known as *otkhod*, leaving their villages seasonally to look for wage labor.[25] The Russian worker's connection to the land became a particularly important ideologeme in public discourse, and its traces are visible, for example, in Levin's insistence in *Anna Karenina* that the abstract calculations of Western political economy do not pertain to the Russian peasantry, with its special relationship to the land. Even as industrialization intensified toward the end of the century, periodicals were filled with voices calling for policies to arrest the growth of a Russian proletariat.[26] Even Sergei Witte, the future finance and transport minister under Alexander III, whom contemporaries would remember as "the creator of state capitalism in Russia" for his role in financing the expansion of the Russian railroad network, was initially no advocate of large-scale industrialization.[27] In 1885, before the start of his government career, Witte published an article in Ivan Aksakov's newspaper, *Rus'*, titled "The Serfdom of Manufactures." Witte argued that if the Russian state hoped to prevent the consolidation of a political threat from the "millions of machine-people . . . now joined together not by an artistic, or religious [*veruiushchei*], but by a destructive idea," it would have to ensure that each worker retained ownership of a plot of land large enough to support him and his household.[28] At the time that Witte's article appeared, these "machine-people" were less likely to appear in literature as a united and dangerous proletariat than as disturbing glimpses at the edges of awareness and as pieces of larger and even more frightening machines.

Debates raged in newspapers and journals about the possibility of industrial capitalism in Russia well into the 1880s. Some, like the *narodnik* economist Vorontsov, argued that a backward country like Russia would not be able to follow the developmental path of the Western countries and that its version of capitalism, no matter how well supported by the state, would be malformed. "Not having the opportunity to develop in the way that the nature of capitalism demands, the latter, having appeared, must remain a guest, dragged in almost by force, feeling itself not at home and therefore incapable of exerting that great influence on all spheres of life, which it had in the country of its natural conception and flourishing."[29] Nevertheless, industrialization was proceeding, if haltingly. For the International Centennial Exhibition, held in Philadelphia in 1876, Russia contributed hundreds of exhibits. The catalogue of the Russian section lists dozens of factories and plants that exhibited their products, together with information about the number of workers employed and the output of their steam engines, measured in horsepower. These industrial goods demonstrated Russia's accomplishments alongside the paintings of Ivan Aivazovsky and Vasily Vereshchagin.[30] While arguments about the possibility or desirability of industrialization raged in the press, its real expansion was becoming increasingly apparent throughout the empire.

In this discursive context, when virtually everything pertaining to capitalism and industrialization was subject to debate, it is not surprising that the representation of the factory would be particularly fraught. When it comes to literary treatments of factories, these political ramifications would be modified and mediated by existing techniques of representation. The tendency of fictional works to filter their descriptions of the factory interior through the terrified and overwhelmed observer was a literary convention. In the same period, other genres offered entirely different ways of writing about the factory. A good example is I. I. Kolyshko's travelogue *Sketches of Contemporary Russia*, published in 1887. In one section, the young traveler has occasion to visit a large calico mill in Tver' *guberniia*. This mill, notes Kolyshko, is notable both for its extraordinary scale—he observes that it "should be counted among the most gigantic factories not only of Russia, but of Europe as well"—and for its state-of-the-art manufacturing techniques.[31] Kolyshko and his traveling companion arrange a tour of the whole mill complex with the interim manager. From the very beginning of the tour, everything about the mill impresses Kolyshko by its orderliness and attractiveness, from the outbuildings neatly surrounded by wooden fences to the pleasing appearance of the young manager. Over the following pages, the travelers tour the interior of the factory, and the manager provides detailed information about all of the machines and their functions in the manufacturing process. We are treated to extensive descriptions of the various spinning and weaving equipment, the kinds of threads and textiles they work with, and the impressive quality of these Russian manufactures compared to those of other countries. We also learn about the mill's integration into the global economy: it receives the majority of its cotton from the United States, and it imports its machines from England, but these will soon be manufactured in the mill's own workshop. Its calico is so highly regarded that manufacturers in Manchester counterfeit this mill's trademark to sell their textiles in Asia.

We learn of these operations in the abstract. The descriptions are full of terminology provided by the manager, and it is this that we read, rather than the presumably less informed observations of Kolyshko himself. The impression that this account produces, despite the evident pride its author takes in the quality of Russian manufactures, is decidedly dry. Kolyshko explains how the various processes work primarily via third-person reflexive verbs, as if the machines carry out the work on their own. A reviewer of the travelogue in the journal *The Cause* (Delo) complained that Kolyshko seemed to have seen everything, save for one triviality: the workers, many of them children, who operated these machines.[32]

Factory workers likewise play a very limited role in literary scenes that feature factories. In contrast to Kolyshko's sketch, however, these scenes also lack the calm enumeration of technical details. Instead, it is the space of the factory interior itself, as experienced by an observer unfamiliar with such spaces, that is the primary object of representation in literary scenes of the factory. Over the course of half a century, characters would repeatedly experience the terrifying otherness of the factory, an environment seemingly out of place in the Russian landscape and whose meaning and etiology were often impossible to explain.

FROM GOGOL'S OFFICE TO TURGENEV'S MILL: SERIAL DESCRIPTION AND *SKAZ* NARRATION

For most of the second half of the nineteenth century, descriptions of the factory in works of literature remained both consistent with each other and distinct from ostensibly nonfictional accounts of factories. Even as other genres, such as the works of reportage or travel writing by Blagoveshchensky and Kolyshko discussed above, provided readers with considerably more detailed information about Russia's industrial plants, imaginative literature continued to emphasize characters' inability to extract any meaningful information from the factory interior. By the early 1850s, the major conventions of the literary representation of the factory were in place, in particular the mediating function of a particular character's consciousness (and, occasionally, that character's own words, conveyed as *skaz* narration). The prevailing internal focalization of these scenes motivates the chaotic seriality of their description. The peasant who has just wandered into the cavernous interior of the factory cannot make sense of what she sees, so the reader gets an itemization of strange and disturbing sense impressions rather than a detailed technical report from a manager or engineer. This serial description should not be regarded merely as a failure to integrate the factory into the register of established locations in Russian realist fiction, such as the peasant hut, the gentry estate, and the big city. Rather, as Scarry observes about labor in general, the factory presented a particular challenge: the work that took place within was unceasing and difficult to visualize. A static description—or a literary daguerreotype, to borrow the popular midcentury metaphor—would not capture the key feature of this environment: its constant but rigidly circumscribed activity. That this activity took place in an interior that was itself historically novel and unfamiliar to most readers added to the difficulty. The bewildered observer, staring uncomprehendingly as machines roar while workers dart around them, could at least convey the sheer strangeness of this environment for which an adequate language did not yet exist.

Fortunately, the Russian literary tradition supplied some techniques that could be adapted to the representation of such an environment. In particular, another busy interior that had recently entered Russian literature could serve as a model for the factory: the paper machine of government bureaucracy. Scribbling civil servants had been performing monotonous and often inscrutable work since the early 1840s in the service of vast systems for organizing human activity. The central figure in the literary history of the bureaucratic scribe is, of course, Gogol, and it is in his brilliant descriptions of paperwork that we can discern an antecedent of the factory scene. One scene of *Dead Souls* in particular exhibits the techniques that Grigorovich and others would employ in writing about factories: in chapter 7 of volume 1, Chichikov joins the landowner Manilov and proceeds to the chancellery of the provincial town of NN to make out his deed of purchase of his dead souls. As in the novel's earlier episodes where Chichikov had entered the homes of provincial landowners, this scene begins with a description of what they see inside the office. However, this scene differs from the others in one important respect: the vast accumulation of details inside this office constitutes an intricate *process*:

Our heroes saw a great deal of paper, both for rough drafts and of the purest white for final copies; they saw heads bent over their work, and broad napes of necks, and many frock coats, and dress coats of a provincial cut, or simply some sort of short jacket of light gray that stood out quite sharply. . . . And one could hear, in snatches, brief remarks uttered in a hoarse tenor: "Lend me, Fedosei Fedoseevich, the file on Number Three Hundred and Sixty-Eight!" . . . At times a voice, more majestic and beyond a doubt belonging to one of the higher officials, would ring out imperiously: "There, transcribe that!" . . . Great was the scratching of quills, and the sound thereof was as if several carts laden with brushwood were driving through a forest piled with dead leaves a yard deep.[33]

Several of the definitive features of the factory description are already here in this description of the provincial bureaucratic apparatus: the series of fragmentary objects—papers, heads, napes, coats—enumerated consecutively; the reliance on similes of questionable explanatory value; and the snatches of characteristic sound. The temporal organization of the scene is especially significant. In contrast to the static capsule descriptions of each landlord's home in the early chapters of the novel, here Gogol's narrator presents a scene in perpetual motion. In the endless operation of this paper machine, the constant activity of the clerks is combined with what seem to be momentary and singular events (like a fragment of conversation), which are raised to the level of illustrative generalizations. Instead of explaining this process, the scene offers an accumulation of details. In place of people performing actions, we see body parts in motion. Unlike visitors to the factory, Chichikov is not bewildered by what he sees, but then, he is not the type who gets bewildered easily. What this scene provides is an adaptable framework, a method for describing a chaotic process whose disorder is paradoxically repetitious and whose parts refuse to cohere into a visible (or legible) whole. A space qualitatively different from its surroundings, in which constant activity does not generate the kinds of events that can produce actual narrative, the Gogolian chancellery anticipates the factories, mills, and foundries of subsequent decades.

The chancellery scene in Gogol also identifies the activity described with the perceptions of particular characters (the phrase "our heroes saw" signals the beginning of the description). Along the way from the government office to the factory, internal focalization of the narration (that is, what we read is, mostly, what a particular character experiences) emerges as a key feature of the factory scene. In some cases, writers emphasize the mediating function of a character's perceptions by relating the factory scene through idiosyncratic first-person narration. We can see an example of this employment of *skaz* narration as a means for incorporating the operations of the factory into literary discourse in Turgenev's "Bezhin Meadow," first published as a separate sketch in *The Contemporary* in 1851 and included two years later in *Notes of a Hunter*. By leaving the description of the paper mill to a peasant boy, Turgenev manages to translate this industrial site's disturbing effects on its workers into the register of folklore.

"Bezhin Meadow" is remarkable for the complex arrangement of genres through which it fixes the factory within its brief narrative. The itinerant narrator, having lost his way after a day of hunting, encounters a group of peasant boys sitting around a campfire, where they are whiling away the nighttime hours by exchanging stories of the supernatural. As Katherine Bowers has pointed out, the first portion of the story, in which the narrator realizes that he has gotten lost in the night, conveys his anxiety by means of gothic commonplaces. This gothic framing, in turn, blurs the boundaries between the supernatural tales of the peasant boys and the ostensibly realist outlook of the educated narrator.[34] In the second part of the story, the narrator purports to reproduce what he has heard from the boys. Their tales are rich in fixtures of the "peasant occult," such as the *domovoi* (house spirit), the *leshii* (wood spirit), the *rusalka* (mermaid), and the *vodianoi* (water spirit), and each boy characterizes himself through his manner of telling and his response to the other tales.[35]

Many of the boys' tales feature typical locales of Russian folklore, such as forests and bodies of water. However, a boy named Pavlusha recounts a tale that takes place inside a paper mill, where a number of the local boys work. In this story within a story, the mill supervisor makes the boys spend the night at the factory instead of going home, since there is so little time between their shifts. During the night, they start to hear mysterious sounds, as if someone is walking around in the superstructure above them. Then the waterwheel starts turning, and water pours over it although the lowered sluice gates should prevent it from doing so. The doors to their room mysteriously open, and some invisible force then starts to carry out the tasks performed by these child workers in the light of day: a net for scooping paper pulp starts moving as if some invisible laborer has gone to work. Throughout this episode, the boys can hear, but they cannot see what is happening. They attribute this to the invisible *domovoi*, but what they have narrated is a ghostly rehearsal of the factory's daytime operations. Turgenev's project of humanizing the serfs and condemning serfdom is on display here as the child naively reveals the labor that consumes his life by projecting it onto an unseen spirit. The text supplies helpful footnotes explaining the terms he uses for various mill components in "our" local idiom (T 3:92–93). To make sense of his work at the mill, Pavlusha uses the words and speech genres he knows. His stylized account brings this site of industrial production into Turgenev's sketch together with a clear, if subtle, political message, but his distinctive way of telling the story competes with the mill as the primary object of representation. Later in this chapter, we will see another example of a factory scene conveyed through *skaz* in the work of Nikolai Leskov. By contrast, the more common approach to the description of the factory rendered a particular character's experience of its interior in the unmarked language of the narrator.

These two techniques—Gogolian itemization and quasi-folkloric *skaz*—remained the major options for factory scenes in Russian literature until the 1890s. In both cases, the description of the factory interior remained distinctly subjective—that is, outside the factory, the narrator could range freely from one character to another and provide information unavailable to any of them; but on entering the factory, objective narration ceased and the perspective of the narrator narrowed to coincide with that of a bewildered observer. Furthermore, descriptions of the factory interior remained conventional, that is, reliant on preexisting devices to capture the novelty of this space and the social relations it entailed.

As Aleksei Vdovin has convincingly demonstrated, one of the major innovations of Russian literature in the early 1850s, and in the work of Turgenev and Grigorovich in particular, was the development of new techniques for representing the complex interiorities of serfs and the concomitant expansion of the range of subjective experiences accessible to literature.[36] Yet even as the mental life of serfs entered Russian literature, the factory—and, in many cases, its occupants—remained in obscurity. The paper mill in "Bezhin Meadow" is the home of invisible supernatural forces. As we will see in the following section, the calico mill in Grigorovich's novel of peasant life overwhelms the senses of the peasant who looks through its windows. In other words, the sensory experience of factory labor remained outside representation. In this way, the factory posed an epistemic problem partially distinct from the long-standing problem of the representation of peasant consciousness in Russian literature.[37] However, in certain cases, literary treatments of the unknowable world of the peasant and the bewildering factory interior drew on a shared reservoir of tropes. For example, Anne Lounsbery has drawn attention to such a scene in Tolstoy's early story "A Landowner's Morning" (1856). The titular landowner visits a village, which "is presented to us as repellently alien—a broken, crooked, fragmented, *illegible* space that reflects less the peasants' reality than the landlord's despairing sense of 'his' people's impenetrability."[38] One of the emphases of this story, as Lounsbery shows, is the gap between the well-meaning landlord and the peasants whom he fails to understand. In some works of literature from the same period, notably in other stories from *Notes of a Hunter* such as "Khor' and Kalinych," both peasant interiors and interiorities became available to the narrator's investigation. Yet in Turgenev's work and elsewhere, landlord and peasant remained equally baffled by the factory. In effect, in scenes involving factories, the separation between nobles and peasants is temporarily effaced in favor of another separation between the epistemic boundaries of traditional Russian experience and the factory, which proves unassimilable to it.

THE TEMPLATE: GRIGOROVICH'S *FISHERMEN*

Dmitri Grigorovich's *The Fishermen* (1853), one of the first works of Russian realism to feature a factory scene, already exhibits the major conventions of these scenes that developed over the following decades. As Greta Matzner-Gore has demonstrated, this novel is "haunted by epistemological uncertainty" and makes the limits of empirical observation one of its central preoccupations.[39] In the course of illustrating the dangers of rural industrialization, the narrative takes the peasant Grishka to a calico mill located in an industrial village. On his approach, the narrator observes that the differences between ordinary villages and those that house factories are apparent from a long distance, especially at night. Whereas a normal village goes to sleep relatively early, factory villages remain brightly lit and noisy late into the night, radiating their activity into the surrounding landscape. As Grishka draws nearer to the factory—"the center of the novel's illusions"—the previously informative narrator retreats.[40] When Grishka comes to the factory window, we see mostly what he sees, and narratorial commentary providing additional information is limited. What Grishka witnesses will be echoed in subsequent descriptions of factories, both in terms of the descriptive techniques employed and the scene's notable silences:

> Gradually there opened up before him an endless view of joists, beams, pillars, and poles, crossing each other in every possible manner, a veritable wooden spider web. . . . Through all the gaps in this wooden spider web could be glimpsed rapidly spinning wheels, which were operated by boys and girls covered in streams of sweat. They must have been suffocating. There was nothing remarkable in that: even the strongest worker, after spending a year in this stifling air, began to weaken and dry up. The wood was drying and cracking; the ceiling and walls were glossy with condensation like in a banya. The still flames of tallow candles were surrounded by gloomy, yellow circles; the light had a hard time penetrating this dense atmosphere. . . . People were crowded like pickles in a barrel; it was impossible to point a finger without running into a joist, a stretched-out warp, or the back of someone's head. The heads of women, girls, and weavers of all ages would pop out everywhere: red and blue headscarves, black and red hair and beards, pale faces, pink

and white shirts dazzled one's eyes like the glass of a kaleidoscope aimed at a candle. All of this moved in the light of a few dozen tallow candle ends in tin holders. . . . The deafening clatter of shuttles, the pounding of battens, the hiss of wheels, voices, laughter, and songs filled the whole building.[41]

The focalization is incomplete here: it is seemingly the narrator, not Grishka, who knows that even those workers who are endowed with the heartiest constitution begin to "dry up" after a year of working in this mill. Nonetheless, the visual and aural disorder of this paragraph suggests that we are reading the impressions of an observer who is as unfamiliar with the scene as Grishka would be. The peasant is bewildered by what he sees, and together with him, we encounter a chaos of individual objects: joists, beams, pillars, and poles. Almost immediately, the text turns to rhetorical figures to establish analogies with familiar objects and make sense of these intersecting materials—the assemblage of crossing lines is likened to a wooden spiderweb. The darkness of the factory interior contributes to the murkiness of the visual impression. Rather than seeing human beings at work, the observer sees only fragments of human bodies in constant and inscrutable motion. The densely packed workers are likened to pickles in a barrel, and the dazzling arrangement of heads of hair and scarves brings to Grishka's mind the geometric shapes seen through a kaleidoscope: once again, in order to make some sense of what the peasant sees, the narrator has to leave the factory and return to a more familiar inventory of objects.

When Grishka gazes through the window into the mill, he repeats the procedure of earlier urban physiologists carefully observing the life of the city through its windows. But the window into the factory does not function as a framing device for the kind of rigorous visual analysis that characterized the work of those physiologists, Grigorovich included, in the 1840s. In Molly Brunson's explanation of this analytical procedure, "the window lends itself well to a perception of the city as a picture gallery, as a labyrinth of streets that contains a countless number of framed everyday scenes," which are "neatly sectioned out of a larger and more chaotic urban environment."[42] In *The Fishermen*, the "fusion of text and illustration" that, according to Brunson, distinguishes the Natural School from subsequent Russian realism can be seen in the process of its disintegration.[43] Like the narrator in Grigorovich's contribution to *The Physiology of Saint Petersburg*, "Petersburg Organ Grinders" (1845), the narrator in *The Fishermen* conveys what Grishka sees as a sequence of details, but the latter scene of chaotic movement resists synthesis into an informative image.[44] Grishka tries to gain some purchase on the ceaseless noise and motion with a series of analogies to more familiar objects—webs, barrels of pickles, kaleidoscopes—but these all seem insufficient. Finally, in an attempt to sum up the image before the reader, the narrator, acknowledging in advance the inadequacy of the comparison, offers a corporeal approximation, which abandons all attempts to encompass the empirical detail of the scene: "At that moment, in the absence of another, more precise, comparison, this lower floor could resemble something like a gargantuan stomach experiencing serious inflammation."[45] By now, the narrator has offered comparisons drawing on the natural world, the typical products of a peasant economy, and the malfunctioning of human physiology, but has suggested that all of them are insufficient. What remains is a lengthy description stymied by its object's apparent indescribability. The key features of this scene—the factory's ceaseless and pointless motion, visual and aural chaos, fragmented human forms that fail to coalesce into whole bodies, and, more than anything, the observer's confusion and bewilderment—remained fixtures of descriptions of factory interiors.

The profusion of rhetorical figures that seek to translate the observer's experience into a more readily comprehensible idiom was not limited to Russian literary treatments of the factory, nor is the narrative focalization. In both respects, a comparison to contemporary American literature is revealing. Three years after *Notes of a Hunter* and two years after *The Fishermen*, Herman Melville published a short narrative diptych called "The Paradise of Bachelors and the Tartarus of Maids." The second half of the title refers to an episode that offers a more sustained focus on the factory interior than almost any work of Russian literature in the nineteenth century. In Melville's story, a businessman travels to a New England paper mill in search of a wholesale supplier of packaging paper. Along the way, his encounter with the mill is prepared by a whole series of inauspicious toponyms, which he lists as he recounts his journey: Woedolor Mountain, a "Dantean gateway" called the Black Notch, a hollow called the Devil's Dungeon, through which flows Blood River, named for its mineral-colored waters.[46] By the time he suddenly hears the factory's piercing whistle in this wilderness, there can be little doubt about the meaning of the title's reference to the lower depths of the Greek underworld.[47] From this moment on, however, Melville's story takes a different path than the factory scenes in contemporaneous and later Russian fiction. At the mill, the traveler receives a tour from a guide named Cupid, who explains the various manufacturing processes and demonstrates the machines. The narrator's movement through the factory is clearly punctuated by expressions of time—"for a moment," "previously," "now"—which establish a clear sequence of events (1276). Within this sequence, he pauses to observe various factory operations. First he sees women cutting up scraps of cloth and observes the pallor of their faces. Then he uses his watch to time the movement of a piece of paper through a set of rollers and marvels at the precision of this "multitudinous and mystical" machine (1274). He ponders all the things this freshly manufactured paper will become: "sermons, lawyers' briefs, physicians' prescriptions, love-letters, marriage certificates, bills of divorce, registers of births, death-warrants, and so on, without end" (1276). As he contemplates the machine, he feels a sense of dread at its "metallic necessity" (1277). While the narrator struggles to comprehend this "miracle of inscrutable intricacy," he does find a language adequate to it in Melville's signature blend of archaisms, puns, and wide-ranging allusions (1278). In the end, the traveler recalls the story's earlier episode, the "Paradise of Bachelors," where he had dined with London lawyers, and considers the connection of these two ends of a global economy.[48] For all the marvel this factory elicits in the visitor, for all the evident psychological stress it causes him and the physical harm it inflicts on the workers, the factory is firmly incorporated into the formal design of this story and into a conception of an economy operating on national and global scales. The Russian factory, by contrast, would remain strikingly resistant to this kind of narrative integration. In the age of realism and reform, when literature confronted historical change in all its social, cultural, political, and economic ramifications, the factory remained stubbornly beyond the range of normal experience.

A NEW KIND OF NOVEL: RESHETNIKOV

Over the course of 1868, *Notes of the Fatherland* published a long novel by a young *raznochinets* writer named Fyodor Reshetnikov. This son of a poor postal worker had already attracted the attention of critics in 1864 for his harrowing "ethnographic sketch" of the abject poverty of a group of state peasants in *The People of Podlipnaia* (Podlipovtsy).[49] In this new novel, *Where Is It Better?* (Gde luchshe?), Reshetnikov attempted a sweeping account of the social and economic aftermath of the emancipation, as a result of which millions of freed serfs were forced by the burden of redemption payments and dwindling land allotments in the face of a rapidly growing population to leave their villages in search of work. Standing in for this massive population on the move is an extended family that crisscrosses Russia in search of a place where "it's better."[50] *Where Is It Better?* takes its characters through a range of employment options in Russia's industrializing economy. As the group disintegrates over the course of its journey, the focus of the narrative shifts to just one of its members, a young peasant woman named Pelageia Mokronosova, who eventually arrives in Saint Petersburg. She finds the city overflowing with newcomers from all over the country and quickly learns that the range of occupations available to women is limited. Every morning, masses of peasant women gather in Haymarket Square (where, around the same time, Raskolnikov does not make note of them) to fight over the handful of people who come by looking to hire cooks, laundresses, and sex workers.[51]

But the city is not merely a conveyor belt propelling country women into urban misery; it also exerts a progressive influence on the new arrivals. Pelageia eventually meets a factory worker who exposes her to culture (they attend a performance of Ostrovsky's *The Storm*), but she falls ill from her exhausting work as a washerwoman and dies. In the novel's conclusion, two characters gesture subtly that the answer to the question "Where is it better?" is not a place so much as a social order where working people could live free of their exploiters. Scholars have noted that this is one of the very few nineteenth-century Russian novels to focus on an emergent industrial working class and to hint at organized labor unrest.[52] Pelageia has ample opportunity to experience the deprivation and misery of urban life, but she also undergoes a transformation under the influence of these new, metropolitan conditions. And around her, a new, more confident, and better-educated class of workers is emerging. It would seem, then, that this is the place to look for a more extended and explicit engagement with the emergent industrial civilization that haunts the margins of works like *The Idiot* and *Anna Karenina*.

Reshetnikov's novel, now almost forgotten, was widely seen by contemporaries as an important sign of major new developments in Russian literature. The novel appeared shortly before the author, succumbing to his own dire poverty, died at the age of twenty-nine. His collected works appeared shortly thereafter, followed a few years later by a second edition. Responding to this flurry of news and publications, most of the major writers of the period commented on Reshetnikov's work and compared it to that of leading contemporaries. The critic Viktor Burenin contrasted *Where Is It Better?* favorably with *The Idiot*, identifying the former with new tendencies.[53] Dostoevsky himself acknowledged that Reshetnikov was trying to do something new and important by going beyond "landowner's literature," although he was sharply critical of the results.[54] Saltykov-Shchedrin, who had edited Reshetnikov's novel as it was serialized in *Notes of the Fatherland*, criticized its excessive length and meaningless details but nonetheless argued that it represented a fundamentally new kind of literature. In a review published in the same journal the following year, he credited Reshetnikov with two major innovations. First, and contrary to the long-standing view that the life of the common people could only yield up "curious anecdotes," Reshetnikov demonstrated that the lives of peasants were also capable of producing "drama."[55] Furthermore, Saltykov-Shchedrin argued that the introduction of peasants as narrative subjects necessitated changes to the character system of the novel. Basing his argument on the sociological writings of Nikolai Mikhailovsky, he claimed that the peasant was wholly occupied by the struggle for survival and thus could not develop the kind of individuality of more privileged groups. Therefore, in order to bring the peasant into literature, Reshetnikov had to introduce a new kind of mass protagonist, a "totality of indivisibles" whose individual stories were inseparable from the condition of the common people as a whole.[56]

The movements of Reshetnikov's mass protagonist extended the setting of his novels to encompass the entirety of Russia. In its epic ambition to represent the collective life of an entire people, *Where Is It Better?* bore some historically significant similarities to *War and Peace*, which was published in full in 1869. According to Lidya Lotman, both novels are structured by the "movement of huge masses of people in space, which expresses the conception of an explosion of humanity's historical activity."[57] A number of contemporaries also felt the need to compare Tolstoy and Reshetnikov. Turgenev, in a retrospective glance at developments in Russian literature since the death of Belinsky, included both authors in a list of the most important works of these years: "What joy he [Belinsky] would have felt at the poetic gift of L. N. Tolstoy, the power of Ostrovsky, Pisemsky's humor, Saltykov's satire, the sober truth of Reshetnikov! Who, if not he, should have borne witness to the germination of those seeds, many of which were planted by his own hand?"[58] The poet Afanasy Fet evidently found this juxtaposition of Tolstoy and Reshetnikov rather jarring, since he referred to Turgenev's remark about "Reshetnikov's sober truth" while praising *Anna Karenina* in a letter to Tolstoy seven years later. Fet, whose preference for "pure art" and reactionary politics put him at odds with both the style and the message of Reshetnikov's works, compared Reshetnikov's novels to the "stupid flaring of enraged nostrils" (that is, to the mindless resentment of the low-born and uncivilized) and contrasted them to the "rose gold" of *Anna Karenina*.[59] On the other hand, in an assessment of Reshetnikov's legacy published a few years later, Mikhailovsky arranged the hierarchy of authors in the opposite manner, praising the authenticity of Reshetnikov's works, rooted as they were in the author's intimate knowledge of the life and suffering of the common people, and noting that Reshetnikov, unlike Levin, could rightfully claim to be one with the people.[60]

Whether offended by Reshetnikov's aesthetic carelessness or convinced that his focus on the common people heralded a momentous expansion of the novel's representational capacities, numerous commentators regarded the output of Reshetnikov's brief career as sufficiently important to discuss it alongside works that are much more famous today. In contrast to most of those works, *Where Is It Better?* places working people at the center of the story, so it is not surprising that the novel deals extensively with the kinds of labor that migratory peasants perform. Members of Pelageia's group stop at several work sites, including a salt plant and a gold mine. In the novel's second part, set in Saint Petersburg, Pelageia tries to look for work beyond Haymarket Square. At one point, she visits a sugar refinery, where her experience is reminiscent of Grishka's in *The Fishermen*:

This factory was extensive, about four stories high, and when she arrived, it was working at full steam. Pelageia Prokhorovna marveled at many things here: the machines surprised her, as well as the huge crucibles and furnaces. Machines were pounding, wheels were turning, somewhere, a whistle could be heard, somewhere, steam was visible, so that it seemed a little frightening to her, even though she had grown up in a mining plant [*v gornom zavode*].[61]

Pelageia's surprise is itself surprising, given the narrator's comment that she is familiar with industrial infrastructure. Nevertheless, the internally focalized description is characteristically fragmented: in place of process, or indeed of any narrative, there are individual fragments, pieces of machinery carrying out repetitive motions. The various details in these scenes tend to accumulate in long series of clauses where each object, accompanied by its own verb, performs its discrete action between commas. Likewise typical is the alignment of the narrator with the observing character in terms of uncertainty regarding the source or meaning of various events: steam appears from "somewhere," as does some sort of whistle. In a novel concerned with the detailed elaboration of the plight of migrating Russian workers across the countryside—a novel that goes into great detail explaining the social mechanisms that lead to massive poverty and inequality—the factory remains a confusing, menacing, almost literally indescribable object. There is, to be sure, also room for individual variations in these scenes. Among the machines and the disorienting noise, Pelageia sees how "the workers walked from one object to another confidently, spoke loudly, whistled, joked about the German technicians, who were pacing beside the machines and crucibles with short pipes in their mouths, and this enlivened her."[62] This novel narrates the gradual formation of a confident, experienced working class capable of organizing a strike. For all their suffering, these workers also undergo an empowering transformation, whose traces Pelageia observes in their confident movement among the machinery. Nevertheless, we do not encounter the factory through the eyes of these men, who will perhaps eventually grow strong enough to take it over. Pelageia is a newcomer to this world, and she—and the reader along with her—must first overcome the sensory shock of the factory floor before she can even notice this nascent proletariat.

Pelageia's experience in the Saint Petersburg refinery is especially interesting because the novel in which it occurs also features a very different labor scene—one that is in many ways comparable to Levin's mowing in *Anna Karenina*, discussed in the next chapter. In an earlier episode that takes place in the novel's first part, "In the Provinces," Pelageia and her fellow travelers find temporary employment at a saltworks, where women are employed to carry heavy sacks of salt. Here the reader encounters a lengthy and detailed description of their labor, and Pelageia's gradual acclimatization to the difficult work. Rather than offering a dry description of the work, Reshetnikov focuses on the songs the women sing. At first, Pelageia, who is observing the scene, "did not understand this labor song about the hard working life, from which the only way out was the swift river [*bystraia rechen'ka*], carrying [the worker's] little will [*voliushku*] to her dear sweetheart [*milomu druzhochku*], who had sailed away somewhere on the ocean-sea [*more-okean*], to a grain-bearing isle [*ostrov khleborodnyi*]."[63] This song is redolent with the locutions and rhythms of folklore, which translate the experience of these itinerant laboring women in postemancipation Russia into the register of traditional agricultural life. The oppressive conditions of wage labor at the saltworks are identified with the ritualized lamentations of folk tradition, and the very modern consequences of an oversupply of workers, low wages, and brutal disciplinary regimes in an economy of "free" laborers are personified and rendered comprehensible as the activity of unidentified "cruel people–evildoers" (*zlye liudi-likhodei*) from which the worker's "little will" seeks escape.

In its way, this scene, and in particular the work song that features prominently within it, is as concerned with the temporal relationships between manual labor and Russian history as Levin's mowing scene is. However, the two scenes differ significantly in both their poetics and their politics. Whereas Levin's synchronization with the mowing of his peasants effects a temporary reconciliation of master and worker into an organic social whole, in Reshetnikov's novel the laboring peasant women synchronize themselves through song. Levin and the peasants mow in silence, and Levin eventually enters an eternal present in which he gets a reprieve from the problems that plague him. While he works, the novel's various threats to the world of gentry estates—railroads, factories, consumerism, the peasants' inability to understand contracts and self-interest—are left behind. In *Where Is It Better?*, the women's song, with its folkloric devices, highlights the collision of multiple temporalities in Russia's economic present. These women draw on the cultural resources of the deep past while laboring in the service of an emerging capitalist world economy. Their labor is not a reprieve from the outside world's pressures but a direct consequence of them. Levin's workers, referred to as *rabochie* (workers) outside the mowing scene, become *muzhiki* (peasants) within it. Reshetnikov keeps these two groups rigorously separate. As Rose Glickman notes, the *muzhiki* "are never referred to as workers, just as the workers are never referred to as *muzhiki*."[64] Finally, like Levin, Pelageia is initially unused to the work, worries about lagging behind, and finds carrying the heavy sacks of salt difficult, but over time she adjusts to the work and to the other peasant women.

Where Is It Better? thus offers a clearer contrast than almost any other work of nineteenth-century Russian literature between the poetics of outdoor manual labor, even if performed under new, capitalist conditions, and the experience of the factory. The former scene is described in detail, and Pelageia quickly grows accustomed to the unfamiliar environment, which is itself readily incorporated into the Russian realist novel's balance of narration and description. The factory, however, remains strange and frightening. If Pelageia is less overwhelmed by the factory than Grishka in *The Fishermen* is, if the narration spends less time dwelling on her inability to come up with an adequate analogy to what she witnesses, it is due to this novel's relatively greater emphasis on the growing confidence of the factory workers, which Pelageia clearly notices. Nevertheless, the environment in which she observes this process is still conveyed through familiar conventions. As we will see in the following section, those who own and manage factories will react in a similar way to their possessions.

BEWILDERED TOURISTS AND RELUCTANT OWNERS IN TURGENEV, BOBORYKIN, AND MAMIN-SIBIRIAK

In 1876, Turgenev published his final and, by some accounts, least successful novel.[65] *Virgin Soil* was Turgenev's response to the activism of the *narodniki* in the early 1870s, particularly the "going to the people" movement, through which urban populists attempted to raise the political consciousness of the common people in the countryside.[66] The novel thus centers on a cell of Petersburg revolutionaries who attempt to make contact with the peasants in order to foment an uprising. With this plan in mind, Nezhdanov, an illegitimate nobleman's son who has the nobility's education and manners but not its social status, agrees to travel to the country as a tutor for the son of a high-ranking liberal official named Sipiagin. In the countryside, Nezhdanov meets several coconspirators and allies, including the manager of a nearby cotton-spinning mill named Solomin. The manager appears sympathetic to the revolutionary cause, but he forbids any organizing among the workers he oversees. As a result, the mill assumes a curious position within the narrative. It comes to serve as a narrative hub, with characters frequently leaving or returning to it, although most of the major events take place elsewhere. In the second part of the novel, Nezhdanov runs away from Sipiagin's estate with Marianna, a poor relation of theirs who dreams of revolutionary action instead of her humiliating life under her benefactors. The two take refuge at the mill, from which Nezhdanov launches his mission to agitate among the neighboring villages.

As a refuge and a base of operations, the mill assumes considerable importance in the narrative of *Virgin Soil*. As an object of contemplation and a site for work, it reveals the differences between the novel's two major male characters and their social and political visions. Nezhdanov is a well-educated, sensitive man whom Turgenev envisioned as a "romantic of realism," referring here to realism in Pisarev's sense as a disposition toward empiricism and practical action.[67] As his name suggests, Nezhdanov is impatient in his longing to right the injustices of Russian society, but he is also prone to aesthetic contemplation and writes down occasional poems in a notebook that he shamedly smuggles wherever he goes.[68] Although he constantly affirms his commitment to the cause, the aims of this cause and the means of realizing them remain vague for him. He reveals that his attachment to the idea of revolution is at least as much a matter of aesthetics as one of politics by talking about Nikolai Dobroliubov's poetry, rather than his much more influential literary and social criticism.

An early indication that Nezhdanov is perhaps not built for revolutionary work comes when he arrives at the mill for his initial meeting with Solomin. While he waits, he goes up to a window and peers inside the building. What we read next is by now a familiar scene. Nezhdanov encounters—and we read—a series of lists, both of nouns ("machines," "looms," "wheels," "belts") and of verbs ("snorted and clanged," "creaked," "hummed," "slapped") (VA 91/T 9:222–23). He hears shouts, whistles, and the ringing of bells and sees men and women bustling about. As an educated Petersburger, Nezhdanov knows little about factories, and what he sees does not impress him. However, it does not frighten him either, and this scene, unlike most of the others in Russian realism, features a rather calm description of what he glimpses. We learn, mostly, of his disappointment in this factory:

> A thousand-headed human force, stretched taut, droned all around. Everything proceeded in orderly, rational fashion, at full throttle, but nowhere was there any indication of confidence, precision, or even tidiness; on the contrary, everywhere one was struck by carelessness, dirt, and soot. Here a window pane was smashed; there plaster was peeling, boards were coming loose, a door yawned wide open; in the middle of the main courtyard was a large black puddle with an iridescent sheen of decay. (VA 91/T 9:223)

The striking mention of the iridescent puddle reveals Nezhdanov's preference for aesthetic details over careful attention to the workings of the mill. Indeed, his disappointment with what he seems to have expected to be a kind of Chernyshevskian experiment in workers' self-management is an early indication of his cooling revolutionary ardor.

Like the other factory descriptions we have seen in this chapter, this factory scene in *Virgin Soil* is rigorously internally focalized. As a result, Nezhdanov's experience of the mill tells us about him: namely, the description becomes an index of his political outlook and his personality. Nezhdanov demands transformative action immediately, and he has no patience with whatever gradual benefits the factory might bring to the workers. On the other hand, Solomin, the impassive manager, favors hard work and gradual reform over impulsive revolutionary action. He is, furthermore, entirely familiar with factories and mills thanks to his work, and it is therefore logical that he would perceive them differently than the uninitiated observers we have so far examined do. More significant than the difference between Solomin's and Nezhdanov's reactions, however, is the shift in narrative focalization that occurs at the moments when Solomin interacts with the mill. This shift blocks the reader from experiencing the mill as Solomin does.

Virgin Soil does not let us see what Solomin sees. Later in the novel, after a mostly unsuccessful meeting of the revolutionary cell, Solomin returns alone to his workplace, where he is familiar with every machine and where the workers regard him as one of their own (*ikh—i ikhnii*) (T 9:271). But we do not get to see the factory through his eyes. For him, it is already a thoroughly familiar object, long incapable of delivering the sensory shock with which less experienced characters encounter factories. When he walks inside, instead of reading about what he sees, we get a simile, which identifies his monotonous routine with the repetitious movement of the machinery: "And again his life began to turn like a large flywheel" (VA 143/T 9:272). As long as Solomin remains at work, there is nothing to tell about him. However, the smooth operation of his working life is interrupted when Sipiagin, the local liberal landowner, invites Solomin to inspect his own malfunctioning paper mill. Along the way, Sipiagin's neighbor, the landowner Kallomeitsev, decides to tag along. Kallomeitsev is a reactionary and takes an instant dislike to Solomin but insists on taking a tour of the mill because, he says, he loves to learn. At this point, a fork emerges in the narrative path: as we approach the factory, a number of different focalizations become possible. If Kallomeitsev, who is certainly unfamiliar with paper mills, really loves to learn, we could see the mill as he does. But we will not find out what Kallomeitsev learns about the mill. Instead, the mill will be doubly mediated. Throughout the inspection, Sipiagin and Kallomeitsev observe Solomin observing the mill, and what we read are their own impressions, both of him and his impressions of the facility. Sipiagin and Kallomeitsev notice immediately that "Solomin was at home in the factory, that everything in it was known to him and understood, down to the smallest detail, that he was in charge here" (VA 150/T 9:278). We hear no noise, are confronted with no confused jumble of images. Whatever Kallomeitsev and Sipiagin think or feel about the mill is not communicated to us. On the other hand, we see through their eyes how Solomin stops spinning wheels with the touch of his finger and knowingly examines the pulp from which the paper is manufactured.

Solomin refuses to help Sipiagin sort out his mill and returns to his job. Afterward, Nezhdanov takes refuge at Solomin's mill with Marianna and initiates his attempts to go to the people. Eventually a peasant reports the revolutionaries to the police, and Nezhdanov, who is already in despair over the failure of his mission, commits suicide in the mill's yard. In his suicide note, he bequeaths Marianna to Solomin, who, after the events of the novel, carries on with his work. His political sympathies notwithstanding, Solomin has quite a bit in common, in terms of his narrative trajectory, with the indefatigable capitalists of Russian literature, whom he resembles in his relentless work ethic, his association with the world of factories, and in the reticence with which the narrator deals with his inner experience. Like them, he will quietly triumph, evading both the police, who descend on the failed revolutionary movement, and the ensuing despair, which drives Nezhdanov to suicide. Indeed, given his Scandinavian features and apparently un-Russian taciturnity, Solomin seems in more ways than one to be a descendant of Stolz, as well as the idealized British workers found in the pages of nineteenth-century self-help literature. Indeed, Sila Paklin, the novel's truth-telling Dostoevskian joker, suggests the comparison of Solomin to a character from the work of Samuel Smiles, author of the original *Self Help* (1859).[69]

As we have seen, hardworking capitalists appear in a number of works of Russian literature, but they abound in the novels of Boborykin. Alternately praised and denounced for his responsiveness to the social and cultural developments of the moment, Boborykin wrote voluminously about the changing class structure of late nineteenth-century Russia and about the rise of new entrepreneurs from among the merchants and nobility, particularly in such novels as *The Dealmakers* (Del'tsy, 1872–73), *Kitai-Gorod* (1882), and *Vasilii Terkin* (1892). In response to *Kitai-Gorod*, Turgenev ridiculed Boborykin's preternatural timeliness and productivity: "I can easily imagine him atop the ruins of the world, scribbling a novel reproducing the latest 'currents' [*veianiia*] of the dying earth. There is no other example of such hurried fecundity in the history of literature! Look, he will end up re-creating the facts of life five minutes before they emerge!"[70] Tolstoy was more positive in a later assessment, calling him "wonderfully perceptive."[71] In the Soviet period, literary historians tended to consign Boborykin to the status of a chronicler of current events who documented "the history of the development and triumphal procession of the Russian bourgeoisie."[72] Of his prodigious writings, often said to amount to a hundred volumes, only his memoirs and a handful of novels and short stories have been republished since his death in 1921. Two separate twelve-volume editions of his fictional writings appeared in the late nineteenth century, and no even remotely complete edition of his collected works exists. Among the few books that have been republished, *Kitai-Gorod* remains his best-known work of fiction. Named after the traditional merchant quarter of Moscow, this novel was supposed to be, in Boborykin's own words, "a sort of artistic threshold to 'knowing the Old Capital.'"[73]

Kitai-Gorod is as much a collection of elaborate descriptions as it is a narrative. A large portion of the text is devoted to an encyclopedic catalogue of the daily life of the thriving Moscow merchants, who are referred to as *kuptsy* (merchants) and *burzhua* (bourgeois) in a fairly indiscriminate manner, suggesting that nothing like Dostoevsky's distinction between merchants and capitalists (examined in chapter 3) exists for Boborykin. Several of the novel's chapters are extended descriptions of bustling street scenes. The first two chapters feature key locations of Moscow business life, such as shops, a bank, and the stock exchange, and depict the unending stream of horse-drawn goods around the commercial section of the city. The last chapter, shifting abruptly away from the major characters, describes the celebrations attending to the opening of a huge new inn and dining establishment. Between these descriptions, the novel's plot illustrates the social changes that Boborykin had already explored in his "Letters about Moscow," which had been published just a year previously in the same journal as *Kitai-Gorod*, the liberal *Herald of Europe*.

The novel's characteristic spaces are city streets, banks, factories, inns, and the houses of wealthy merchants and declining nobles. Its character system contrasts two Moscow communities. On the one hand, the merchants, who have long accumulated wealth but lack social capital, are now poised to take over the cultural and intellectual life of the city. The old bearded patriarchs are being replaced by a new generation, whose most powerful representatives, according to Boborykin, are ambitious women who run their own factories and manage their own fortunes. In contrast to the ascendant merchants, the nobility in *Kitai-Gorod* are an estate undergoing economic, moral, and physical degeneration. The Dolgushin family is ostensibly representative of the condition of this urban nobility circa 1880: the mother is terminally ill and addicted to morphine, while the father, a retired general, spends his time on pointless financial schemes and refuses an offer of gainful employment as a factory supervisor. Of the family's three children, the two sons are depraved gamblers, while the daughter, Tasia, the only member of the family with the moral potential for a future, dreams of becoming an actress—a career that she is finally able to pursue only because she marries the rising young merchant and soon-to-be factory director Rubtsov. The novel's ostensible protagonist is a nobleman named Paltusov, who declares it his mission to "fight the merchant moneybag" and make the nobility economically competitive.[74] All he ends up doing is embezzling a merchant fortune, and he is saved from prison by Stanitsyna, one of the new powerful merchant women.

Considering its focus on the rapidly changing economic conditions of Moscow, *Kitai-Gorod* has relatively little to say about the workings of the various businesses that are effecting these changes. However, the novel does feature a factory scene. Stanitsyna, who owns several factories, goes to inspect a spinning mill and brings along Tasia, whom she has informally adopted (because the only hope for this young daughter of the nobility lies with the merchants). In what is by now a well-established convention, the factory is presented through Tasia's eyes. She has never seen a factory before, and the ensuing description, structured by her incomprehension, employs a paradoxically familiar defamiliarization. In one room, "some sort of mush" is transformed into cleaned wool. In another, "Tasia felt sorry for the stokers," although it is clear that this episodic sympathy does not stem from any kind of deep understanding of their working conditions.[75] At one point Tasia asks about the workers' wages, but the narrator makes clear that she does not know the difference between good and bad wages. In the midst of the novel's extensive descriptions, in which the narrator ranges freely over various different domains of commercial expertise and adopts diverse social and professional registers, the vagueness of the mill tour stands out. Once again, the activity that goes on inside the mill does not coalesce into a comprehensible or narratable process. Instead, the familiar pronominal adjective *kakaia-to* (some sort of) relegates the factory to a place just outside the novel's depth of field.

In the cases of *Virgin Soil* and *Kitai-Gorod*, factory descriptions are mediated by the sensory experience of people who are unfamiliar with factories and not particularly interested in them. We read about what Nezhdanov and Tasia see and experience, rather than what Solomin and Stanitsyna do. However, there are also cases in Russian literature where those who should know the inner workings of the factory—since they derive their wealth from them—nonetheless exhibit a mixture of indifference and fear when confronted by the factory interior. Chekhov's stories, examined in chapter 5, provided the most extensive examination of such reluctant capitalists, but another novel—Mamin-Sibiriak's *Privalov's Millions* (1883)—had already introduced this type before it developed in Chekhov's later works.

As his name suggests, Dmitry Narkisovich Mamin-Sibiriak gained a reputation as a regional writer whose work focused on the development of capitalism in the Russian east at the end of the century. *Privalov's Millions*, his first novel, tells the story of an heir to an industrial empire in the Urals who does not want anything to do with the family business. The novel is a satire on the greed of the local economic elite, who seek to acquire the fortune of Sergei Privalov, this young owner of the local foundry. Privalov himself despises both the foundry and the legacy of his monstrously acquisitive forebears: he visits the site that manufactures his wealth only once in the course of the novel. Instead, sympathizing with the poor peasants oppressed by industrialists and grain merchants alike, he decides to produce flour and distribute it to the people at minimal cost. The construction and operation of the mill initiate the novel's most Tolstoyan depictions of Privalov's experience of the landscape and the peasants. For much of the novel, Privalov alternates between frustrated idleness, visits to his mill, and his legal struggles with two local luminaries who have schemed their way into controlling the Privalov foundry.

There is only one, albeit striking, scene of workers and industry in *Privalov's Millions*, when Privalov makes his single begrudging visit to the foundry to learn about the conditions there. Inside, he glimpses the mysterious operations of massive machines that seem to function without human intervention. As he follows his guide, Privalov moves among the huge machines. In the midst of a "whole sea of fire" and darkness from which "everywhere red-hot iron could be glimpsed," Privalov catches glimpses of workers' bodies: "Those same burned faces, leather aprons, soft hemp shoes on their feet. Privalov felt himself a totally alien, superfluous person in this kingdom of fire and iron and silently observed everything that was shown to him."[76] Amid the overwhelming sounds and imagery, "out of all the cracks and holes, curious eyes glistened at him." The infernal imagery of this scene recalls descriptions of industrial metalworking by journalists like Blagoveshchensky, but the way the workers disappear into the mass of machinery, appearing only as burned faces and frightening eyes, diverges from nonliterary accounts. Once again, the grammatical expression of Privalov's experience is a list of nouns and verbs: "Somewhere, the sound of water could be heard; dozens of iron wheels, gears, and rollers rotated with a dull thunder; the mouths of furnaces—puddling, welding, reverbatory, and some other complicated kinds—glowed blindingly bright."[77] Privalov catches just enough of the informed commentary of the tour guide to assign names to the objects that bewilder him.

LESKOV'S REFRACTED FACTORY

In the growing literature about Russia's industrialization from the last two decades of the nineteenth century, scenes emphasizing the alien and unassimilable quality of the factory interior predominated. However, alternative paths were also available, and I turn now to one of those: a fictional treatment of the factory that aligned the reader's perspective with that of an experienced worker who knows his way around the factory floor. However, in this case—Nikolai Leskov's "Tale of the Cross-Eyed Tula Lefty and the Steel Flea" (1881)—the primary object of representation is not the factory but the narrator's remarkable linguistic style. Leskov returns to the multiple framing narratives that Turgenev employed in his description of the factory in "Bezhin Meadow" in order to direct the reader's attention to his virtuosic storyteller. As a result, until the stylistically neutral and putatively authoritative narratorial voice reappears at the very end of the story, we are confronted with a narration that is not a transparent window through which to see the factory but a dense, potentially distorting medium that serves as a measure of the linguistic, cultural, and perhaps epistemological remoteness of the Cossack Platov and the unidentified narrator who tells his story.

The story's *skaz* narration demonstrates the superiority of Russian craftsmanship over British industrial production in the words of an unsophisticated storyteller who reverts to folkloric locutions and narrative models for representing a consummately modern and historically specific setting: Russia on the eve of the Crimean War. The disastrous outcome of that war had impressed upon the Russian government that failure to modernize was putting the empire's great power status in jeopardy.[78] Leskov's tale is thus set at a historical breaking point—a moment at which Russia's failure to keep up with the modernization of France and Great Britain had left it technologically and logistically outclassed and incapable of contending with French ironclad warships and British artillery. The tale addresses Russia's technological lag only in passing, however, and the focus remains on Russian triumph in a different theater. What could not happen in a story focused on the course of historical events is realized in this work on the level of style. While the plucky Tula craftsmen overcome the sophistication of British industrial manufacturing with individual mastery, the narrator's verbal performance reverses the process by which Russia was forced to confront its incorporation into a world system on European terms. That is, in "Lefty" European science and technology are absorbed into a Russian folkloric idiom that proves readily adaptable to whatever the outside world can throw at it. But this victory of traditional Russian speech and handicrafts does not extend into the reader's present, from which the tale is separated by an epilogue. The resulting collision of markers of different historical periods and sensibilities that interilluminate each other recalls the singing women workers in Reshetnikov's novel, and it is telling that Walter Benjamin chose Leskov (although not "Lefty") as the focus of his essay on the changing nature of historical experience under modern technological conditions.[79]

The story of "Lefty" is based on a contradiction: on the one hand, native Russian artisans outperform the scientific design and production methods of English industry. However, the same traditional contempt for industrial science and manufacture that produced the Tula craftsmen who were able to make shoes for the English steel flea also causes the Russian military to ignore the intelligence that Lefty brings back with him from the trip to

England.[80] This failure to adopt new methods leads directly to the Russian defeat in the Crimean War: "But if only they had reported Lefty's words in time to the Emperor, the war against the enemy in Crimea would have taken an entirely different turn."[81] The Cossack Platov's native skepticism of reform and foreign innovation is fully justified by the Tula artisans' superiority to the cutting-edge industrial techniques of British engineers, but Count Chernyshchev's refusal to listen to Lefty's report from England about the proper care for weapons is directly responsible for the Russians' defeat by the British in the ensuing war. During his inspection of the British armament factory Lefty makes his most significant discovery: the barrels of old British rifles are smoother than those of their Russian counterparts. Moreover, the Russian generals who had earlier inspected those same facilities had missed this fact because they were unwilling to take off their gloves and examine the weapons in detail. It follows that the Russian technique of cleaning musket barrels with brick dust gouges the metal and makes the weapons inaccurate. This lesson never reaches the Russian military leadership, in part because of Lefty's alcoholic misadventures on his return trip and his untimely death, but also due to that establishment's inertia and hostility to reform.

Furthermore, despite the patriotic pride evident in the story's description of the hardworking, hard-drinking Tula craftsmen, the English industrial workers seem to enjoy a better standard of living. Here, in William Edgerton's brilliant translation, is what Lefty sees when he tours the English factories:

> He looked at all their production: he really liked their metallic mills and their soapy-rope factories, and the way they managed things—especially the way they took care of their workers. Every one of their workmen was always well fed, none was dressed in rags, each one had on a capable everyday jacket and wore thick hard-nail boots with iron caps, so that he wouldn't stump his toes anywhere on anything. Along with his work he got teaching instead of beatings, and he worked with comprehension. In front of each one, hung up right in full view, was a stultification table, and within arm's reach was a racing slate. Whatever any craftsman did, he would look up at the tables, and then check it with comprehension, and then write one thing down on the slate, race another thing, and put it together accurately: whatever was written down in the figures really came out that way. And when a holiday came, they would all get together in couples, each one would take a walking stick in his hand, and they would go for a walk in a proper way, all proud and polite.[82]

This critique of Russian factory conditions, made safer by its presentation in the highly stylized language of the uneducated narrator, looks forward to the superior conditions of the English factory rather than back to the traditional

Russian workshop, although this latter will produce the miracle of craftsmanship at the center of the story. In contrast to the skepticism of British science and engineering expressed both by the patriotic Platov and by Lefty himself, in this passage it appears that the British industrial system has at least one major advantage over the Russian from the perspective of the laboring narrator.

At the end of the story, a marked shift occurs, both in the style of the narration and in the relative belatedness of Russian manufactures. As the *skaz* recedes and a new narrator appears, writing in standard literary Russian, we find ourselves in a world of Russian factories, where labor is regulated by the steady rhythm of machines. The narrator laments the lost glory of the era of heroic handicrafts:

> It goes without saying that Tula no longer has such master craftsmen as the legendary Lefty: machines have evened up the inequalities in gifts and talents, and genius no longer strains itself in a struggle against diligence and exactness. Even though they encourage the raising of salaries, machines do not encourage artistic daring, which sometimes went so far beyond ordinary bounds as to inspire the folk imagination to create unbelievable legends like this one.
>
> Workers, of course, know how to value the advantages they have gained through practical applications of mechanical science, but they still recall those olden times with pride and affection. These memories are their epic—an epic that has a genuinely "human soul."[83]

Clearly, the "artistry" referred to here has a dual meaning. Rationalized factory production is opposed to the artistry of the earlier artisanal industry and, by implication, to the verbal artistry that produced this folk epic. The narrator of "Lefty" sees in the end of preindustrial production the loss of the basis for this kind of folk epic of craftsmanship.[84] Whereas the old labor process could inspire "popular fantasy to compose fabulous legends," such as the tale of Lefty, modern technology has ushered in an age where production is regulated, constant, and incapable of generating narrative. In retrospect, the most striking elements of our tour of the English factory appear to be Platov's brilliant "translations" of foreign borrowings into his folksy idiom and his inimitable description of the English workers.

In its original published form, "Lefty" was preceded by a preface, bearing the name of Leskov himself, which identified the text as a narrative he recorded on one of his many journeys through the Russian Empire.[85] With this preface (whose claims Leskov would later retract) and the story's conclusion, we find ourselves separated from the events in "Lefty" by an additional layer of textual mediation. The conclusion to the story hints that this document may itself be an example of that "artistic boldness beyond measure" inspired by the heroic feats of the Tula craftsmen. We have, as it were, gained access to the factory at the expense of rigorous realism.[86] And now, in the time of the story's conclusion, the historical discontinuity between Russia and the West—a discontinuity that was the very condition of Platov's tour of the English factory—has apparently disappeared. We are left, then, with a world of factories which, like the capitalists we will encounter in *The Idiot*, carry on their interminable tasks, avoiding, as much as possible, the events that are the basis of narrative.

KUPRIN AND THE REFAMILIARIZATION OF THE FACTORY

With Aleksandr Kuprin's *Molokh* (1896), we enter a different phase in the history of the literary representation of the factory. The protagonist of this novella is an engineer who works at a giant steel mill in the south of Russia. This time, the mill is not an incidental detail in the landscape but the focal point of the narrative. The novella begins with a panoramic view of the factory, occasioned by Bobrov's walk to work. As he reaches the crest of a hill, the enormous mill complex stretches out below him, and an extensive description of its design and appearance, complete with technical terminology and helpful authorial footnotes, follows. Much of *Molokh* consists of lengthy descriptions—of the mill and its huge machinery; of Kvashnin, the grotesquely oversized owner; and of the lavish banquet he organizes for the local high society. The steel mill is an essential part of this world, and the speech that Kvashnin delivers at the banquet summarizes its place in a global economy that extends not just horizontally, over the earth's surface ("Is it not we who have entangled the whole globe in a net of railroads?"), but also vertically, into the natural resources under the ground ("Is it not we who cut into the bowels of the earth and transform its treasures into cannons, bridges, locomotives, rails, and colossal machines?").[87] The mill lies at the center of this cruciform structure and concretizes the abstract extension of a whole economy ("Is it not we who . . . bring into motion thousands of millions in capital?").[88] The descriptions of this vast economic engine are no longer focalized through a single character, although Bobrov's revulsion at his job, which he is convinced makes him complicit in modern-day human sacrifice, figures prominently in the narrative. *Molokh* shows that the gap between the workers and articulate intellectuals like Bobrov remains vast. While he agonizes over the terrible effects of factory labor (at one point he calculates that every day the conditions at the steel mill shorten its workers' lives by a cumulative twenty years), the strike that interrupts Kvashnin's banquet takes all of the characters by surprise.

Nevertheless, when we read about the mill in *Molokh*, it is in a style of neutral reportage, full of technical detail that suggests not only the narrator's (and implied author's) expertise but the possibility that the reader can make sense of all this as well. An early work in Kuprin's literary career, *Molokh* appeared soon after the young writer published a journalistic account of his own tour of a steel mill, which served as a study for the novella.[89] In this convergence of journalistic and literary treatments of the industrial site, the conventional separation of factory descriptions in these two genres of writing comes to an end. Kuprin's description of the factory in *Molokh* is similar in its focus on the details of the production process to other contemporaneous writings about Russian industry.[90] Kuprin, together with writers like Maksim Gorky and Aleksandr Serafimovich, both of whom would become classics of socialist realism, were, at the very end of the nineteenth century, paving the way for the production novels of the twentieth.[91]

This was, to be sure, not the only form of literary response to the industrial boom of the 1890s. The industrial stories of Chekhov, which are the focus of chapter 5, combined the old conventions of representing the factory with the new thematic features we find in writers like Kuprin. In these works, industrialists emerge from the narrative shadows, becoming important characters and even protagonists. Nevertheless, they have more in common with Bobrov, who is disgusted by the monster he works for, than with Kvashnin, who appears totally congruent with his role. Chekhov's capitalists experience their own factories as terrified visitors. And as factories become a more normal part of Russia's social and physical landscape, they seem to imbue the whole world with their menacing otherness. But before we return to the 1890s, we need to take a closer look at the works of Tolstoy and Dostoevsky, which display a range of strategies for rendering the myriad changes taking place in Russia intelligible as narrative form.

The Economies of *Anna Karenina*

I skvoz' son mne zheleznyi konek
Govorit: "Ty za delom, druzhok,
Tak ty nezhnost'-to k chortu poshli . . ."

And through my dream the iron horse
Says to me: "You mean business, my friend,
So to hell with tenderness . . . ."
—Iakov Polonsky, "Na zheleznoi doroge" (On
the Railroad)

ANDROID KARENINA

For all the fear and confusion that factories inspire in Russian literature, they are usually harmless to the major characters. In the case of Turgenev's *Virgin Soil*, the factory can even serve as a refuge. Giant factories produce an overpowering impression on those who experience them, but at the same time, the novels and stories in which these factories appear can generally sequester them in isolated descriptive passages and shift the main focus of the narrative elsewhere. But there is no way to take the train out of *Anna Karenina* without turning it into a completely different book. In Tolstoy's novel, the relentless movement of the locomotive and the potentially limitless expansion of railroads play a central role, both as the protagonist's cause of death and as the mechanism that threatens to transform Russia into a misshapen monster, at least as far as Levin is concerned. Anna dies under the wheels of a freight train (*tovarnyi poezd*) that is doing its part to import that foreign civilization of artificially induced desire and superfluous production that is the main polemical target of Levin's theory of Russian agriculture. It is no accident that Anna dies the way she does (killed by the machine that drives so much of her life), nor is it an accident that she in particular is linked to the novel's nightmares of industrialization, since trains and factories constitute the invisible infrastructure of her life. Because the train and all that it entails—the industrialized destruction of Russia's agrarian society, runaway consumerism, and the importation of alien values—loom so large, the stakes in representing now-endangered agrarian Russia become correspondingly higher. It is in the most heavily industrialized of the major nineteenth-century Russian novels that we find the most sustained examination of agricultural life and labor.

Turning from a comparative examination of numerous works of literature to a focused reading of *Anna Karenina* (1875–77), this chapter proposes that the double plot of Tolstoy's novel provides aesthetic resources for imagining Russia's temporal heterogeneity on the cusp of an enormous economic transformation. Anna's and Levin's stories differ in their temporal structures, their prevalent generic features, and the relative visibility within them of, alternately, industrial and agricultural economies. The two plots envision two possible paths for Russia, one advancing relentlessly into the industrial future, the other attempting to resist this process by arresting the movement of history. Within the vast imbricated structure of the novel's "labyrinth of linkages," there are distinct narrative pockets in which the generic implications of these two ideologically charged historical options play out. On the one hand, there is Anna's plot, its rhythm driven by the accelerating train and its social background haunted by terrifying visions of barely human peasants laboring in iron and peeking out of crowds on train station platforms. This is a gothic world of ominous fatidic forces in which dreams reveal the hidden costs of Anna's lavish lifestyle and dimly portend personal and social catastrophe. On the other, there is Levin's plotline, in which the mowing scene assumes prime importance as an act of aesthetic preservation of an older, precapitalist social order. In those uncounted hours spent in the fields with his (hired) peasant workers, Levin experiences a temporary synchronization with the people, which allegorizes a harmonious social order uniting peasant and landlord in an age-old brotherhood of labor.[1] At other times, however, Levin struggles with his peasants, who now live under conditions of free labor—a particularly salient issue in the years after the emancipation transformed some 20 million former serfs into (nominally) paid workers.[2] The novel can only preserve this temporary fragment of the old order by sequestering it inside an idyll, where it can be guarded against the corrosive temporality of historical change. To get to Levin's idyll, however, we will have to take a historical detour, since it is by way of a much later period's response to *Anna Karenina* that certain crucial aspects of the novel become legible.

The early years of the twenty-first century have seen the emergence of a new genre of literary production known as the literary mash-up, which typically takes a canonical work from the nineteenth century and updates it with elements of twenty-first-century popular culture, such as zombies, vampires, or robots. In 2010, Quirk Books, publisher of perhaps the best-known example of this genre, Seth Grahame-Smith's *Pride and Prejudice and Zombies* (2009), issued another notable title: *Android Karenina*.[3] In Ben Winters's reimagining of Tolstoy's novel, postreform Russia is a country whose fundamental social antagonisms have been overcome by the widespread availability of robot workers. *Android Karenina* reduplicates the double plot of the original on the level of its character system. In this alternative Russia, each member of the nobility is accompanied at all times by his or her robotic double—a homunculus that embodies the quintessential characteristics of its corresponding human. The familiar characters, including Anna, Vronsky, Kitty, and Levin, together with their mechanical doubles, now live in a world of deliberately anachronistic technology, at the heart of which is a population of robotic cleaners, servants, porters, miners, and soldiers. The robots are programmed not to protest their condition, but a malevolent force threatens the social order. An organization of renegade scientists, committed to an even faster pace of technological change, terrorizes the civilian population by turning their own robots against them. Thus, in a plot development that actualizes one of the fundamental fears—or hopes, as the case may be—of Russian society in the second half of the nineteenth century, these unemancipated mechanical serfs launch a rebellion against their human masters.[4]

The ensuing details of the plot take *Android Karenina* further from Tolstoy's novel, and they are less significant here than the transformation of elements of the original in Winters's rewriting, which suggests what in the nineteenth-century work has become salient for the twenty-first. In particular, the comparison of these nineteenth- and twenty-first-century novels reveals what is available in the former for appropriation and transformation by the steampunk style of the latter. In this regard, the rich detail of Tolstoy's realism is particularly important. The original novel, with its telegrams, mechanical farm equipment, and, above all, trains, provides ample material for repurposing by an aesthetic that "prizes brass, copper, wood, leather, and papier-mâché—the construction materials of this bygone time," as well as "cogs, springs, sprockets, wheels, and hydraulic motion" and "the sight of the clouds of steam that arise during the operation of steam-powered technology."[5] Steampunk makes use of these materials to furnish a vision of "a past that is borrowing from the future or a future borrowing from the past," with the Victorian era as the center of gravity around which this complex temporal structure bends.[6] As we will see, this intermingling of past and future is a persistent formal and thematic feature of the original *Anna Karenina*.

Scholars have argued that one explanation for the continuing appeal of the Victorian era for steampunk art of the late twentieth and early twenty-first centuries is that the technological change of that earlier age, however rapid and disruptive, was accessible to the senses. Drawing on the material culture of Victorian Britain, the steampunk style constructs an alternative modernity based on "the first Industrial Revolution's utterly knowable gadgetry."[7] Thus, the material infrastructure of the steam-powered late nineteenth century is recovered by steampunk as an aesthetic remedy for the alienating effects of an increasingly monotonous and incomprehensible digital civilization, one of whose defining features, in the view of numerous commentators, is its disorienting illegibility. For example, on the level of sensuous experience, Fredric Jameson takes the inability of visitors to orient themselves inside the Bonaventure Hotel in downtown Los Angeles as a "symbol and analogon" of the impossibility of locating oneself in the world system created by postmodern flows of information and capital.[8] Along similar lines, and again taking Los Angeles as the quintessential site of postmodern disorientation, Kevin McNamara posits that the sprawling freeways and suburbs of Southern California constitute a development of the traditional city that is "no longer imaginable as a whole."[9] In place of an inscrutable twenty-first-century economy in which bankers do not understand the financial instruments they are trading and computer scientists do not know what goes on inside neural networks of their own creation, steampunk offers a technological world that still overlaps with the human sensorium.[10]

On their own terms, such analyses of our ostensibly postindustrial age are incisive and compelling. But the focus on changes taking place in the disorienting present almost inevitably relegates the preceding period to the status of a contrastively comprehensible background, while, as we have seen, witnesses to the first Industrial Revolution's transformation of landscapes, cities, and human beings did not feel the same comfort of familiarity in this emerging civilization. In the late 1890s (continuing the tradition of factory scenes examined in the previous chapter), one of Chekhov's reluctant capitalists steps inside her own steel mill and observes "a multitude of enormous, rapidly turning wheels, belts, and levers, the piercing hiss, the screeching of steel, the clatter of mine carts, the harsh puffing of steam, the faces, pale or red or blackened from coal dust, the shirts soaked with sweat, the glint of steel, copper, and fire, the smell of oil and coal, and the wind, now very hot, now cold": this is hardly a success of cognitive mapping (Ch 8:260).[11] As this chapter seeks to show, Tolstoy's novel already sets up a contrast between an earlier agricultural civilization that was not only a better home for human beings but also more conducive to literary representation than the harmful, confusing, and terrifying world of industrial modernity.

In light of the foregoing discussion, it might seem that steampunk recuperates a distorted, ahistorical version of nineteenth-century technology, which it renders benign and even quaint, like the amusing robots that have replaced servants in *Android Karenina*. But it is important to note how steampunk also underscores a set of similar challenges confronting two different periods: how to assimilate radically new means of production to older ways of relating to, inhabiting, and representing the world. Furthermore, Winters's book hints at the importance of this challenge for Russian literature in particular while also showing how a work of art can supply representational resources in situations profoundly different from the conditions in which it was created. It has been argued that capitalism was far more successful in the fictional Russia of the realists than it was in the real Russia of government ministries and entrepreneurs.[12] This may well be the case, but the imaginative horizon of Russian literature clearly extended beyond currently existing conditions, as Winters's adaptation emphatically demonstrates. In *Anna Karenina*, the society of agrarian landowners and peasants appears to be receding into the past, while a new world of industrial and financial enterprises seems to be on the verge of transforming Russia in every respect. Yet this novel resists this new world not just discursively, as when Levin declares that industrialization is a problem for other places, but also formally, by running narrative simulations, as it were, of what could happen if the world of trains and banks established itself fully in Russia. The consequence of such a development, *Anna Karenina* indicates, would not be good.

THE IRON HORSE

As frightening and disorienting as the factory interior often was in Russian literature, it could generally be isolated to self-contained scenes within larger narratives (the broader ramifications of growing industrial fortunes tended to have greater narrative consequences, as we will see in the following chapter on *The Idiot*). The arrival of the train was more consequential for literature, both due to the greater familiarity of train travel for readers and writers and because the spread of railways effected the "industrialization" of the central representational categories of time and space.[13] Over the course of the second half of the nineteenth century, train travel entered the common experience of larger numbers of the kinds of people who read novels. And as the railroad transformed travel, commerce, and military logistics, it exerted a profound influence on the meaning of time. This transformation extended from travelers' personal experience of time to the timekeeping systems of entire countries and continents. By the late nineteenth century, the expansion of national and international rail networks and the speed of railroad travel along them made local systems of timekeeping increasingly unsustainable. At first railroads instituted their own systems of keeping time, but eventually the needs of global communication drove an international effort to standardize world time. The starting point was the Prime Meridian Conference, held in Washington, D.C., in 1884, although the complicated process of institutionalizing a global conception of abstract and universal time in a system of global time zones stretched well into the twentieth century.[14]

The transformed experience of space and time under the influence of the train (an experience that was augmented by the proliferation of numerous technologies, including the telegraph, the telephone, the cinema, and the internal combustion engine) had profound consequences for literature and, indeed, for a whole range of cultural phenomena.[15] Russian writers noted the consequences of the train's capacity to homogenize vast distances, as when Dostoevsky noted sardonically in *Winter Notes on Summer Impressions* (1863) that, following two days and nights of relentless movement, he arrived in Berlin from Saint Petersburg only to find that the German city looked very much like the Russian capital he had just left (D 5:47).[16] Others complained about the damage done by the speed of railroad travel to the characteristic modes of perception that had previously made it possible to observe life and turn it into fiction. Leskov has the narrator of one of his stories relate a remark by Pisemsky—apparently gleaned by Leskov from personal conversation—that "the observed impoverishment of literature is linked, first of all, to the proliferation of railroads, which are very beneficial for commerce, but harmful to literature."[17] According to Pisemsky, the industrial efficiency of railroad travel deprives the traveling writer of most of his material. He relates, gloomily, all the ways that old-fashioned travel by horse could provide endless material for storytelling: the driver would, naturally, turn out to be a scoundrel; the other passengers would invariably be insolent; the groundskeeper at the inn would, of course, be a fraudster; and the cook would be "as slovenly as they come [*neopriatishche*]."[18] In the tradition of *Dead Souls*, each of these interactions with a miscreant, every bit of filth and disorder encountered on the road or in one's soup, would furnish the writer with abundant detail of Russian life. But now, Pisemsky laments, the train, with its unrelenting industrial efficiency, has reduced travel to a mechanical operation where one adheres to the timetable and gets one's dinner from the buffet without even getting into a fight with anyone. All that had furnished the realist with his firsthand knowledge of Russia has been rigorously extirpated from this new mode of travel, reappearing now, if at all, as mere disruption to a rationalized and perfected procedure.

If train travel could drain the color and feeling from life, it could also replace these with its own content: a new, ruthlessly instrumental attitude toward space and the things that fill it. The post-Romantic poet Iakov Polonsky offered a reflection on the fate of the lyric in the age of the railroad in his 1868 poem "On the Railroad."[19] The poem's narrator rides the train through the Russian countryside and observes a series of scenes. Each one could have afford the opportunity for extended lyrical reflection:

> There is home! There, off to the side,
> The batten-clad roof comes into view,
> The dark little garden, bales on the threshing floor;
> One old woman there, perhaps,

Is pining away for me, waiting for her dear one.
I would take a peek into her little corner,
I would rest in the shade of those birches,
Where so many dreams have been sown.[20]

Von i rodina! Von v storone
Tesom krytaia krovlia vstaet.
Temnyi sadik, skirdy na gumne;
Tam starushka odna, chai po mne
Iznyvaet, rodimogo zhdet.
Zaglianul by ia k nei v ugolok,
Otdokhnul by v teni tekh berez,
Gde tak mnogo poseiano grez.

On each occasion, though, the inexorable movement of the train renders the lyrical pause impossible: the narrator will not return home, will not see his old mother, will not rest in the shade of the birches, recalling his dreams. He cannot stop; he is propelled forever onward by the mechanical movement of the train, and this movement changes his relationship to the landscape as well as to his own inner life. More scenes flit past as he fleetingly contemplates various counterfactuals. He might have loved a woman he glimpses through the window, he might have stopped in a nearby village to talk to an old friend. But each stanza of the poem ends with a reiteration of the inevitable: "The iron horse hurries on, hurries on / and, whistling, rolls hundreds of wheels" (*Mchitsia, mchitsia zheleznyi konek / I, svistia, katit sotni koles*). A century later, Michel de Certeau would observe that the train traveler can see everything but can touch nothing, as the world outside the window becomes a mere object of "abstract ocular domination."[21] Although nineteenth-century trains were considerably less comfortable than the clean, air-conditioned train de Certeau's traveler takes through twentieth-century France, the relationship between observing passenger and observed world seems much the same in Polonsky's poem. Wherever he is at any given moment, Polonsky's lyric persona is always already leaving, and the train's movement contaminates his inner experience with industrialized ruthlessness: "And in my dream the iron horse / says: 'You mean business, my friend, so to hell with tenderness.'"

While the expansion of the railroad network may have attenuated travelers' observation and hardened their hearts, its increasing ubiquity in Russian life would eventually lessen its most disruptive effects and even, in some cases, provide new opportunities for storytelling. As Anne Dwyer has observed, both Dostoevsky and Leskov utilized the railroad car as a space for new encounters between usually segregated social and ethnic groups in Russian society.[22] Myshkin and Rogozhin meet at the beginning of *The Idiot* on a return journey to Russia on the Saint Petersburg–Warsaw Railway. Over time, literature was able to domesticate the railroad. While Lebedev in *The Idiot* interprets the rail network covering Russia as the Star Wormwood from the book of Revelation, some thirty years later the bored provincials in Chekhov's *Three Years* use the regular schedule of the train as a signal that it is time for tea. In contrast to the factory, then, which largely remained a space in which it was hard to do anything besides experience awe, the railroad gradually became a motive force in literary narrative.

When it comes to literary treatments of the railroad, Tolstoy stands out for the extreme hostility of his response. Famous for his resistance to many of the social, political, and metaphysical consequences of nineteenth-century modernity, Tolstoy saw the railroad as the emblematic manifestation of these baleful changes. At various times in his writing life, Tolstoy would draw an analogy between railroad travel and prostitution, versus travel by road and normal love; associate it with inflamed, violent, and unnatural passions; and link it to distorted and harmful economic change.[23] Tolstoy also developed innovative narrative techniques to cope with the sensory assault of train travel. The scenes in *Anna Karenina* that take place aboard the train are famous for their protomodernist narrative perspective, which manages to accommodate Anna's rapidly shifting sensory impressions and affective responses but also complicates the relationship of language to its referents.[24] In these moments, Tolstoy moves away from putatively objective representation in favor of a focus on Anna's embodied subjectivity (in this internal focalization, the train scene recalls the factory scenes discussed above) as it is buffeted in the feedback loop formed by the motion of the train and her latent passion for Vronsky.

As she travels, Anna undergoes a transformation under the influence of the train. On her arrival back in Saint Petersburg, she breathes a sigh of relief in expectation of a return to normalcy. However, it is clear that her experience of the world has changed irrevocably: her husband's ears, formerly unremarkable, suddenly look ridiculous (AKP 104/AKN 92). This will not be the only change. Anna starts to experience nightmares, in which she glimpses disfigured peasants performing mysterious work and muttering in French about iron. She realizes that these recall other nightmares she had in the past. The nightmares induce a kind of hermeneutic anxiety as she looks for other, earlier signs linking her illicit love for Vronsky to the train. With time, the reader might begin to notice that these signs seem to emanate beyond Anna's awareness, both preceding her appearance and persisting after her death. The sections that follow will examine the meaning of these signs in a context that most previous examinations have not considered: the public discourse about industrialization and the workers' question. But why should the protagonist of the quintessential high-society novel have nightmares about trains and workers? In seeking an answer to that question, this chapter will show how the narrative of *Anna Karenina* strains under the pressure of historical forces and how generic fissures develop in this work as it attempts to resist the advance of a nightmarish modernity. In this light, the novel's double plot structure becomes a kind of thought experiment in which two alternative paths, each inflected by a different generic mode, narrate two possible fates for Russia.

It is precisely these moments of historical and generic stress, where *Anna Karenina* depicts the collision of different economic forces, that come to the foreground in *Android Karenina*. At first it may seem that Winters's decision to equip Anna with an android companion has more to do with the punning name than with anything in the original novel. However, if we return to Tolstoy's novel while keeping Winters's version in mind, another android—that is, literally, a being resembling a man—is already there: the strange figure Anna sees recurrently in her nightmares, the "little peasant"—referred to repeatedly in the novel as a *muzhichok*—who mutters strange words while moving his hands incessantly inside a sack. Here again, the twenty-first century affords crucial perspective. In a review of *Android Karenina* for the *New Yorker*, Elif Batuman argues that Tolstoy's novel already anticipates the technologized world of Winters's adaptation. In particular, "Anna's nightmare, one of the most famous passages in Anna Karenina, clearly anticipates the 'steampunk-inspired' atmosphere of *Android Karenina*, incorporating a steam locomotive, a peasant-workman repetitively hammering at some metal, and his sinister French mumbling: 'Il faut le battre, le fer, le broyer, le pétrir' ('One must beat the iron, pound it, knead it')."[25] From the perspective opened up by *Android Karenina*, then, the muzhichok who keeps showing up throughout *Anna Karenina* gains new significance: he is pointing toward a future, perhaps one among many alternative futures, that is most fully realized in a science-fictional world where laborers have become mechanical automata. That said, the muzhichok is certainly more than a precursor to the robotic laborers of *Android Karenina*. He also points back to the past—the preindustrial past that persists in the novel's agricultural spaces, but also the labor that went into the construction of the railroads that keep characters and commodities circulating in the novel. The muzhichok's sinister French mumbling is one of the links joining him to an unnatural and alien presence in the midst of Russia's villages and fields.

OMENS AND PEASANTS

True to Tolstoy's famous description of the novel's architecture as an "endless labyrinth of linkages" in a letter to Nikolai Strakhov, the scenes in which the muzhichok appears in *Anna Karenina* form a dense structure of situation rhymes and fatidic implications for both Anna and the reader.[26] The muzhichok practically demands interpretation, so much so that Anna is the first to undertake this hermeneutic operation. It is she who sees an ominous link—"a bad omen," she calls it—between the gruesome train station accident, in which a railway worker is run over by the train from which she disembarks in Moscow, and her incipient relationship with Vronsky (AKP 65/ AKN 61). Scholars are divided on the extent to which Anna is the source of a self-fulfilling prophecy that seems to join her fate to that of this unfortunate worker.[27] At the moment of the disaster, however, the text itself provides an important clue about this connection. As Eduard Babaev has observed, the narrator insistently refers to this accident victim as a peasant (*muzhik*), although, in terms of the work he performs at the station, he is a shunter, in Russian a *stsepshchik*.[28] The true name of the man's occupation is tabooed, to borrow Olga Meerson's apt designation of this technique in Dostoevsky.[29] And it is precisely in this hidden word that we observe how the labyrinth of linkages—*stsepleniia*—and the complex machinery of social and fatidic determinations, in turn linked metaphorically in *Anna Karenina* to trains and rails, shows through.[30] One of these links is the mutilated shunter himself, transmogrified into a mysterious and terrifying muzhichok who will continue to lurk in dreams and shadows throughout Anna's plot.

Numerous readers have identified connections between Anna and the muzhichok. His appearance at key moments and in spaces particularly connected to her—the train, her bedroom—as well as certain details—his tendency to speak French; his sack, which can be read as a grotesque transformation of Anna's red bag; their isolation from the social whole to which each ought to belong—all this suggests their deep connection.[31] Indeed, the muzhichok can be read as Anna's gothic doppelgänger.[32] Given the early connection, sanctioned by Anna herself, between her fate (and her transgression) and the muzhichok, it is understandable that most commentators have interpreted the peasant nightmares and visions in terms of the central psychological and moral dilemmas of Anna's relationship with Vronsky. The muzhichok has therefore tended to function in these accounts as a metaphor for Anna's and Vronsky's actions or for their moral states. For example, Vladimir Nabokov interprets the series of dreams and encounters thus: "The muffled up conductor covered with snow on one side and the stove-keeper whom she sees in her half-dream gnawing the wall with a sound as if something were torn apart, are nothing but the same crushed man [killed by the train that brings Anna to Moscow] in disguise—an emblem of something hidden, shameful, torn, broken, and painful at the bottom of her new-born passion for Vronski."[33] Likewise, Edward Wasiolek associates the images of the train and iron with the "impersonal power of sex" and the inexorability of Anna's fate.[34] For Gary Browning, the dreams and other appearances of the muzhichok amount to "a *symbol* of a dehumanized grotesquery, disinterestedly wielding malicious, cruel, emotional violence, in this instance, upon Anna."[35] Readers have further noted the absurdity of the peasant speaking French and associated this linguistic anomaly with the unnatural, chimerical quality of Anna's moral transgression or read it as a mythical representation of the fatidic force that consigns Anna to death in the end.[36]

Convincing as these readings are, their tendency to fold the muzhichok into Anna's personal story occludes an important aspect of the novel's engagement with contemporary social tensions, and an examination of those tensions shows that the muzhichok is connected to Anna in another, more historically specific way. Concrete economic links join the muzhichok and Anna, insofar as she is an excessive consumer of the very goods produced by the modern economy of factories and railroads that also, inevitably, produces the social and physical catastrophe the muzhichok embodies. It is important to note here, however, that the muzhichok does not "reflect" the workers' question or any other social issue in the sense of appearing in the novel as a slice of contemporary life. His effects on other characters and his distribution within the narrative signal that a more complex process of mediation is taking place here—a process dependent on the stylistic and generic capaciousness of the realist novel. In other words, when the muzhichok appears, he brings with him a whole panoply of tropes that integrate him into longstanding traditions of literary representation. The muzhichok resembles representations of industrial workers that were widespread in the public discourse of the time, but his function in the narrative of *Anna Karenina* also draws on gothic devices that accentuate his status as the unacknowledged remainder of the economic transformation that encompasses all the major characters in the novel.

Although interpretations focused on Anna's and Vronsky's psychological or moral condition have often overshadowed readings of the muzhichok in terms of industrialization and the condition of the Russian worker in the 1870s, some commentators have drawn attention to the concrete historical meaning of this figure. Nabokov describes the muzhichok as "a Russian proletarian in appearance."[37] Michael Katz likewise writes that "Anna's urbanized, alienated peasants have left their traditional pursuits to work on the railway."[38] According to Alexei Pavlenko, peasants in *Anna Karenina* reveal the novel's "political unconscious": "The subject of Anna's and Vronsky's nightmares, and the object of Levin's persistent religious and economic quest, represents the unconscious presence of history in Tolstoy's novel: specifically, the Russian peasant's historical trajectory from an unskilled agricultural serf docilely tilling his master's land to a skilled industrial worker capable of standing up for his or her own economic interest."[39] Pavlenko makes a compelling case for reading the peasant in terms of the inescapable force of history in *Anna Karenina*. However, as I argue below, the transformation of the peasant (who is superhumanly capable in this novel, rather than unskilled) into the figure of the enfeebled industrial worker is precisely what the novel attempts, albeit ultimately unsuccessfully, to arrest by containing these two figures in distinct temporal and generic zones. Most recently, Thomas Newlin has offered an insightful interpretation of the peasant dreams as a manifestation of the larger "category crisis" in *Anna Karenina*, which in turn is linked to the breakdown of "traditional boundaries, categories, and social structures . . . with the accelerating incursion of modernity into Russia."[40] Newlin sees the muzhichok as a mirror of Anna, who is another contradictory victim of Russia's "category crisis." Indeed, while Vronsky and Anna both see the peasant in their dreams, most of the occurrences of the muzhichok are linked to her. The reason for this, I argue, is that she, more than Vronsky, is the novel's exemplary consumer.

As Mina Magda has recently pointed out, Anna's adultery is accompanied by her transformation into a consumer. As she sinks deeper into the transgressive relationship with Vronsky, her consumption of luxury goods increases, so that "the objects that accumulate alongside her fall . . . turn Anna's tragic bedroom into a spectacle of consumption."[41] As she gives herself over to the gratification of the body, as symbolized by her red bag, Anna also acquires more and more expensive goods.[42] Dolly marvels at the luxury and material abundance of the Vozdvizhenskoe estate when she visits Anna. In her final stream-of-consciousness moments before her suicide, Anna notices a husband and wife gazing at her dress and overhears women commenting on the fineness of her lace. As she prepares to fall under the train, her little red bag encumbers her for a moment. All these bad and superfluous things have to come from somewhere, and it is hardly subtle that Anna is crushed by the vehicle of all this material excess. Levin confidently declares that "there can be no workers' question in Russia," but of course there is, both in Russia and in *Anna Karenina*. If Levin can make this claim, it is because the workers are rarely seen and because Anna, not Levin, is the primary beneficiary of the products of their labor.

In his book about Russian agriculture, Levin contends that Russia's poverty stems in large part from the "alien civilization abnormally grafted on to Russia, particularly by the means of communication—the railways—entailing a centralization of the cities, the development of luxury and, as a result of that, to the detriment of agriculture, the development of factory industry, of credit, and its companion—stock-market games" (AKP 484/AKN 408). The centrality of women's consumption in this system became something of a literary theme over the following years, including in Zola's *Nana* (1880) and in Tolstoy's own "The Kreutzer Sonata" (1889), where Pozdnyshev expands on Levin's argument and posits the existence of an industrial-sexual economy in which women's consumerism is coupled with a manufacturing system that exploits countless factory workers (including, as Pozdnyshev does not make clear, hundreds of thousands of women). He claims that women gain "frightening power over people" by turning the vast majority of Russian industry to the creation of huge quantities of consumer goods. The only purpose of these is to adorn women as they themselves circulate in the sexual economy. "Millions of people, generations of slaves, perish at hard labor [*v etom katorzhnom trude*] in factories merely to satisfy women's caprice" (LNT 27:26). It is not necessary to read Pozdnyshev's argument back into Levin's, but doing so helps make clear what is already latent in Levin's social theory: we can imagine a Russia dotted with factories that produce these useless women's things and crisscrossed by railroads that ceaselessly transport them to the cities and towns. The cost of this production is the physical destruction of countless industrial workers. Anna, as one of the greatest consumers of luxury goods in *Anna Karenina*, is the one who glimpses the consequences of this lifestyle. The muzhichok speaks French because he, too, is a fragment of that artificial Western civilization whose incursion into Russia has torn peasant laborers from their communities and turned them into unnatural railway and factory workers. Everything that is wrong with him—his enervation and poverty, his social isolation, his strange and incomprehensible labor, his presence at railway stations and in the homes of the rich, his French speech—points to his identification with invasive capitalism. The reason Anna sees him is that, in effect, he works for her, since she helps drive this infernal economy. In the culminating step of the process, she too will be crushed by the icon of this terrible machine.

"IL FAUT LE BATTRE LE FER": INDUSTRIALIZATION AS NIGHTMARE

Of the nine appearances of the muzhichok or his metonymic attributes in *Anna Karenina* that Browning has enumerated, the first is effectively invisible on an initial reading of the novel.[43] In the middle of part 1, as the train carrying Anna pulls up to the platform in Moscow, the narrative pauses on a few other passengers who are also getting off the train. Among these is a little peasant, carrying a sack, who leaps off the train. At most, anyone reading the novel for the first time might take the five words devoted to the peasant in the original—"a peasant with a bag over his shoulder"—as a quintessential example of what Roland Barthes called the "reality effect," a pure signification that what is being offered here is "reality" itself. Yet on closer examination, even at this first appearance the muzhichok seems to violate plausibility and introduces the destabilizing, fantastic element that will accompany all his subsequent appearances. The narrator mentions the muzhichok disembarking the train just behind the young conductor, who, a moment later, will go back inside the first-class cabin. As Yusuke Sato and V. V. Sorokina have observed, these sentences suggest that the muzhichok exited the first-class cabin, where his presence would have been unrealistic. This in turn suggests that the muzhichok's "reality remains incompletely clarified."[44] The text is not totally clear on this account, but if the muzhichok is, indeed, in the wrong cabin, then this is just the first of his many appearances in places where he does not belong. In any case, the narrative gives no clear indication whether Anna or Vronsky notice him at this moment. The veridical status of the muzhichok—that is, whether he is "really there" in the novel's diegesis, or whether he is a product of the inner states of Anna or Vronsky—is therefore ambiguous from the start.

This uncertainty remains in force in the most famous scenes featuring the muzhichok: Anna's and Vronsky's partially shared dreams. The details vary from one dream to the next, and there are significant differences between the versions that Anna and Vronsky see. Anna encounters a "muzhik, small and frightening, with a disheveled beard." She describes to Vronsky how "he keeps rummaging [in his sack] and suddenly says something in French, very fast, and, you know, rolling his r's: 'Il faut le battre le fer, le broyer, le pétrir . . .'" In another dream, "the little old man is doing something, bent over some iron, muttering meaningless French words, and, as always in this nightmare (here lay its terror), she felt that this little muzhik paid no attention to her, but was doing this dreadful thing in the iron over her. . . . She woke up in a cold sweat" (AKP 361, 752/AKN 307, 630). Here again, Anna privileges the interpretation of the muzhichok as dark portent of some personal calamity. And while Vronsky tries to dismiss the dream and Anna's attempts to interpret it as a bad omen related to her approaching childbirth, the narrative offers no explanation for the dream that would be plausible within the epistemic conventions of nineteenth-century realism.

While Vronsky is eager to dismiss Anna's concerns, his physiological response to what she tells him belies his speech. As Anna recounts her dream, he feels "the same horror filling his soul" as he recalls his own version of the dream (AKP 361/AKN 307). This sense of horror, which, the text underscores, is shared by Anna and Vronsky, might be somewhat surprising to the reader. In the published version of the novel, Vronsky's dream differs from Anna's in significant details. He sees how a "muzhik tracker . . . , small, dirty, with a disheveled beard, was bending down and doing something, and he suddenly said some strange words in French." Furthermore, before we are shown the contents of Vronsky's dream, the narrator offers the reader a reassuringly plausible explanation for what Vronsky has seen: "After lunch he immediately lay down on the sofa and in five minutes the memories of the outrageous scenes he had witnessed over the last few days became confused and joined with the thought of Anna and the muzhik tracker who had played an important role in the bear hunt" (AKP 355/AKN 302). Based on this narratorial explanation, it would seem that each sees a dream based on his or her daily impressions—Vronsky recalls the tracker, while Anna sees traces of her hallucinatory train journey. However, Vronsky nonetheless recognizes a basic and evidently very disturbing similarity between the dream he had seen and the one Anna describes to him.

The drafts of *Anna Karenina* lack this reassuringly naturalistic explanation of the link between the events of Vronsky's day and the content of his dream. In the first complete version of the novel, Anna and Gagin, the character who would become Vronsky, already share a dream, although Gagin's version here more closely resembles Anna's:

> Once, in the middle of winter, he was more late than usual. He had been at dinner, seeing off a comrade who was leaving the regiment. He had drunk more than usual and—this rarely happened with him—fell asleep. Having woken up, he hazily recalled some sort of frightening dream, which had stunned him. In his room there had stood a *muzhik*, small, dirty, with a disheveled little beard, and he had been doing something, bent over, and had suddenly started to speak French, he kept quickly muttering some strange words. And he woke from horror. There was nothing horrible. But in the dream it had been horrible. "What nonsense," Gagin thought, doused himself with water, got dressed, and rode off to her. (AKN 739)

In the published version, Vronsky's dream reflects his day with the visiting foreign prince, including the bear hunt. But at this stage, the little peasant, already displaying his distinctive features, performs inscrutable work while bent over and mutters incomprehensible words in French. Vronsky's reaction, like Anna's a few pages later, is horror, despite the narrator's reassurances that "there was nothing horrible."

While the final version of the novel offers more material for a naturalistic explanation of the apparent dream coincidence, Vronsky and Anna nonetheless react to it with overwhelming, visceral fear. The word the narrator uses repeatedly to describe their state is *uzhas*, a word that Tolstoy favored when describing states of extreme experience, such as a character's proximity to death. Robert Louis Jackson brilliantly traced how a phonic pattern based on the sound cluster *uzh* develops in "The Death of Ivan Ilych" (1886). This pattern evolves from the banal commonplace *neuzheli* ("You don't say?" or "Really?"), uttered by the deceased Ivan Ilych's colleagues on learning of his death, to Ivan Ilych's own *uzhas*, as he realizes he must die.

In the process, we become aware of the horror of death concealed within the coworkers' platitudes. As Ivan Ilych's suffering progresses, his attempts to communicate are reduced to a postverbal scream of pain—conveyed by the single letter *u*.[45] Horror, a prerational, corporeal experience of mortality, thus lingers just beneath the surface of meaning, like the skeleton of language, which will inevitably be revealed in time. It is this *uzhas* that Anna and Vronsky experience when they wake. Yet they are not dying. Unlike Ivan Ilych in his moments of *uzhas*, Anna and Vronsky experience something more distant and obscure than impending death. They cannot articulate it, and the Tolstoyan narrator, so often noted for his omniscience, is also silent on this matter and offers us no insight into the meaning of their terror. This terror at a dream, at fantastic coincidences, at ominous fatidic patterns that form what Helena Goscilo has called a "motif-mesh" threatening to ensnare Anna—all of this points to the muzhichok as a visitor from another world and, in a sense, a different kind of fiction.[46].

If the muzhichok is interpreted as an omen of Anna's dark fate, his appearance contributes to the impression that Tolstoy's novel deviates from the strictly empirical basis of the ideal type of realist novel. Although *Anna Karenina* has often been seen as the supreme achievement of the realist writer par excellence, Tolstoy scholars have also made important qualifications to its putative realism. Richard Gustafson has argued that in Tolstoy's fiction, objects serve as emblems of deeper moral or spiritual truths, so they "tend not to be verisimilitudinous but baldly emblematic."[47] According to Amy Mandelker, "*Anna Karenina* is not a realist novel, although it has come to be read that way. Rather, it reflects on every level, both thematic and formal, Tolstoy's polemic with realism and with Victorian literature, and his quest for mythopoesis as an alternative."[48] The muzhichok in particular has also been read in light of mythological precedents and as a sign of the "subliminal presence of pandemonium" in the novel.[49] Nevertheless, Anna's and Vronsky's reactions to their visions suggest that, even if they inhabit a world filled with fatidic linkages and symbols, they find the irruption of this metaphysical structure into their lives extremely disturbing. Even if the world they inhabit is not strictly governed by natural laws, their reaction to the dreams suggests that they think it is, and they react to the muzhichok as they would to an intruder from a world of gothic horrors.

As a realist fiction with supernatural elements, Tolstoy's novel is in good company. Scholars have traced the persistence of gothic elements throughout realist literature, where it enabled the articulation of a wide range of social, economic, and other anxieties.[50] As Katherine Bowers has put it, "The gothic genre enabled writers to access an array of tropes and conventions that combine melodrama, enhanced fear, and a backdrop of social breakdown to portray this feeling of overwhelming anxiety."[51] Scholars have shown that the gothic was particularly important for Dostoevsky, who learned much from Ann Radcliffe and Charles Maturin as he developed his own narrative technique.[52] Anne Hruska has also written about the importance of Radcliffe's gothic novels for the early Tolstoy.[53] It would appear, then, that many, perhaps most, of the Russian realists sometimes turned to the affective resources of the gothic.

Returning to *Anna Karenina*, Michael Holquist has argued that the vast network of social conventions against which Tolstoy's characters struggle spreads through the narrative like a supernatural force. Characters find themselves in a setting "layered-over with hierarchically stacked fields of force that are invisible in themselves, but whose effects are everywhere present, transforming random movements into meaningful gestures that are signs."[54] It is in the context of this semiotic hypertrophy, where everything seems to mean something, that Anna interprets the peasant in terms of her personal fate. But beyond Anna's conscious awareness, Holquist suggests, the novel registers what Monika Elbert and Wendy Ryden, writing about the gothic in American naturalism, have called "the horror of the real."[55] In this case, the real that the muzhichok dimly suggests is Russia's industrialization. As the embodiment of the destruction and violence that remain otherwise invisible to people like Anna and Vronsky, the muzhichok embodies a gothic "return of the repressed." Valdine Clements describes this fundamental dynamic of the gothic as "something—some entity, knowledge, emotion, or feeling—which has been submerged or held at bay because it threatens the established order of things" and which "develops a cumulative energy that demands its release and forces it to the realm of visibility where it must be acknowledged."[56] The "intense creature-terror" that Anna and Vronsky experience following their convergent dreams points to the uncovering of the buried human costs of industrialization.[57]

RUSSIA'S INDUSTRIAL GOTHIC

The plausible explanation of Vronsky's and Anna's dreams as reactions to events from their waking lives leaves a residue of uncertainty. The coincidence of the images they see suggests another, more distant source. Images of brutalized laborers working to implement Russia's state-directed program of industrialization and infrastructural development were widespread in the public discourse of the postemancipation era. In the context of that discourse, what Anna and Vronsky glimpse in their nightmares begins to resemble the "horror of the real." As we will see, Levin theorizes that runaway modernization is causing Russia to become desynchronized, creating monstrous distortions in its social structure. The muzhichok expresses in the plot what Levin proposes in theory.

Beyond the confines of the novel he haunts, the muzhichok resonates with numerous representations of the costs of industrialization. Within the plot, he is linked especially to the train, a source of many anxieties and baleful associations in the nineteenth century generally, but perhaps especially in Russia. Tolstoy's novel joins a number of other prominent literary responses to the railroad in the 1860s and 1870s. From one side of the political spectrum came Lebedev's interpretation in *The Idiot* of the network of Russian railways as a fulfillment of apocalyptic prophecy from the book of Revelation.[58] From the other, Nekrasov's 1865 poem "The Railroad" depicts the catastrophic labor conditions under which the railways were built, as well as the conventional repression of these human costs:

> The road is nice and straight, the embankments narrow,
> Mileposts, rails, and bridges.
> But to the sides lie Russian bones . . .
> How many there are! Vanechka, do you know?
>
> Hey! Listen to those fearsome exclamations!
> The stamping of feet and grinding of teeth
> A shadow has come over the frosty windows . . .
> What's there? A crowd of corpses!
>
> At times they overtake the iron road,
> At times they run along the side.
> Do you hear the singing? "On this moonlit night
> We like to admire our work!
>
> We wore ourselves out in the heat and the cold,
> With backs always bent,
> We lived in dugouts, struggled with hunger,
> Froze and were drenched, suffered from scurvy.
>
> The literate overseers robbed us,
> The bosses whipped us, need crushed us . . .
> We endured everything, soldiers of God,
> Peaceful children of labor!"
>
> Priamo dorozhen'ka: nasypi uzkie,
> Stolbiki, rel'sy, mosty.
> A po bokatom-to vse kostochki russkie . . .
> Skol'ko ikh! Vanechka, znaesh' li ty?
>
> Chu! vosklitsani'ia poslyshalis' groznye
> Topot i skrezhet zubov;
> Ten' nabezhala na stekla moroznye . . .
> Chto tam? Tolpa mertvetsov!

To obgoniaiut dorogu chugunnuiu,
To storonami begut.
Slyshish' ty penie? "V noch' etu lunnuiu
Liubo nam vidit' svoi trud!

My nadryvalis' pod znoem, pod kholodom,
S vechno sognutoi spinoi,
Zhili v zemliankakh, borolisia s golodom,
Merzli i mokli, boleli tsingoi.

Grabili nas grometei-desiatniki,
Seklo nachal'stvo, davila nuzhda . . .
Vsë preterpeli my, bozhii ratniki,
Mirnye deti truda!"[59]

Vanya, the young general's son, asks his father who built the railroad. His father answers: Count Fyodor Mikhailovich Kleinmichel. That night, the earth itself discloses the truth, as the countless laborers who died to achieve Russia's infrastructural modernization return to the surface, where Vanya sees them as he looks out the window. The devastating human consequences of economic and technological progress materialize as the reanimated bodies of those who really built the railroad, and what was rendered invisible in the abstractions of state rhetoric and economic calculation becomes monstrously concrete. In order for the poem to accomplish this concretization of the social costs of the railroad, it draws on the tradition of the early nineteenth-century Russian gothic, such as the reanimated dead of Vasily Zhukovsky's ballads.[60] Still, for the passenger safely protected by a pane of glass, these horrifying undead workers remain an image beyond reach, like Polonsky's village. In a sense, they can get no closer to Anna, even if she is one of the primary beneficiaries of their labor. She has no contact with these workers in her life, except when she chances to observe the body of one left on the tracks. It is only in dreams—which frequently permit more explicitly symbolic systems of meaning into the realist novel—and related states of semiconsciousness that Anna encounters these *muzhichki*.

In many nineteenth-century accounts, both literary and nonliterary, to both those welcoming progress and those condemning its destructive effects, the train appears as the quintessential icon of modernity and the most powerful image of industrial civilization. As a railway worker, the muzhichok in *Anna Karenina* is thus encoded in a matrix of highly charged details, including iron, trains, bodily disfigurement, foreign technologies and ideologies, and distorted sensory perception, all of which are linked to trains and death by networks of motifs in the novel. Beyond the text of *Anna Karenina*,

84

these details link up with contemporary public discourse for which the railroad stood for modernization and Russia's convergence with the West, while the financing of railroads and the spread of railway commerce were identified with the new financial institutions of capitalism. Moreover, the muzhichok himself is endowed with a number of attributes that, considered in the context of contemporary writing about industrial labor, posit him as a kind of embodiment of the baleful consequences of industrialization in general. In fact, the peasant, taken together with the dead watchman at the beginning of the novel and the drunk factory worker whom Anna glimpses near the end (AKP 762/AKN 639), constitute a kind of inventory of the harmful effects of industrial work, as against the healthy, perfectly functioning workers whom I discuss below in the context of the mowing scene.

The muzhichok displays the kinds of damage and degradation that contemporary social critics observed in industrial workers. To them, industrial labor and the disciplinary and administrative regimes imposed by owners and foremen on the workers destroyed the bodies, minds, and morals of peasants who came to work at industrial sites. Throughout the late 1860s and 1870s, investigative journalists and researchers published accounts of the horrific conditions endured by factory workers, as well as the economic and social havoc wrought by industrialization. For example, in 1869, the radical sociologist, writer, and critic V. V. Bervi, writing under the pseudonym N. Flerovsky, published *The Condition of the Working Class in Russia*, modeled on Friedrich Engels's *The Condition of the Working Class in England* (1845). Flerovsky documents his travels throughout Russia and combines his personal observations with extensive statistical data to paint an unremittingly bleak portrait of the lives of all types of working people in Russia, from wandering peasants performing odd jobs to factory workers. In the course of the book, he deploys detailed statistical data recording the impoverishment of the Russian population and condemns the abnormality of profit-driven activity.[61] This book generated widespread discussion in the Russian press and even implicit comparisons to *War and Peace*, whose final serialized installments appeared in the *Russian Herald* that same year.[62] Flerovsky devotes the last section of his book to the "worker of industrial Russia" and to the empire's industrial regions. Although these appear at first glance to be the most prosperous places he has yet visited, Flerovsky soon confronts the massive exploitation of the workers by the "capitalists" and discovers that the people here are in fact even poorer and more miserable than in the rest of Russia, as attested by their massive mortality rates:

> Out of twelve industrial *guberniias*, in ten the mortality rate is greater than in the most terrible quarters of London, where there are only thieves and paupers. A patriot who gets his hands on such data could lose his mind. Industry, this source of prosperity and happiness for peoples, becomes among us a

scourge which nails [people] into their coffins, a misfortune with which neither plague nor cholera can be compared. The division of labor, which allows the worker to increase his production tenfold, becomes for him a source of starvation, poverty, and death to such a degree that out of the ten industrial *gubernias*, the population shrank in three of them, and did not increase at all in one.[63]

Industrialization was supposed to ensure the prosperity of nations according to economic theory, but in the Russian case, it has apparently proven to be a disaster.

Other observers purported to document the effects of industrial labor on the bodies of workers. Blagoveshchensky's sketch about the iron foundry, discussed in the previous chapter, expresses admiration of the colossal energy of industrial ironworking but also dwells on the damage the labor does to the workers' bodies:

> These heroes of labor do not at all resemble powerful men. They are all slight and thin like skeletons, with exhausted expressions on their faces, with swollen eyes and uneven, angular motions. As one can see, they have all adapted so thoroughly to the hellish conditions of their labor that they carry out their task almost mechanically. From boredom they sometimes carry out various pranks and amuse themselves as best they can. I witnessed how a metallurgist, in the very heat of work, noticing that a worker was coming up behind him with a wheelbarrow . . . , quickly turned and under a hail of sparks managed to smear the man's whole face with soot, for which he received the angry nickname of "devil."[64]

Another contemporary investigative journalist, F. D. Nefedov, wrote a series of historical and ethnographic studies of the textile factories of the Ivanovo district. These studies, published in the 1870s in the newspaper *Russian News*, combined detailed statistics on the horrifyingly inadequate volume of air per worker inside the mills and the insufficient hours made available for workers' rest with harrowing details about their physical suffering. As part of an examination of child laborers at the factories, he asks one worker about the children's fates:

> On one occasion I asked a factory worker what kind of people these boys who work at the drying drums, in the steam vats, and the racks grow up to be.
> He, giving it a bit of thought, responded in the following way:
> —God knows, where they disappear to, we somehow don't see them afterwards.
> —What do you mean, you don't see them?!
> —Just like that, they dry up.
> I took his response for a pure metaphor.

—You mean to say that they subsequently change their line of work and move to another factory?—I asked again.

—No, they just dry up, totally dry up!—the factory worker answered seriously.[65]

The scrawny, bedraggled figure of the muzhichok in *Anna Karenina* resonates with these depictions of industrial workers, suffering from lack of air, intense heat, and the stress of unendurable labor. Through him, Anna gets to witness, like Vanechka in Nekrasov's poem, the hidden truth, buried beneath the railroad tracks, disclosing itself.

AFTER ANNA

I have argued above that the muzhichok is overdetermined by the fatidic forces operating on Anna's life inside the novel and by representational conventions prominent in 1870s Russian public discourse more broadly. If the muzhichok is indeed linked, in something like Anna's and Vronsky's "political unconscious," to the dangers of industrialization, he also seems to be contained by the ambiguous status of their dreams and visions. After all, the little peasant with a sack on his shoulder who jumps off the train at the beginning of the novel could be just an ordinary peasant who somehow managed to get into the first-class carriage. However, things get much stranger and more ominous after Anna's death.

In part 8 of the novel, in the wake of Anna's suicide, history takes over the novel as the plot responds to events that had not yet occurred when Tolstoy began to serialize the novel in 1875. Following Mikhail Katkov's refusal to publish Levin's negative attitudes toward the Russo-Turkish War of 1877, Tolstoy decided to release the final part of the novel as a separate edition.[66] In response to that separate publication, the *Russian Herald* published an editorial essay, where Katkov points out that Anna's name does not even appear in the final part of her eponymous novel. Having been crushed under the wheels of the "juggernaut of our time," having committed suicide "in the new manner," Anna vanishes from the narrative.[67] In her absence, life goes on largely unaffected. At the beginning of the final part of the novel, the narrative shifts to Koznyshev, who is disappointed by the slight interest his book has generated in the press. Burdened by stress, he decides to travel to Levin's estate for a vacation. Since he has to take the train to get there, he has ample opportunity to witness the outpouring of patriotic fervor leading up to the war. On the train station platform, he encounters Vronsky, who is going off to fight in the Balkans. As Vronsky boards the train, the narrator cursorily describes a few other people on the platform. Amid cries of "God save the tsar" and "Hurrah!," a volunteer is bowing. And then at the very end of chapter 2, a tiny detail flits by that the reader is likely to overlook on account of the overabundance of such details in the final part of this massive novel. Behind the young man who was bowing "very conspicuously," there "peeped two officers and an elderly person with a big beard, in a dirty peaked cap" (AKP 775/AKN 650). This is none other than the muzhichok, perhaps in a slightly different guise, but unmistakably part of the same cluster of associations as the previous *muzhichki*. The chapter ends with the words *v zasalennoi furazhke*—in a greasy peaked cap. This cap links the man to the ugly worker, again labeled a *muzhik* by the narrator, whom Anna sees bending down to the wheels of the train, and whom she herself associates with her nightmares. Until this point, there existed the possibility of ascribing these various dreams and visions to Anna herself, but now she is gone. Nor does the text give any indication that Vronsky might have noticed this man and linked him to his own nightmare. As Vronsky departs, apparently oblivious to the people on the platform, the elderly man remains behind. It now seems that the ambiguous reality of the muzhichok in part 1 has been resolved in favor of his independent existence, and the ominous, supernatural force to which he is linked persists even after Anna and Vronsky have both departed the narrative. The nightmare of industrialization, which Anna and Vronsky had glimpsed in transmogrified, oneiric form, is coming true.

In chapter 17 of part 7, Stiva Oblonsky, burdened by debts, overcomes his aristocratic disdain for capitalist moneymaking and gets a remunerative job with an agency whose name translators have tended to render excessively comprehensible. A more literal translation of this preposterous organization is the "United Agency for the Credit-Mutual Balance of the Southerly-Rail Roads and Banking Institutions" (AKP 719/AKN 602).[68] The agency's name breaks Russian grammar, while the organization itself deforms the social fabric of Russia by putting aristocrats like Stiva to work further dismantling the traditional way of life with railways and banks. The muzhichok is the quintessential laborer employed by this monstrous enterprise, its own chimerical name echoing the inscrutable French that he so improbably mutters. Beyond Tolstoy's intransigent opposition to modernity, both the monstrous company and the terrifying peasant draw on the robust associations between industrialization, violence, and horror circulating in Russian public discourse.

THE SYNCHRONY OF LABOR

At the beginning of part 8, it is the train that temporarily unites Vronsky, on his way to the war, and Koznyshev, on his way to Levin's estate of Pokrovskoe. However, to traverse the distance between the train station and Levin's estate, Koznyshev and Katavasov, his university friend and companion on this visit, have to travel in a tarantass on the country road. They arrive at Pokrovskoe "dusty as Moors" (AKP 781/AKN 655). As Kliger has observed, the difference between the railroad, with its deterministic path and inhuman motion, and the slow, meandering country road expresses the division of *Anna Karenina* into two narrative zones, two modern conceptions of time, and "two key truth shapes of modernity . . . at war."[69] The dualistic structure that Kliger identifies also accommodates two different visions of Russia's economic path. The first, which links Anna to the conventional life of the Europeanized Saint Petersburg gentry and the forces of industrialization, imparts its ineluctable rhythm to her life and ultimately destroys her. Levin, as the novel's other protagonist, mostly inhabits an altogether different world, one structured by the temporality of country life and agricultural labor. Whereas the muzhichok, as a figuration of the industrial gothic, suggests the vast social and political consequences of industrialization without articulating them explicitly, the agricultural scenario is developed in considerable depth in the great scene in part 2 where Levin joins his peasants in mowing, and in his various reflections on Russia's agricultural economy.

In one of the most sustained reflections on Levin's mowing scene, Gary Saul Morson observes that this extended description of labor seems unique, not just in Russian literature but in Western realist literature generally:

> If one surveys the European novel, one may reflect that people do not seem to work very much. Who ever works in a Jane Austen novel? Some novelists describe work as hell. Only rarely does it define a life: *Adam Bede* impresses because George Eliot describes carpentry as creativity as well as drudgery. But only Tolstoy, as far as I know, gives us anything like the mowing scene in *Anna Karenina*, where we get, step by tiny step, the strain and pleasure, the merged mental and physical effort, the self-consciousness and loss of self, of a difficult job we are in the process of learning. Tolstoy understood what we have come to call "flow."[70]

This scene is rich in ramifications both for the novel's ideological presuppositions and for its poetics. In contrast to illegible industrial labor, which can only be glimpsed through oneiric screens, agricultural labor turns out to have a great capacity for generating descriptive and narrative interest. In this extraordinary scene, narrative and description, subjective experience and objective detail, combine in perfect sync. The flow of narrative time coexists with temporally suspended subjective experience so perfectly in this scene that it seems to exemplify the balance of destiny and the eternal present that Fredric Jameson has defined as the condition of literary realism.[71] It would be hard to imagine a more striking contrast to all the factory scenes in which the workers and their labor disappear into a chaos of random details.

As Morson puts it, Levin experiences "flow" as he labors together with the men (one could say *his* men, although the meaning of this possessive pronoun is particularly significant here, as I will discuss below). The ultimate effect of this communal labor is a temporary reconciliation between landowner and hired agricultural workers in what appears, for a moment, to be a reconstitution of the prereform relationship of master and serfs. Furthermore, as several readers of this scene have noted, it takes on the characteristics of an idyll from which the social conflicts present throughout the rest of the novel are temporarily excluded. What enables the preservation of an idyll in the midst of a realist novel—moreover, one particularly concerned with the effects of modernization—is one of the most notable structural features of *Anna Karenina*: its relativistic time.

Scholars have long drawn attention to this phenomenon in Tolstoy's novel, as well as the steadily increasing divergence that it creates between the Anna and Levin plotlines. Nabokov observed in his *Lectures on Russian Literature* that the novel groups the principal characters according to their differentiated temporality, so that over the course of the novel, Stiva Oblonsky, Anna/Vronsky, and Levin/Kitty come to inhabit incompatible timelines. The intersubjective temporal flow of the narrative adapts to the personalities and lifestyles of characters. Nabokov notes in particular how "the quality of Lyovin's highstrung and moody nature is reflected in the curious jerks given here to the thread of the chronological web Tolstoy is weaving."[72] Georg Lukács considered the structure of time in *Anna Karenina* one of the most important aspects of the book, particularly with respect to its place in the history of the European novel. According to Lukács, Tolstoy's works are riven by three contradictory temporalities: the time defined by social convention; natural domestic life; and, finally, the moments of potential transcendence, such as the scene of Karenin and Vronsky at Anna's deathbed. While the first two forms of time devolve into mere monotony in the experience of the alienated modern subject, the third remains apart—"mere moments, isolated from the other two worlds and without constitutive reference to them"—as the promise of a different, integrated existence, but one which cannot be part of the lived experience of the novelistic protagonist.[73] "Thus," Lukács concludes, "the three concepts of time are not only mutually heterogeneous and incapable of being united with one another, but moreover none of them express real duration, real time, the life-element of the novel."[74] For Lukács, the world of nature, as it appeared to modern (that is, novel-reading) people, could only be nature perceived from within culture (which congealed into a seemingly immutable structure that Lukács referred to as second nature). For people entrapped in second nature, any glimpses of reconciliation could only be fleeting and incapable of reintegration into the temporal flow of lived experience.

Lukács's analysis elucidates the importance of *Anna Karenina*'s heterogeneous time, but his tripartite division is not sufficient to capture the full range of the novel's temporal variations. Considered as a whole, the novel's temporality is composed of numerous individual rhythms linked to particular characters and their distinctive professional and social activities. Minor characters are subsumed by the rhythms of their ways of life, while Anna and Levin exceed their environments. Stiva Oblonsky and Karenin are integrated into the temporal organization of their work and the prevailing rhythms of their parts of the novel, so that the pace of the narration mirrors, in Nabokov's words, Oblonsky's "routine of animal existence which his wife's misfortune cannot mar." His work, first at the government ministry but also, it is strongly implied, at the railway/bank, will likewise consist of imperturbable routine. Karenin, for his part, inhabits his "series of committee meetings and other administrative chores [as] he quietly and steadily makes his way toward bedtime and its lawful joys."[75]

As the novel's two protagonists, Anna and Levin are associated with the two most ideologically significant forms of labor in the novel. Of course, Anna is not directly involved in industry, but it is precisely the rhythm of industrial, Westernized civilization—exemplified by the motion of the train—that propels her to her doom. As critics have observed, her emotions are linked to the disorienting and unnatural (for Tolstoy) effects of travel by train.[76] Anna becomes overstimulated by the various excesses of artificial civilization, as demonstrated most vividly in her hallucinatory train ride from Moscow back to Saint Petersburg at the end of part 1. These psycho-physiological effects of the railroad are in turn linked to Anna's frightening visions of the muzhichok. Indeed, the driving force of the narrative, her act of adultery, is closely linked to the train both as the site of crucial interactions between Anna and Vronsky and as a powerful influence on her state of mind. In anticipation of "The Kreutzer Sonata," the effects of the train are both physiological and moral, distorting perception and deforming judgments. In the end, the train destroys Anna and carries Vronsky away to his probable death. As Vladimir Alexandrov puts it, "Vronsky and Anna appear to be rushing through life toward the end of their time, which is death, whereas Levin and Kitty linger in slow time, which is life."[77]

Levin's own relationship to time is certainly not untroubled, however. At the end of the novel, the closest he comes to a resolution of his temporal predicament is to realize that

> I'll get angry in the same way with the coachman Ivan, argue in the same way, speak my mind inappropriately, there will be the same wall between my soul's holy of holies and other people, even my wife. I'll accuse her in the same way of my own fear and then regret it, I'll fail in the same way to understand

with my reason why I pray, and yet I will pray—but my life now, my whole life, regardless of all that may happen to me, every minute of it, is not only not meaningless, as it was before, but has the unquestionable meaning of the good which it is in my power to put into it! (AKP 817/AKN 634)

Given Levin's many oscillations between hope and despair, conviction and doubt throughout the novel, the reader may be left with a degree of lingering skepticism about the permanence of this transformation. On his way to this moment, Levin has experienced a number of other transformative moments, all of which have nonetheless dissolved in corrosive everyday time, which, as Lukács argues, invariably reasserts itself following moments of transcendence in Tolstoy. Within this temporal configuration, the "gentry nest, radically closed in upon itself," seems perpetually under threat.[78] Nevertheless, the novel seems intent on articulating this idyllic vision as the nucleus of an altogether different conception of Russian life. The temporal and representational balance mediated by the rhythm of labor in the mowing scene radiates out as a conception of the proper relationship of the different parts of the Russian economy.[79]

The entirety of the mowing scene is punctuated by references to time. Just as Levin is beginning the work, a peasant warns him that once he begins, there can be no stopping: Levin will be integrated into the rhythm of the work and will have to move at the uniform pace of all the mowers working in concert across the field. The peasant's warning not to "lag behind" (*otstavat'*) echoes Levin's earlier concern that he will not be able to keep up with the mowers. As he begins the work, this concern recurs insistently. Tolstoy's characteristic repetition here achieves a formal modeling of Levin's thought process as forms of the verb *otstavat'* occur six times over three pages, most frequently in terms of the danger of Levin lagging behind the peasants (AKP 248–50/AKN 213–15). But Levin does not lag behind the others, and as he becomes engrossed in the labor and gives himself over to the rhythm of the work, he begins to experience moments in which he does not notice time. Meanwhile, the grammatical aspect of the verbs shifts from perfective to imperfective as Levin enters the continuous time of the agricultural labor.

The reader is treated in these pages, as Morson notes, to an exquisitely detailed description of the mowing and all its sensations: the exhaustion of muscles, the feeling of one's back drenched in sweat, and the heat of the sun on one's skin. While Levin ceases to sense time, the narration lingers on this scene. Supplementing the rhythm of the mowing itself is the pattern of intervals between the mowing of individual paths. As Levin completes a path, he and the reader are afforded a view of the surrounding scene and a respite from the work. The mowing provides the narrator opportunity for the detailed enumeration of the natural objects that the mowers encounter, including branches, quails' nests, and snakes (AKP 253/AKN 217). This labor, requiring the full effort of both body and mind, generates vast quantities of sensory data for the novel to record. Yet the work is also calm enough to allow Levin to observe the surrounding landscape. In a word, mowing supports both narration and description. In place of the monotony of industrial labor, which is both physically devastating to the workers and so meaningless as to be illegible, agricultural labor allows both the human being and literary representation to flourish. But beyond its salubrious effects, this mowing scene serves as a microcosm for a particular vision of Russian social organization and economic life.

Decades later, Tolstoy would provide a theoretical statement that corroborates what this scene puts into practice. In his polemic against factory labor, "The Slavery of Our Time" (1900), Tolstoy takes issue with the political economists, who, he argues, are solely interested in the condition of factory workers because they regard industrial labor as the inevitable culmination of the evolution of economies toward capitalism. His own critique is more fundamental than that of the economists. As far as Tolstoy is concerned, the chief problem with industrial labor is its "monotony" (*odnoobraznost'*). Monotony appears to be the key feature distinguishing healthy, meaningful work, such as existed before industrialization, from that which has no meaning to the person performing it and is likely to have deleterious effects. In the course of the essay, Tolstoy repeatedly contrasts the effects of "free, healthy, varied, and meaningful" agricultural work with the unhealthy, repetitive, and stupefying conditions of industrial labor: "All the sages and poets of the world always saw the realization of the ideal of human happiness only under the conditions of agricultural labor." For their part, "working people whose habits have not been perverted prefer and have always preferred agricultural labor over all other kinds." Furthermore, "factory labor is always unhealthy, monotonous, whereas agricultural [labor is] the healthiest [and most] varied; . . . agricultural labor is always free [*svobodnyi*], *i.e.* . . . the worker alternates labor with rest according to his will, whereas labor at the factory, even if it belonged to the workers themselves, is always unfree, dependent on the machine" (LNT 34:158). In this fascinating passage, which bears traces of Tolstoy's quarrel with Marx, the temporality of industrial labor, governed by machines, rather than the rhythms of the human body, makes it fundamentally incompatible with human flourishing.[80] Not only are the intervals of agricultural labor better synchronized with the natural rhythms of the human body and therefore able to accommodate periods of labor and rest, but this synchronization also corresponds to the appropriateness of that kind of work to the demands of human freedom.[81] In speaking of *svobodnyi* labor, Tolstoy implicitly distinguishes the freedom of the worker to control the pace of labor in the field from the question of "free labor" (*vol'nonaemnyi trud*)—that is, wage labor—that was vigorously discussed in the years of Russia's postemancipation industrialization. What is more, Tolstoy explicitly associates agricultural labor with literary representation by noting that "all the sages and poets of the world" had incorporated praise of agricultural labor into their works.

In *Anna Karenina* agricultural labor is already shown to support temporal balance in both social and aesthetic terms. The language with which the narrator describes Levin's integration into the work of mowing parallels Levin's own theory of how the Russian economy ought to develop. Levin argues elsewhere that the economy should develop in such a way that "the other branches of wealth do not outrun (*operezhat*) agriculture, that, in conformity with a given state of agriculture, there should exist corresponding means of communication," and that the railroads, rather than helping agriculture,

> had outrun agriculture and halted it, causing the development of industry and credit and therefore, just as the one-sided and premature development of one organ in an animal would hinder its general development, so credit, the means of communication, the increase of factory industry—though undoubtedly necessary in Europe, where their time had come—here in Russia only harmed the general development of wealth by setting aside the main, immediate question of the organization of agriculture. (AKP 484/AKN 408)

Just as it is essential for all the mowers to work together in synchronized rhythm, Levin argues that the entire economy of Russia must develop as an organic whole, its various interrelated components moving at the correct pace. Otherwise, industry, "credit," and other branches of Western-style modernization threaten to cripple agriculture and encourage the formation of a dangerously lopsided civilization.

Levin's argument takes its place among diverging views of Russian economists about the proper pace and rhythm of economic development. Economic liberals like Boris Chicherin argued that economic development was governed by universal laws, so that the only task of governments was to avoid interfering in the natural process. In such a view, national particulars were artificial impediments to the operation of the law of political economy. For example, as I discussed in the introduction, the preface to the first volume of Gorlov's *Foundations of Political Economy* argued that the "former, artificial organization" of Russian economic life—that is, serfdom—was giving way to the "natural laws" of the national economy, which it was economists' job merely to observe.[82] However, numerous other groups, from government ministers favoring protectionism, to populists and slavophiles who thought that Russia's economic path would be distinct from that of Western

Europe, argued that the pace and direction of Russian economic development would differ from that of Europe.[83]

Levin himself clearly sides with the latter group. At one point, he boldly declares to Stiva that "there can be no workers' question in Russia" (AKP 375/AKN 319). He tells Stiva that he has traveled to the industrial cities of "Germany, Prussia, France, and England" (AKP 375/AKN 318). When he runs into Shcherbatsky, Kitty's cousin, the latter mockingly invites Levin to see the other Europe—to join him in Paris, rather than the industrial city of Mulhouse (AKP 351/AKN 299). These visits have reinforced his idea that, unlike with Europe and its economic laws, the key consideration for Russia's economic development is the relationship of the (Russian) peasant to the (Russian) land. Levin's argument closely resembles the views of protectionist economists of the time, who argued that the geographical and cultural conditions of Russia favor an agricultural economy rather than European-style industrialization. In particular, the passage from *Anna Karenina* just quoted is very similar both in substance and even in its vocabulary to an argument made by Ludwik Tęgoborski, a Polish-born economist, diplomat, and Russian government official who between 1852 and 1855 published a vast study titled *On the Productive Forces of Russia*. In this detailed analysis of the Russian economy, Tęgoborski argued that, because Russia was not geographically or culturally equipped to compete with the countries of Western Europe in industrialization, it should focus on the development of its agricultural production and local small-scale (*kustarnyi*) industry:

> From all this we think it may fairly be inferred that Russia, not being in a position to equal or outstrip [in the French original, *dépasser*] other countries in the career of manufacturing industry—not combining the requisite conditions for becoming a great manufacturing country—we should rather seek to stimulate those branches of industry which are best adapted to the situation of our eminently agricultural country, and best combine with the industry of our villages; and that, as a general rule, we should endeavor to protect those manufactures of which our own soil supplies us with the raw materials.[84]

In Levin's vision, it is precisely the relative pace at which different elements of the Russian economy develop that is of crucial importance. As this argument about the pace of economic development is incorporated into the narrative pattern of *Anna Karenina*, it changes into a series of rhythms, in which form it is contrasted with the unnatural rhythm of modern industrial civilization, whose metonym—the train—claims both Anna and a number of peasant workers throughout the novel. The ideal pace of Russian economic development, with its agricultural focus, is isomorphic with the synchronization of movement that Levin and his workers experience in the mowing scene.

LEVIN'S LABOR IDYLL

The novel performs a double sequestration of Levin's (and Tolstoy's) vision of social reconciliation. First, Levin's estate of Pokrovskoe is isolated from the surrounding world of railroads and *muzhichki*. On the inside, the Levin household represents an economy in its premodern sense—that is, a self-sufficient household unit. Like idylls in the age of the novel generally, Levin's estate preserves this autonomous *oikos* against the incursion of a larger economy mediated by market forces. Resisting the relentless acceleration of a technological economy and its attendant perpetual obsolescence, the idyll tries to stop history. Inside the idyll, production balances consumption, while outside it, the economy either undergoes continuous growth or suffers the catastrophe of contraction. One of the most representative scenes of idyllic self-sufficiency comes in chapter 2 of part 6, when representatives of the Shcherbatsky and Levin households meet and Kitty introduces a new method for making jam. In this moment, despite Agafia Mikhailovna's suspicion of this innovation, the scene radiates abundance and well-being as the women come together around the estate's bumper crop of berries. Indeed, compared to the wrenching questions of modernization that Levin confronts in the industrial cities of Europe and even in his relations with hired peasants on his own estate, this debate about innovations in jam-making begins to look like a domesticated reduction of the crises confronting the world beyond the boundaries of the estate. Two decades later, Chekhov seems to gesture at the impossibility of maintaining this atemporal vision of self-sufficiency when, in "In the Ravine," he illustrates the pointless abundance of the Tsybukin family with the image of Varvara's jam, which accumulates too fast to be consumed (Ch 10:179).

However, even the inner world of the Levin estate is threatened by modernity. As I have already noted, there is always a distance, both spatial and more broadly chronotopic, separating Levin's estate from the world of railroads and urban civilization. Yet even on Levin's estate, problems stemming from the new economic conditions frustrate his plans. Before the mowing scene, Levin struggles with a new, hired workforce. Amid the inefficiency and disorder caused by the peasants' seemingly eternal resistance to the master's commands, the narrator notes that "the hay was to be got in not on half shares with the peasants but by hired workers [*rabotnikami*]" (AKP 155/AKN 135). When Levin tries to hire enough workers to plow the fields, he finds out that the steward cannot hire enough: the men demand too high a payment. "Again this force opposed him," we read (AKP 156/AKN 135). A major obstacle to the realization of Levin's plans is the changing nature of labor relations between peasants and landlords in the wake of the emancipation.

Discussions of the problems posed by free labor (*vol'nonaemnyi trud*) were common amid the broader discourse about the peasant question. Tolstoy's longtime friend Afanasy Fet published a series of essays in various periodicals in the 1860s and 1870s, in which he reflected on his own experiences as a new landowner. The first of these, which appeared shortly after the emancipation, was titled "Reflections on Free Labor." Here Fet considers the difficulties he encounters when he tries to draw up a contract with his hired workers. He signs a contract with one former serf, only to receive a visit from the man's uncle that night. "No, the young one cannot receive money, because I am his master [*khoziain*]," says the uncle.[85] "In vain did I try to explain to Gavrila that now, on the contrary, there was no law that allowed someone to make another work," Fet recalls.[86] The peasants, still living according to the old order, have no concept of a legally binding contract—or *kundrakh*, as Uncle Gavrila calls it—between an employer and an employee. More than a decade later, Levin finds that his workers have still not adjusted to this new state of affairs. When he tries to explain to the peasants how they can enter into a mutually beneficial relationship with him, he finds that they refuse to trust the landlord (AKP 339/ AKN 289). There seems to be no place for the kind of rational economic calculation between former serf and former master that could make the new system of free labor function. It is only during the mowing scene that the work seems to effect a reconciliation between landlord and laborer.

This is why a second concentric circle is necessary, in which the old, patriarchal relations can be temporarily reconstituted. It is notable in this regard that in the mowing scene the narrator refers to the hired workers as mowers and *muzhiki*, while elsewhere in the novel, Levin has to deal with recalcitrant and uncomprehending "workers" (*rabochie*), a word with connotations of low-prestige unskilled labor.[87] Earlier in the novel, Levin despairs at the incompatible motivations guiding him—the employer—and the workers, whom he has to pay, but in the mowing scene these incompatibilities seem to fade away as the postemancipation conflict between wage laborers and bosses is suspended. A much older, more stable form of social relations seems to reemerge, in which the painful adjustment to a new system of free labor and relations mediated by contracts and payment is temporarily suspended.

That this reconciliation had to come at the cost of generic consistency was a feature of the novel already noted by its first reviewers. In May 1876, while the serialized installments of *Anna Karenina* were in the process of being published in the *Russian Herald*, a review of the novel in progress appeared in that journal. The author (probably the novelist V. G. Avseenko) defended the novel against detractors who criticized its remoteness from the topical concerns of the day, but found fault with Levin's character and with the scenes focusing on his estate.[88] The reviewer observes an aesthetically unsatisfactory shift in the generic mode in those moments of the novel. He writes: "In those parts of the novel where Levin emerges as the main character, it is as if the dramatic tension wanes, and the reader enters the realm of idyll. This pertains in particular to the chapters devoted to Levin's country life. Here the interest concentrates not on the collision of characters, but on the epic representation of the halted flow of time."[89]

The reviewer's association of the mowing scene with the idyll is suggestive. Mikhail Bakhtin identified one of the chief characteristics of the idyllic chronotope in a kind of temporal condensation, whereby time and place become fused in a stable unity. "This unity of place in the life of generations weakens and renders less distinct all the temporal boundaries between individual lives and between various phases of one and the same life."[90] Each time the reader is introduced to one of the peasants alongside whom Levin labors, the text offers a laconic encapsulation of the man in which his physical characteristics seem to express his essence. Thus we read about Prokhor Ermilin, "a famous mower, a huge, swarthy man," or Tit, a "small, skinny muzhik" who cuts down wheat in "his wide swath" (AKP 255, 249/AKN 219, 214). Notably, Tit is identified in the original as a muzhichok, yet he bears none of the disturbing characteristics of the muzhichok associated with the railroad and Anna's nightmares. These men do not tire as they work: it is as if the divide between struggling subject and unyielding object has been suspended and the labor these men perform belongs to their essence. Despite his own considerable physical strength, Levin struggles to keep up with the peasants, even the old ones, until the moment when he becomes integrated into the work and seems to acquire their inexhaustible energy. These same peasants baffle Levin with their resistance to his attempts at rational management, but they mow perfectly with their simple traditional implements, rest while eating their simple food, and seem entirely content in their world. It is only here, in this moment that Bakhtin aptly describes as a labor idyll, that Levin is able to withdraw from the problems afflicting his estate.[91] For a few hours, the socioeconomic tensions of this new historical moment are resolved, and worker and landlord are united in a community where social distinctions have been suspended.[92] Not long after, however, Levin's estate returns to its desynchronized condition, like Russia itself.

There is another, more specifically literary reason that the mowing scene requires sequestration in an idyll. Tolstoy manages to fuse agricultural labor with novelistic narration and description in this scene, but in the long term, over the course of a lengthy narrative, the connection between repetitive labor and the fundamentally biographical form of the realist novel begins to break down. For all the effort *Anna Karenina* puts into distinguishing between beautiful agricultural and terrible industrial labor, the endlessness of any kind of manual labor contradicts one of the basic features of novelistic narrative: its foundation in a human life that changes over time. Russian literature is full of agricultural estates, but there are few examples of peasants laboring in the fields in these works, including earlier works by Tolstoy.

Lounsbery, discussing "A Landowner's Morning," notes that the serfs in that early story bear the physical traces of their unremitting toil, but the narrative does not show them laboring:

> Labor that marks the body in this way does not, it seems, lend itself to artistic representation. If there are virtually no well-known nineteenth-century Russian novels that are primarily about peasant life, this is largely because the kind of work peasants most often do—hour upon hour of backbreaking, monotonous tasks performed alongside others who are engaged in the same work—is not well suited to a narrative form that evolved to represent an individual's progress in life and the compromise this individual must reach with society in order to develop.[93]

The labor in the fields is never-ending, but Levin's participation in it is occasional. After the mowing scene, he goes on to other things, including his relationship with Kitty, and the novel moves on with him. The resolution of the temporal and ideological conflicts temporarily achieved by the mowing scene cannot extend to the novel's narrative as a whole.

Nevertheless, for all his troubles Levin does not experience the consequences of Russia's transformation with nearly the same force that Anna does. He holds to his gentry ways, while around him Russia moves ever further into the world of credit, banks, and railroads. It is especially significant that the railroad is banished from Levin's estate, because it is precisely the railroad that threatens the isolation of this agricultural community and its strictly local economy. As long as Pokrovskoe is separated from the railway by the country road, the temporal split between Levin's estate and the capitals and their inhabitants can be maintained. For the time being, the novel can maintain its antithesis between the agricultural community and the technological civilization of iron and steam that was in reality incorporating Russia into a system of international grain trade. Agriculture, taken out of isolation, was becoming part of an increasingly integrated economic system in which the sale of grain, made possible by those "means of communication" that Levin criticizes, was becoming a major component of the Russian economy. During the terrible famine of 1891–92, Tolstoy blamed the railroads for exacerbating the crisis by enabling profiteers to transport grain to more profitable markets.[94] Other critics would emphasize the government policy of exporting grain to finance industrialization as one of the causes of the disaster.[95] In the public discourse, the railroad represented the imposition of the laws of international capitalism onto the localized agricultural production of the Russian countryside.

In *Anna Karenina*, at least for the time being, Levin's peasants remain safely removed from both the railroad and their monstrous double, the industrial muzhichok. Multiple protective barriers separate them from the train cars and cities he inhabits. Pokrovskoe is sequestered from the outside world, and within the estate, the mowing scene preserves social forms and representational capacities that are absent from the rest of the novel. Inside this circumscribed space, where the forces pulling Russia in different directions come to a temporary halt, agricultural labor accrues extraordinary narrative and descriptive interest, thereby expanding the range of human activities available to literary realism.[96] It is remarkable, in the final analysis, that this is the most famous scene of people laboring in nineteenth-century Russian (or perhaps any) literature. The mowing scene represents a rearguard action against economic and social forces threatening to destabilize or destroy the world that Levin, a proud member of the landed gentry, is eager to defend. This scene's vividness also reminds us that forms of activity particularly associated with economic change, such as factory labor and capital accumulation, remained obscure and difficult to represent in numerous works of Russian literature from this period.

As we have seen, *Anna Karenina* appeared in the midst of a long series of works that confronted the factory as a particularly difficult object of representation. Even more than the railroad station or the train car, the factory embodied the submission of human activity to economic logic. The factory floor was a space that encumbered most of the activities that constitute the substance of realist novels—speaking, thinking, even observing. Of course, the factory could not remain a self-contained space, striking in its sudden appearance in the midst of fields or villages. Factories could only exist within networks of production, transportation, exchange, and consumption. Whereas the factory scenes in the works of the various writers examined in chapter 1 tended to remain isolated from their surrounding narratives, in *Anna Karenina*, where factories do not appear, the broader consequences of the industrial civilization heralded by those factories comes to the forefront, both for the structure of Russian society and, perhaps, for the shape of Russian literature. Although the events that fill the pages of *Anna Karenina* have much more to do with Paris (or Saint Petersburg and Moscow) than with Mulhouse, the world that the trains and factories were creating already reached far beyond those distant factory towns. In this respect, Tolstoy's novel forms a thematic bridge to the two chapters that follow. *Anna Karenina* is balanced between the expanding railroads and Levin's stubbornly resistant domestic *oikos*. In *The Idiot* and *The Brothers Karamazov*, it is not the railroad but the cash nexus that exerts its force on each novel's narrative dynamics and economic imaginary. And as powerful as Tolstoy's railroad is, Dostoevsky's money—protean, mobile, alternately undetectably abstract and indestructibly concrete—proves to have even farther-reaching effects on the shape of his novels.

Myshkin among the Merchants:
Forms of Money and Narrative Form in *The Idiot*

> He advanced the following Paradox, That it
> required much greater Talents to fill up and
> become a retired Life, than a Life of Business.
> Upon this Occasion he rallied very agreeably
> the busie Men of the Age, who only valued
> themselves for being in Motion, and passing
> through a Series of trifling and insignificant
> Actions. In the Heat of his Discourse, seeing a
> Piece of Money lying on my Table, I defie (says
> he) any of these active Persons to produce half
> the Adventures that this Twelvepenny-Piece
> has been engaged in, were it possible for him
> to give us an Account of his Life.
> —Joseph Addison, "Adventures of a Shilling"

"THEY STOKE FIREPLACES WITH MONEY"

More than any other of Dostoevsky's fictions, *The Idiot* (1868–69) depicts the lives of the Russian financial elite. To give some sense of the wealth of characters like Totsky and Rogozhin, who together are worth several million, it is useful to consider that a skilled Russian factory worker in the industrial center of the Shuisky district in the late 1850s—a time of relatively high wages—could expect to earn 11 or 12 silver rubles a month, while the entire budget of the Russian government in 1867 was about 415 million rubles.[1] From the perspective of the first generation of the novel's readers, the wealth so suddenly conjured up and squandered in this novel is particularly striking given that parts of the contemporary press attributed the weakness of the Russian economy throughout the early to mid-1860s to an insufficient supply of capital (*bezdenezh'e*).[2] Events of the preceding years—including the government's massive borrowing during the Crimean War (1853–56); a speculative boom followed by a banking crisis in 1859, which greatly com-

101

plicated the government plan to subsidize former serfs' purchase of land; and a general economic downturn linked to the global Panic of 1857— made debates about Russia's economic future nearly ubiquitous in the print media.[3] The combined impact of lingering financial crisis, economic upheaval, and the massive human cost of the Crimean War led to a decline in living standards in the Russian population as a whole between 1856 and 1865, as the social historian Boris Mironov has shown.[4] Dostoevsky experienced the consequences of the economic crisis directly: in the summer of 1865 his journal, *The Epoch*, went bankrupt amid a widespread decline in periodical subscriptions and revenues.[5]

While commentators offered explanations of, and solutions to, Russia's ongoing economic difficulties, reviewers of the first chapters of *The Idiot*, sometimes writing in the same periodicals, ridiculed the colossal sums that kept appearing in the novel. For example, D. D. Minaev included an epigram about the novel in his feuilleton for the satirical journal *The Spark:*

> In your pocket, poor man,
> A penny has a place of honor, and a big one,
> While in the ingenious novel
> Millions are worth nothing.
> We Slavs endure cold
> In our homes not for the first month.
> While in the wondrous novel,
> They stoke fireplaces with money.

> U tebia, bedniak, v karmane
> Grosh v pochete—i v bol'shom,
> A v zateilivom romane
> Milliony ni po chem.
> Kholod terpim my, slaviane,
> V dome mesiats ne odin.
> A v prichudlivom romane
> Topiat den'gami kamin.[6]

The abundant wealth, which strained the credulity of reviewers, comes not from the landed property of noble protagonists, as in so many other nineteenth-century Russian novels, but from social groups that remained mostly peripheral to the Russian literary canon: merchants and *raznochintsy*.[7] Most of the noble characters, on the contrary, are impoverished, and their economic dependence on members of other social groups becomes a major motivation for the plot. Indeed, the novel's financial plot captures Prince

Myshkin in its orbit (and even necessitates complicating his aristocratic title, as we will see). Contrary to the etymological suggestions of the novel's title, Myshkin himself does not remain an isolated and idiosyncratic figure separated from society.[8] A web of financial ties define his relationships with other people and with the material world as long as he inhabits the narrative space of the novel.

This chapter on *The Idiot* focuses on an ongoing struggle between two moneyed factions, characterized as modern capitalists and backward merchants, which runs alongside the main plotline of the novel. The rich men who vie to control Nastasia Filippovna generally fall into these two categories based on their biographies, the sources of their wealth, and the degree to which their attitude toward money can be characterized as either capitalist or fetishistic.[9] While the capitalists earn their money by means of various business ventures and gain social status through their successful investments, the merchants attempt to keep their fortunes sequestered within their families and transfer wealth through inheritance. The sums of money that appear in *The Idiot* bear traces of their origins wherever they circulate. The following pages will track the movement of the inherited money of the merchants, which proves very difficult to spend and also unprofitable to those who possess it: both of the prominent characters associated with the merchantry—Rogozhin and, as I will argue, Myshkin—benefit little from their money and ultimately end up penniless. Moreover, Myshkin's fate mirrors Rogozhin's in that both end up exiled from Russia, with their narratable lives effectively over, while the capitalists Totsky and Epanchin continue living their successful professional and social lives beyond the concluding chapter. The novel thus offers its prognosis of Russia's economic future by eliminating the merchants and providing the capitalist entrepreneurs with an unobstructed path to continued success, although it does not follow them into this future, which appears to lie beyond the limits of what the novel can narrate. Furthermore, while the merchants and capitalists compete for economic dominance, the transactional logic that characterizes their economic activities infects the plot involving Myshkin and Nastasia Filippovna.[10] While she attempts to elude commodification by threatening to become a wage laborer, Myshkin's epileptic vision reveals that he has accepted a quasi-ontological connection between material objects and their monetary value. Nastasia Filippovna's status as the potential prize in a contest between merchants and capitalists indicates that the nobility are economically marginal in this novel. Although Myshkin descends from an old aristocratic family, he is able to enter the novel's social world and join the competition for Nastasia Filippovna thanks to his connection to the merchantry.

While *The Idiot* has most often been interpreted in terms of breakdown and separation, of historical rupture and formal fragmentation, I argue that a model of the economy *avant la lettre*, operating in the background of the novel and occasionally irrupting into major episodes, functions as a countervailing force to the centrifugal tendency of *The Idiot*.[11] Despite the apparent ethical and cultural gulf separating Myshkin from the world of Saint Petersburg society, the plot, based on Dostoevsky's meticulous attention to contemporary events, implicates the prince in the economic excesses that have seized Russian society.[12] Moreover, the novel is driven by two somewhat incompatible narrative impulses: to depict Myshkin's path through contemporary Russian society, on the one hand, and to provide a synthetic view of Russia's economy by tracing financial relationships and flows of capital between estates and social groups, on the other.[13] While the first narrative thread depicts Myshkin's failure to find a place in society, the second demonstrates his embeddedness in economic networks. If, as Dostoevsky claims in a letter, Myshkin's character was supposed to represent the unreal quality of the ruling class in its current state of separation from the Russian people, the novel into which he is incorporated emphasizes instead the monetary relationships that link the nobility horizontally and connect it to other moneyed groups in a society from which nearly all representatives of the working class and the poor are absent.[14] In its depiction of the struggle between capitalists and merchants and the effects of this struggle on representatives of a declining nobility, *The Idiot* does not scrupulously reproduce empirically verifiable sociological types or economic conditions.[15] Rather, it arranges its competing interest groups in a way that underscores the evolving and heterogeneous nature of Russian economic life of the period. In the process, *The Idiot* employs the generic resources of the realist novel—intersecting plotlines, networks of major and minor characters, terminological heteroglossia—in contributing to the elaboration of an economic imaginary in the era of the Great Reforms.[16]

A NARRATIVE ECONOMY

In the mid-1860s, discussions of Russian state finances, growing public interest in the stock market, the changing composition of society, the development of industry, and the balance of trade seemed to call for the conception of Russia as an economic whole. While economists wrote about a market society as an "ungraspable system of exchanges," novels like *The Idiot* contributed to the multigeneric representation of just such a system by offering readers a legible model of a society constructed out of innumerable economic relationships.[17] The fictional world of *The Idiot* is populated with "ordinary" people such as moneylenders, factory owners, merchants, and providers of inheritances (IPV 461/D 8:383). As the narrator observes in his characteristic manner, these "ordinary people are constantly and for the most part the necessary links in the chain of everyday events; in bypassing them we would thus violate plausibility [*pravdopodobie*]" (IPV 462/D 8:384). "Plausibility" in the novel is therefore linked to the presence of a community of minor characters (perhaps more narratively consequential in this novel than in most of Dostoevsky's works) engaged in the economic life of Russia, such as the moneylender Ptitsyn and Gania, who works for Epanchin's joint-stock company (IPV 78/D 8:67).[18]

There is, however, a major difference between the economic relations in *The Idiot* and Gorlov's vision of limitless exchange. In Dostoevsky's novel, a great deal of money is kept sequestered and inert. Instead of participating in the broader economy and bringing together disparate people and commodities through continual circulation, it accumulates within families of merchants. Although one can trace all the fortunes in *The Idiot* to various kinds of commercial and industrial enterprise, rather than to the estates of noble families (the Myshkins, Barashkovs, and Ivolgins are all impoverished, and even the rich Polish count who seduces Aglaia at the end of the novel turns out to be a penniless fraud), the novel distinguishes between a mysterious, traditional merchantry and a rising class of capitalist entrepreneurs, which prospers while the merchants stagnate or decline. The contrast between merchants and capitalists, in turn, is linked to the different ways in which these two groups regard and utilize money. Merchant characters are associated with the nonproductive accumulation of money and with its transformation into an unconvertible fetish imbued with personal value that exceeds or defies calculation. For the capitalists, on the other hand, money is capital: infinitely convertible funds that circulate perpetually, linking people and objects together.

The economic imaginary of *The Idiot* is complex and historically uneven, as in *Anna Karenina*, but the emphasis is on two money economies rather than two regimes of labor. The expanding operations of new entrepreneurs coexist with the traditional mores and occupations of merchants, and not all money is handled in accordance with capitalist rationality. This use of money, in turn, is part of a larger cultural divide. The novel represents conservative merchants as religious schismatics and misers, suspicious of the outside world and unwilling to participate fully in the economy. The association of merchants with a closed-off, mysterious culture at odds with the rest of society was not unusual at the time. For example, Aleksandr Ushakov, a chronicler of merchant life in the 1860s, writes cryptonymously in his serial publication *Our Merchantry and Trade* that the merchantry has long since been "driven by some kind of unknown forces, incomprehensible and somehow in contradiction to all the developments of recent history, [and] persists in its stubborn indifference, avoids all social concerns in business—

even to the extent of harming that business—and lives and grows wealthy and goes bankrupt in isolation."[19] Nevertheless, Ushakov, like many writers of the period, including Tolstoy, Saltykov-Shchedrin, Ostrovsky, Melnikov-Pechersky, Boborykin, and Pisemsky, depicted the merchants as a thriving group whose economic power in Russia was growing. Dostoevsky, while drawing on the shared representations of merchants found in other writers, places special emphasis on their moribund condition, as opposed to a separate group of flourishing capitalists of nonmerchant origin.[20] In contrast to Gorlov's society of buyers and sellers, the merchants in *The Idiot* inhabit a world where money rarely functions as a facilitator of exchange. Instead, their illiquid wealth congeals into indestructible and unexchangeable cash whose worth depends not on its face value but on its connection to unique personal experience. The most vivid demonstration of the nonmarket value of the merchants' money comes in one of the novel's most famous scenes: Nastasia Filippovna's name day celebration.

INDESTRUCTIBLE BANKNOTES

Rogozhin bursts into the gathering at Nastasia Filippovna's apartment in part 1 holding a "strange object" in his hands. "It was a big stack of paper, about five inches high and seven inches long, wrapped firmly and closely in *The Stock Exchange News,* and tied very tightly on all sides and twice crisscrossed with the kind of string used for tying sugar loaves" (IPV 159–60/D 8:135). We soon discover that the package contains 100,000 rubles in 1,000 hundred-ruble bills, which Rogozhin, as the presumptive heir to a rich merchant, was able to borrow from moneylenders at the last minute.[21] Once conjured out of these credit institutions, this stack of cash concentrates the various meanings that accrued to money in 1860s Russia. The bundle's packaging is very important in this regard. A product of the first period in Russian history when the stock market became an object of public interest, the *Stock Exchange News* (Birzhevye vedomosti) allowed a reader in Saint Petersburg to learn about economic processes taking place all over an increasingly interconnected world.[22] The newspaper contained the latest information from the growing number of Russian regional trading floors, such as commodity prices, as well as other important information for mid-nineteenth-century investors—it is, in a word, something that a capitalist like General Epanchin would read. The newspaper contained various signs of the "stock market games" and "fevers" that in the eyes of many commentators characterized the economic culture of the mid-1860s.[23] For example, a reader of the *Stock Exchange News* in January 1868 would find a table listing the winners in the January 2 drawing of lottery bonds. These were government bonds with a nominal value and a regular rate of return, which were entered into a lottery. The lucky holder of a bond with the right serial number could win far more than the bond was worth. A 100-ruble investment could potentially yield a 200,000-ruble return: a colossal sum seemingly conjured up out of nowhere.[24] The package as a whole would also have suggested the unstable value of paper currency (*kreditnye bilety*, following Finance Minister E. F. Kankrin's reform of 1839–41).[25] Although the paper ruble was nominally worth its face value in silver rubles, its devaluation was so undeniably a fact of daily life that Dal' included a mention of it in his dictionary definition of the preceding series of paper money, the *assignatsiia*.[26] In all these respects, the wrappings of Rogozhin's money associate it with the contingency of value in the modern marketplace.

Despite these associations with abstract figures and unstable currencies, what Rogozhin drops on the table is striking in its materiality, and the narrator draws attention to the sensuous qualities of the money. The package's dimensions are carefully enumerated, and even the manner in which it is held together receives attention. The reader can almost feel the weight of the package as Rogozhin places it on the table: unlike the sums of capital discussed on the pages of the *Stock Exchange News*, this money is undeniably, physically present in the scene and will exert a hypnotic power over the people assembled in the room. The guests gaze at the bundle of money in fascination, especially when Nastasia Filippovna orders that it be thrown into the blazing fireplace. However, the money does not burn, as if asserting its unyielding materiality: "The outer paper was nearly all charred and smoldering, but it could be seen at once that the inside was not damaged. The packet had been wrapped in three layers of newspaper, and the money was untouched" (IPV 173–74/D 8:146). The narrative is distended by the characters' prolonged emotional reactions to the burning package as it seems to linger in the flames. Yet despite the perceived span of time, when it is finally pulled out of the fire, the money is almost unharmed—"Maybe just one little thousand is damaged a tiny bit, but the rest is untouched," notes Lebedev (IPV 173–74/D 8:146). Only the newspaper—the association with abstract capital and the fluctuation of value—is burned away, having been replaced by the concrete image of a stack of bills with a handful of singed notes on top. The merchant's stack of cash is now fully separated from the abstractions of modern economic life. The physical presence of the money induces powerful emotions in the gathered characters, particularly in Gania. After the package is hurled at his feet, he faints, and the 100,000 rubles suddenly disappear from the novel. No further mention is made of them for hundreds of pages, until the beginning of part 4, but the sum lingers on in the margins of the narrative.

Before Rogozhin produces his bundle of cash, Nastasia Filippovna refuses another generous offer—75,000 from Totsky if she marries Gania. But that money, described as "capital," is explicitly offered "to ensure her fate in the future" (IPV 47/D 8:41).[27] This is invisible money: the existence of financial institutions is its condition of possibility, and given their normal functioning, it exists virtually and thus cannot be thrown into a fire.[28] By contrast, Rogozhin's bundle, passed between two characters who are far removed from utilitarian calculation, is decidedly not capital, and the novel seems to offer no possibility that it will ever be spent. When it is saved from the flames, the entire sum goes to Gania, who, against his own acquisitive nature, returns it to Myshkin. The prince, it is implied, returns it to Nastasia Filippovna, who, the narrative has made quite clear, will not use the money that she has failed to destroy. The bundle, "thrown to him [Gania] by a mad woman, to whom it had also been brought by a madman," thus manages to circulate without being exchanged for anything, not given as a gift, but passed on because it is unwanted (IPV 465/D 8:386). The packet of money is a fetish, not in Marx's sense of an infinitely convertible commodity that conceals its material origins, but in the way the notion is employed in the writings of Georges Bataille, for whom "fetishism is an absolute realism: it unleashes real desires, in real spaces, with real objects. Not for an instant does Bataille oppose, as Marxists do, fetishism and use-value (for him there is no fetishism of the commodity); when he evokes fetishism, it is, on the contrary, always against merchandise. The fetish is the irreplaceable, untransposable object."[29] The Bataillean fetish cannot be exchanged; it can only be consumed. Rogozhin's money is likewise irreplaceable; it cannot be spent because it cannot be separated from its original context, where Nastasia Filippovna proved willing to destroy it to demonstrate her opposition to her own commodification. Having survived the fire, the money continues a kind of ghostly circulation outside of exchange because, being invested with the desires and defiant pride of Rogozhin, Nastasia Filippovna, and Gania, it can no longer be equivalent to anything. It is possible that the money ends up in Rogozhin's possession again, considering Nastasia Filippovna's emphatic refusal to spend it. In any case, to the extent that the novel traces its movement, this money retains its emotionally charged particularity. Wherever it goes, it retains a connection to its source: the pathologically passionate Rogozhin, who has invested it with an incalculable emotional value. Despite his willingness to sacrifice a fortune for Nastasia Filippovna, Rogozhin is fundamentally a miser, that is, a person for whom money has a personal, unconvertible value.[30] In this he resembles the rest of his family and, the novel makes clear, the merchant estate as a whole.

As the most prominent representative of the merchantry in the novel, Rogozhin exemplifies the characteristics of the estate, with his cultural conservatism and emotional investment in money. Introducing the Rogozhin family home, the narrator observes that it has proven peculiarly resistant to the rapid transformation of the Saint Petersburg cityscape: of the old houses like the one Rogozhin's family has long inhabited, a few, "built at the end of the last century, have survived precisely on these Petersburg streets (where everything changes so quickly) almost without change" (IPV 204/D 8:170). The exterior of the house seems to stand outside historical time, while the interior, in its gloomy and disordered stability, is a kind of metonymy of merchant life. Myshkin observes to Rogozhin, "Your house has the physiognomy of your whole family and of your whole Rogozhin life" (IPV 207/D 8:172). The room in which Myshkin finds Rogozhin is dominated by a faded portrait of Rogozhin's father, which reveals him to have been an Old Believer, a group often associated in nineteenth-century Russian culture with business acumen.[31] The father's ascetic restraint was made clear by the fury with which he had earlier reacted when Rogozhin squandered a sum of his money on a gift for Nastasia Filippovna. The portrait, with its "suspicious, secretive, and somewhat doleful gaze," reinforces the hostility of the father, the Rogozhins, and the merchant estate toward the outside world and the new economy (IPV 172/D 8:173). The semantic associations of the Rogozhin name strengthen the connections between the merchantry, hoarding, and lifelessness. The name Rogozhin probably comes from the traditional Old Believers' cemetery in Moscow (D 9:407). It also recalls the Rogozhskoe neighborhood of Moscow, which, according to an urban physiologist contemporary to Dostoevsky, was a doorway to the merchant quarter of the city, a "dark and mostly unknown smithy where Moscow capital is forged."[32] The associations of insularity and stasis extend to Rogozhin's given name and patronymic as well. Rogozhin's name is Parfyon (derived from the Greek *parthenos*, or "virgin") Semyonovich; his father was named Semyon Parfyonovich. This onomastic chiasmus joins father and son in a closed loop that suggests stasis and sterility, as if the former begat the latter and vice versa.[33] As if to underscore this implication, Rogozhin's brother, who had demonstrated his own extreme avarice by cutting the gold tassels from the cover of their father's coffin, is named Semyon Semyonovich (IPV 11/D 8:12). After Rogozhin's sentencing for the murder of Nastasia Filippovna, the vast Rogozhin fortune passes to this brother, who in all likelihood will continue to hoard it.

As the diametrical opposite of the capitalist and an opponent of monetary circulation, the miser frequently played a role in nineteenth-century social analysis: one economic theorist of the 1860s argued that precious metals, as opposed to credit, are always implicated in people's psychological compulsion to hoard. He thus sought to explain the shortage of capital in terms of widespread miserliness: "Only economists can refer to the noble metals as commodities and consider them no higher than tar, lard, hemp, or any other product. What profanation!"[34] Karl Marx, writing at the same time as Dostoevsky was working on *The Idiot*, proposed that the hoarder, although a seemingly atavistic figure in a modern economy, unwittingly regulated the money supply by taking excess gold out of circulation. Marx's hoarder thus plays a part in the operation of the economy despite trying to stay out of it.

Marx interprets hoarding as a transformation of a religious ascetic impulse: "The hoarder therefore sacrifices the lusts of his flesh to the fetish of gold. He takes the gospel of abstinence very seriously."[35] Dostoevsky implies such a connection as well; when Myshkin visits Rogozhin's house, the narrator observes that it is of a certain type that is generally populated by merchants and that the lower floors of such houses are routinely occupied by *skoptsy* running money-changing businesses. Nastasia Filippovna later makes the connection between the ascetic moneylenders and Rogozhin explicit. Insisting that he will follow his father's path, she predicts: "You'd start saving money [*kopit'*], and you'd sit like your father in this house with his *skoptsy*; perhaps you'd adopt their beliefs in the end, and you'd love your money so much that you'd save up not two but ten million, and you'd starve to death on your moneybags" (IPV 214/D 8:178). In her words, the *skoptsy* are linked graphically to the verb *kopit'*, implying a link by false etymology between the accumulation of money, religious asceticism, and sexual sterility.[36] The miser's millions remain immobile, sequestered in his hoard instead of circulating in the economy and reproducing themselves. Although Rogozhin in his wild expenditures does not seem to be the model of the ascetic miser, he is surrounded by signs that this is indeed his fate.

MERCHANT MYSHKIN

The Rogozhins are the most prominent example of merchant-misers in the novel, but there is another merchant family that plays an important role (although this is revealed only later) at Nastasia Filippovna's gathering. There, amid the succession of shocking deeds and revelations, Myshkin announces, to the surprise of everyone present, that he too is very rich and can vie for Nastasia Filippovna's hand in marriage. This is a striking reversal of the earlier depiction of Myshkin; in the first chapters of the novel he appears to be so removed from economic life that other characters consider it impossible that he should have money at all. At their first meeting, Gania tells Myshkin that "it would be better for you to avoid pocket money and generally carrying money in your pocket" (IPV 35/D 8:30). It becomes clear, though, that Myshkin's fortune has come to him by way of a convoluted inheritance. In order to justify the appearance of this new fortune in the novel, Ptitsyn is deployed to explain the circumstances of Myshkin's unexpected wealth. It takes him a long paragraph to relate all the twists of the story. The reader learns that Myshkin had an aunt, previously unknown to him, who had died recently and who was the daughter of a Moscow merchant named Papushin, who himself had died "in poverty and bankruptcy" (IPV 165/D 8:139). However, Papushin had an older brother, also recently deceased, who had a great fortune. In the recent past both of the rich Papushin's sons had died, leaving him no heirs. "This so shocked the old man that soon afterwards he himself fell ill and died" (IPV 165/D 8:139). Since this rich merchant was a widower, his only surviving relation was the old woman, Myshkin's aunt, who despite her own illness managed to find Myshkin and made him the beneficiary of her will before becoming the last casualty of this complicated transaction. It seems that the novel strains against its own imperative to plausibility as it attempts to provide Myshkin with his money: five people are introduced only to die in the proper succession, and the fatidic force of melodrama has to be deployed in the form of the unknown relation and the sudden inheritance for this fortune of an obscure Moscow merchant to reach Myshkin. Yet as improbable as his inheritance is, it nonetheless traces a financial and legal link between the prince, ostensibly far removed from the practical side of modern Russian life, and a merchant fortune.

Myshkin's sudden enrichment gives him access to the novel's major conflict, but it also underscores his temporal heterogeneity. Although for many readers scenes like the one in which Myshkin reveals his wealth are quintessentially Dostoevskian, the sudden appearance of large sums of money is more typical of literature from the 1830s–40s, when Dostoevsky was just beginning his career. Works of that period were filled with gamblers, grifters, and aspirational seekers of fortune, such as Germann from "The Queen of Spades," Chichikov from *Dead Souls*, or the pathetically ambitious heroes of Iakov Butkov, such as the protagonist of "One Hundred Rubles," an impoverished civil servant who wins the titular prize in a lottery and promptly goes mad from joy.[37] To be sure, people grow rich in the novels of the second half of the nineteenth century, but they tend to do so thanks to success in business, like Totsky and Epanchin in *The Idiot*, rather than through gambling or inheritance. Myshkin's merchant fortune therefore serves as a further indication of the atavistic character of his social position and strengthens the link between him and an archaic social structure. Indeed, it is particularly significant that Myshkin's wealth comes in the form of an inheritance. Inherited wealth links Rogozhin and Myshkin to each other and dooms them both to obsolescence. Their dependence on inheritance allegorizes their status as members of a hereditary estate. All the same, this intrusion of sudden wealth has to be updated for the age of realism: multiple causal links take the place of a sudden stroke of fortune. On the other hand,

Epanchin and Totsky do not depend on any kind of hereditary links with the past for their status and their domain of social action; only their control of capital matters. As members of a class defined primarily by its economic power, these ascendant capitalists are propelled by the novel's narrative trajectory into the future, while the merchants, burdened by their hereditary ties to the doomed past, are consigned to oblivion.

Ptitsyn's painstaking account of how the money got to Myshkin reveals that Myshkin is himself the grandson, on his mother's side, of a merchant, albeit a minor one, belonging to the Third Guild.[38] In this context, Myshkin's nobility associates him with the other impoverished noble families and their state of dependency on other estates in the novel. Since nearly all money in *The Idiot* originates with either the capitalists or the merchants, Myshkin too has to be enfolded into this typology in order to gain money and, with it, agency in the narrative. In some sense, Myshkin's linkage to the merchants is predetermined by the novel's very first scene, in the train returning to Saint Petersburg, where he meets Rogozhin. Once this connection is secured by the merchant inheritance, it also integrates Myshkin into the larger structure of the novel's subplot of economic struggle. Together with the merchants' money, he inherits their fate.

To be sure, the parallels between Myshkin and Rogozhin have their limits. The prince is no miser, for instance, and Myshkin's nobility aligns him with the other representatives of the disempowered and rapidly obsolescing nobles of the novel, many of whom linger on in states of economic dependency on merchants or capitalists. Indeed, his socially heterogeneous genealogy is only one part of his fundamental ambiguity, which is central to the novel's design. Many readers of *The Idiot* have drawn attention to this, whether emphasizing, like Linda Ivanits, Myshkin's "incorporeity," or the vast accumulation of incomplete and contradictory details and rumors, whose cumulative effect is, in Robin Feuer Miller's words, "that the narrator's description and explanation prove to have been misleading in the end; the sparsely scattered facts and abundant mysteries are the stuff out of which the reader must form his understanding of the meaning."[39]

Nevertheless, in one of the key scenes defining Myshkin's character, his connection to the merchantry and their noncapitalist relationship to money attracts particular attention. As soon as word of Myshkin's unexpected inheritance gets out into the novel's public sphere, which is maintained by a steady exchange of rumors, an article appears about him in a "weekly newspaper of the humoristic sort" (IPV 261/D 8:217). This parodic paraphrase of Myshkin's story stresses that "a relation of his mother (who, naturally, was of merchant stock), a childless old bachelor, a merchant, bearded, and a schismatic [*staryi bezdetnyi bobyl', iz kupchikh, borodach i raskol'nik*]" was the source of his fortune (IPV 263/D 8:218). The characteristics of this person, not all of which are apparent from Ptitsyn's ostensibly true account of the inheritance, bring him into the same semantic field as Rogozhin's family. Myshkin's money is, according to the article, the product of yet another sterile Old Believer who stored up his millions in cash without any apparent economic use for them. While Myshkin is not doomed to starve to death on his moneybags like Rogozhin, his fate is also to be burdened by a vast amount of money that cannot be spent.

Likewise, in a minor episode, Myshkin's relationship to incommensurably material banknotes echoes Rogozhin's connection to his bundle of cash. Early in the novel, as he has just arrived at the home of the Ivolgins, Myshkin meets Ferdyshchenko, who asks him for his sole twenty-five-ruble note. "The man unfolded it, looked at it, turned it over, then held it up to the light. 'Quite strange,' he said, as if pondering. 'Why do they turn brownish? These twenty-fivers sometimes get terribly brown, while others, on the contrary, fade completely'" (IPV 93/D 8:79). These seemingly throwaway lines, uttered by one of the novel's loquacious buffoons, forces the narration to pause on the material quality of the note.[40] Rather than allow the money to dissolve into sheer liquidity, as yet another twenty-five-ruble note, the description here makes the money reveal its physical presence: some notes are different from others. Ferdyshchenko's words prefigure the scandal at Nastasia Filippovna's where Rogozhin produces his bundle of 100,000 rubles. In both scenes, a sum of money loses its functionality as a general equivalent and takes on the solidity of matter. Myshkin, of course, is not prone to Rogozhin's excesses, but in his hands, too, money slows down, grows denser in details, and resists being put back into circulation.

UNSEEN FACTORIES

Both Rogozhin and Myshkin can afford to vie for Nastasia Filippovna, the daughter of a ruined nobleman, because they are heirs to merchant fortunes. Both are linked to sexual sterility, which in turn implies the unproductivity of their wealth. By the end of the novel, both are destroyed: Myshkin, having reverted to his earlier condition of "idiocy," is sent back to Switzerland into the care of a certain Dr. Schneider, and Rogozhin is sentenced to hard labor in Siberia. On the other hand, the novel's two major capitalists—General Epanchin and Totsky—meet with an altogether better fate. Totsky, after making his exit from the party at Nastasia Filippovna's in part 1, disappears from the novel, presumably to go back to his business dealings with his reputation intact, and by the end of the novel General Epanchin has seen at least one of his daughters profitably married (Adelaida to Prince Shch.).[41] And while it turns out that Aglaia has quarreled with her family and fallen for a

Polish charlatan posing as a wealthy count, the tone of the narrative in the last pages suggests that this too is a temporary setback for the Epanchins. Finally, Gania and Ptitsyn, both younger men with great financial ambitions, are "living as before, have changed little," and the narrator has "almost nothing to tell about them" (IPV 612/D 8:508). This means, presumably, that they have entered what Ilya Kliger has called the "homogeneous empty time of a career," which is defined by the steady accumulation of money and is lacking in narrative interest.[42]

In contrast to their surreptitious exit from the novel, the capitalists occupy considerable space in the early chapters, which offer a comprehensive list of their entrepreneurial activities and the sources of their wealth. Both Totsky and Epanchin are active participants in a distinctly modern economy. Totsky is introduced to the reader as an "arch-capitalist [raskapitalist], a member of companies and societies," in the words of Lebedev, and the dowry of 75,000 rubles he plans to offer along with Nastasia Filippovna is described as "capital" on several occasions (IPV 12/D 8:11; IPV 49/D 8:44). He is particularly associated with the verb "exploit" (ekspluatirovat'), a word that was so gratingly novel in the mid-1860s that Dal' described it as "exceedingly awkward."[43] In the preparations for Nastasia Filippovna's marriage announcement, Totsky and Epanchin plan to "exploit" Gania's passion "for their own advantage, and to buy Gania by selling him Nastasia Filippovna as a lawful wife" (IPV 50/D 8:43).

The exact nature of Totsky's capitalist activities is evidently less important than their status as markers of his involvement in the world of corporations and stock-market wealth. This wealth, in turn, is the real source of Totsky's status, although he presents himself as a prominent landowning nobleman. His claim to descend from a prestigious lineage turns out not to be altogether trustworthy. The narrator relates that Totsky acquired the young Nastasia Filippovna when her father, a man whose noble status was "rather more certain [pochishche] than Totsky's," was destroyed by debts and other misfortunes (IPV 40/D 8:35). The implication is that the wealthy Totsky might have gained his nobility rather recently, while Nastasia Filippovna's father fell victim to the general decline of the old nobility as it failed to adapt to new economic conditions.

General Epanchin, the novel's other big capitalist, has likewise benefited from the social mobility made possible by wealth. The general may indeed be taken as a representative of a nascent Russian entrepreneurial class: having risen from very modest origins (he belongs to the official category of soldiers' children), he has become a respectable member of the "middle circle," as his wife, Lizaveta Prokof'evna, describes the family's milieu: "We have always been people of the middle circle [srednego kruga], as middle as can be" (IPV 525/D 8:435).[44] This is a surprising thing for her to say, however, since she comes from an old noble lineage. Like her distant relative Prince Myshkin before his inheritance, Lizaveta Prokof'evna lacks independent means, and the family depends on the general's business activities for their income. As the reader learns in the novel's first pages, the general derives his wealth from a variety of sources:

> Besides this (excellent) house, five-sixths of which was rented out, General Epanchin owned another enormous house on Sadovaia Street, which also brought him an extraordinary income. Besides these two houses, he had quite a profitable and considerable estate just outside Petersburg; and there was also some factory in the Petersburg district. In the old days General Epanchin, as everyone knew, had participated in tax farming. Now he participated and had quite a considerable voice in several important joint-stock companies. He had the reputation of a man with big money, big doings, and big connections. (IPV 15–16/D 8:14)

The narrator observes that it is widely known that the general had in the past participated in the disreputable activity of tax farming, but this fact has apparently not affected his status, and, like Totsky, he has adapted well to the economic and legal conditions of the postreform period.[45] Now Epanchin has a large and profitable estate, which he evidently purchased after achieving prosperity: land ownership, the source of the old nobility's wealth and prestige, is now an aspirational target for the upwardly mobile. Besides being a farmer, the general is also an industrialist, but the narrator displays little interest in the factory that the general owns. It is never mentioned again in the novel, and the reader never learns what kind of factory it is. Yet in the novel's diegesis, it continues to exist somewhere on the outskirts of Saint Petersburg, employing workers and generating profit for the Epanchins. Like those industrial cities that Levin visited in *Anna Karenina*, this factory exerts a narrative force much greater than its marginal location might suggest. In general, the business activities of both Totsky and Epanchin largely go on behind the scenes of the novel; nonetheless, they link these characters to various aspects of the Russian economy, including industry, agriculture, real estate, and finance. Contrary to the common perception that Dostoevsky's fictions are populated by those who do not work, these two men are constantly busy, as is their money. At no point in the novel does the money of the capitalists take on the densely material quality of Myshkin's or Rogozhin's cash. Instead, it seamlessly links their varied business activities together as sources of income and, in its visible traces, helps to map Russia as an economy.

The contemporary reviewer quoted at the beginning of this chapter, responding to the outsized emotions and enormous sums of money on display at Nastasia Filippovna's, complained that "inheritances in the millions fly about in the novel like so many bouncing balls. . . . That is why money in *The Idiot* is absolutely worthless, cheaper than wood shavings. . . . To read such stories in our penniless [*bezdenezhnoe*] and hungry times is very amusing."[46] As the preceding discussion has shown, the fortunes that bounce around in the novel's scandals and rumors belong to the merchants, while the wealth of the capitalists is quietly engaged in the generation of profit outside the novel's major episodes. The effects of the capitalists' money are less directly visible, but it proves far more destructive than the localized and concrete wealth of the merchants. Totsky's wealth ensnares Nastasia Filippovna in a condition that the novel associates with serfdom. Her father, the narrator relates, had struggled against a rising tide of debts and misfortunes with "penal, almost peasant labors [*katorzhnykh, pochti muzhich'ikh trudov*]" before succumbing to his fate, at which point Totsky assumed predatory guardianship of his daughter (IPV 40/D 8:35). When she confronts Totsky, she threatens to discard his financial support by becoming a washerwoman, that is, a worker who must sell her labor for a wage. It would seem that she could escape from an individual capitalist, but not from the broader capitalist system. With the disempowerment of the nobility and the confinement of the merchants to their limited, largely familial spheres, the rest of society is left open to conquest by the capitalists. *The Idiot* does not go into great detail about the economic future of Russia, but it does point toward the grim consequences of this development. Social reality in the novel is already saturated by money. It is so ubiquitous that Nastasia Filippovna has nowhere to escape from it. But perhaps the fullest indication of its dilated sphere of influence is that it even invades the ostensibly transcendent realm of Myshkin's epileptic visions.[47]

METAPHYSICAL PRICE TAGS

In part 2, Myshkin experiences a sense of spatial and temporal disorder in advance of one of his ecstatic visions. Suddenly, his perception is arrested by the recollection of a shop window. "He now wanted to make absolutely sure: had he really been standing in front of that shop window just now, perhaps only five minutes ago, had he not imagined it or confused something? Did that shop and those goods really exist?" (IPV 224/D 8:187). In this display window, he recalls, "despite all his absentmindedness and anxiety," a "thing" worth sixty kopecks in silver (IPV 225/D 8:187). The unmentioned object, as David Bethea observes, is a knife.[48] But the legible sign of this weapon, whose decisive importance for subsequent events Myshkin seems to foresee in his quasi-mystical state, is a very specific price, and it is the existence of the shop and its commodities that serves as reassurance to Myshkin that he is still in the real world. Throughout this scene, what Myshkin regards as his anchor in space and time is indeed a sign that he exists in this age of prices and commodities and no other. Rather than focusing on the materiality of the knife in the display window, Myshkin seeks reassurance of his sanity in the fact that this "thing" has a reliable monetary value—sixty kopecks, as he reiterates three times. Even in the midst of his visions of transcendent harmony, a very different kind of harmony shows through: the total adequacy of a price to its object.

THE END OF THE STORY

What Myshkin glimpses in his vision remains true for the secular world of *The Idiot*: fluid, universally fungible capital is in the process of becoming the measure of reality. The narrative form of Dostoevsky's novel complicates Moretti's claim that "all that money can do [in Russian and other peripheral realist novels] is generate hyperbolic distortions of modern economic behavior."[49] On the contrary, money in *The Idiot* flows calmly and rationally into the accounts of capitalists who live unobtrusively on the margins of the main plot in which Myshkin, Rogozhin, and Nastasia Filippovna enact their tragedy. This invisible capital—such as that generated by Epanchin's factory, which must go on producing wealth even during the six-month gap between parts 1 and 2 of the novel[50]—generates an economy: a whole in which the parts are bound together by the circulation of money, which, in its shifting forms, yokes commodities and people together in a network that is empirically undetectable but nevertheless real. In this context, Rogozhin's bundle of money—money that refuses to transform itself into other things, that resists becoming anything other than its durable, paper self—is useful to the novel in inverse proportion to its economic utility.

The systematic defeat of the merchants by the capitalists leaves the world of *The Idiot* open to conquest by the latter. This has profound consequences for the continued representation of this fictional world. Notably, what disappears along with the merchants' noncapitalist money is their outsized personalities. If Rogozhin and Myshkin, with their tortured interiorities, are among Dostoevsky's most memorable characters, it would be hard to say the same for pallid, unimpressive Totsky or Epanchin. Their failure to be interesting is part of their success in business. After the scandal at Nastasia Filippovna's name day party, Totsky and Ptitsyn walk away unscathed, unencumbered, and free to reflect on what just happened. "Let's say everything that happened there just now was ephemeral, romantic, indecent, but, on the other had, it was colorful, it was original, you must agree. God, what could have been from such a character and with such beauty!" (IPV 175/D

8:149) The answer to Totsky's hypothetical question is what takes place over the remaining three parts of *The Idiot*, full of "ephemeral, romantic, indecent," but "colorful" and "original" events. The result is a novel of extraordinary power and devastating consequences for Nastasia Filippovna, Myshkin, and Rogozhin. The capitalists will have as little to do with it as possible, but they will be there when it is all over.

There are other nineteenth-century Russian novels in which capitalists exhibit greater complexity and stand closer to the center of events, such as Privalov in *Privalov's Millions* and Stolz in *Oblomov*, but these are people who refuse to be *mere* capitalists. Privalov, the descendant of larger-than-life Ural industrialists, is wracked with guilt over what his ancestors took from the workers, and Stolz carries the imprint both of his German father's discipline and thrift and of his Russian mother's poetic nature. But the very peripherality of the capitalists in *The Idiot* makes their example particularly telling. The comparison with Stolz suggests the deeper meaning of the capitalists' ultimate victory in *The Idiot*, as well as the structural consequences of that victory for that novel and perhaps for Russian realism generally, insofar as he does share one key feature with Totsky and Epanchin. As Anne Lounsbery has shown, the portions of *Oblomov* that focus on Stolz favor narration over description to such a degree that generations of readers have found these parts of the novel uninteresting in comparison to the extensively detailed descriptions of the immobile Oblomov.[51] The cause of Stolz's excessive narrativity, Lounsbery argues, is his association with "an explicitly modern conception of geographic space—a landscape thoroughly knowable, mappable, and traversable, aimed at facilitating the circulation of people, goods, and money."[52] The representation of the capitalists in *The Idiot* likewise suggests that they are linked to a particular temporality, which their incessant economic activity is bringing about. In the context of Dostoevsky's views on capitalist development in the West, the sheer boringness of the capitalists is telling, insofar as it offers an indication of a future for Russia that lies beyond the representational capacities of the novel.

It is highly significant in this respect that Myshkin and Rogozhin, the representatives of a vanquished merchantry, also exhibit the most elaborated interiorities among the novel's characters. The reader learns about Myshkin's and Rogozhin's physical appearance and gains considerable insight into their inner lives, as well as the correspondence between these two aspects, so that each man's appearance becomes a signature of his complex inner existence; they are, in a sense, exemplary novelistic protagonists. Their economic role is likewise maximally legible; the form that money takes in their hands is visible and tactile to the extreme. As such, it is ideally suited for representation by a genre that privileges the data of the senses.[53] On the other hand, what defeats the merchants is a power that is considerably less vivid and, as a result, less legible. The economic power that Totsky and Epanchin wield is mostly invisible, as is their money, and their triumph shifts the novel's economy into a mode from which little empirical data can be extracted. Like Epanchin's factory and Totsky's estate, the financial operations of the capitalists remain invisible in the novel. The two capitalists eventually withdraw into an altogether different temporality, in which, by the narrator's own recognition, very little happens that can be told.

Dostoevsky suggested elsewhere that this unnarratable temporality is characteristic of modernity. The narrator of *Winter Notes on Summer Impressions* (1863) maintains that the privileged locus of modernity and its corresponding temporal order is Western Europe, as Kliger has pointed out.[54] Observing Paris, the narrator summarizes the French bourgeoisie's sense of time: "I'll do a little business today in my stall, and God willing, tomorrow I'll do some more business, and perhaps the day after tomorrow, if God is so merciful . . . Well, and after that, if only I can save up just a bit, then—*après moi, le déluge!*" (D 5:74–75; ellipsis in the original). The beneficiaries of fully developed Western capitalism think that they stand at the end of history, in an eternal present in which no further events will occur. Such a temporality is diametrically opposed to that which predominates in the plot of *The Idiot*, in which, as numerous commentators have observed, traces of apocalyptic or messianic time occasionally irrupt into the everyday time of the novel. This messianic time, charged with transformative potential, gives way at the end of *The Idiot* to the empty, unnarratable time of the capitalists and their perpetual accumulation. Once the capitalists have won, they enter a time that marks the cessation of narrative events as such. Earlier in the novel, Lebedev offers an allegorical interpretation of Russia's railroad network as the fulfillment of apocalyptic prophecy (IPV 304/D 8:254). However, this interpretation is not in keeping with the unfolding of capitalism on the level of the narrative. The real triumph of the capitalist economy in the novel inaugurates a temporal order that spells the end of novelistic—and, perhaps, historical—events, not the end of secular time.

Whereas in *Crime and Punishment* the narrator had announced the continuation of the story beyond the epilogue, in this novel all that remains after the ending is a bad infinity beyond the reach of novelistic narrative: there is no suggestion that we can follow Rogozhin to Siberia, the Epanchins back to Saint Petersburg, or Totsky to France. Likewise, the novelized economy, rendered vivid by the conflict between the merchants and capitalists within the main portion of the novel, enters its next, invisible stage in the epilogue. In contrast to so many accounts, both in the nineteenth century and today, that stress, alternatively, capitalism's creativity, dynamism, or violence, *The Idiot* posits that a fully capitalist world is one in which nothing can happen and about which nothing can meaningfully be said.

Of course, this does not spell the end of Dostoevsky's own investigations into the meaning of Russian capitalism for the Russian novel. The next chapter turns to *The Brothers Karamazov*, in which, if anything, money is even more ubiquitous than in *The Idiot*. As we will see, Dostoevsky's final novel pursues the hypertrophy of the money economy to a reductio ad absurdum: not only does everything in that novel have a price tag, but it is exactly the same price. As the money economy disintegrates under the accumulated weight of its own posited equivalences, the possibility of novelistic narrative reemerges once again.

Heterogeneous Money in *The Brothers Karamazov*

> I could not understand what a promissory
> note was until I read Balzac. How Nastasia
> Filippovna threw the money in the fireplace—
> that I can see clearly. But what else one could
> do with it—that I can't understand. How
> Raskolnikov whacked Lizaveta with the axe—
> that I can imagine. But how, exactly, did the
> old pawnbroker work, where did she get her
> interest rates? What is a pledge? What is a
> mortgage? Why is a silver ruble not equal to
> an *assignatsiia*? Not one of the Russian writers
> condescended to explain this to me.
> —Tatiana Tolstaia, "Kuptsy i khudozhniki"
> (Merchants and Artists)

A WOODLOT FOR SALE

There is a woodlot in *The Brothers Karamazov* in which—and to which—nothing happens. Characters cluster around it in different configurations: Fyodor Pavlovich, Mitia, Ivan, and Smerdiakov all talk about it, Fyodor Pavlovich and Mitia both try to sell it, and Fyodor Pavlovich and Smerdiakov both try to convince Ivan to travel to the village of Chermashnia, where the woodlot is located. While nothing comes of any of these plans, the frequent recurrence of the woodlot, as well as the place that conversations about the woodlot occupy in this novel's intricately structured narrative, suggests its importance. Of the two scenes that include the most extensive discussions of Chermashnia and the woodlot, the first takes place in chapters 6 and 7 of book 5, between the two most ideologically weighty books of the novel, in which Ivan poses the problem of evil and Zosima offers his theodicy. Moreover, after the second half of book 5—containing "The Grand Inquisitor" and the two chapters in which Chermashnia comes up—was published in June 1879, a gap of nearly two months followed before the appearance of book 6, leaving readers to dwell on the conversations about Chermashnia as Dostoevsky prepared his response to Ivan's rebellion.[1] In chapter 6, Ivan, returning from the tavern where he paraphrased to Alesha his poem of the Grand Inquisitor, runs into Smerdiakov, who strongly hints that Ivan should get out of the way so that something might happen to Fyodor Pavlovich. Then, a few pages after Ivan's first refusal to go to Chermashnia, Fyodor Pavlovich himself repeats his own request that Ivan travel to the village to handle the sale of the woodlot. The reason Fyodor Pavlovich wants Ivan to go, as readers of the novel will remember, is that the local father-and-son merchant team is willing to pay 8,000 rubles for the sale of the woodlot, but an alternative buyer, Liagavy, alias Gorstkin, has arrived from out of town. Fyodor Pavlovich, apprised of this development by a local priest, learns that Liagavy is willing to pay 11,000. Fyodor Pavlovich is eager to net the additional 3,000. However, he cannot go to Chermashnia to negotiate the deal on his own because he is waiting for Grushenka, so he asks Ivan to go in his place. After a night of indecision, Ivan silently acquiesces to the trip, but on the way there he changes his mind and boards the train for Moscow. The way is clear for Smerdiakov to murder Fyodor Pavlovich even though neither the future killer nor the victim has succeeded in convincing Ivan to go to Chermashnia.

The larger implications of this episode for the novel's structure of cascading responsibilities are hard to miss. Fyodor Pavlovich, driven by his greed, is trying very hard to arrange the circumstances in which he will be murdered. In addition to all the other things that 3,000 rubles can potentially buy in this novel, it is the price at which Fyodor Pavlovich unwittingly values his own life.[2] The decision to go or not is deeply consequential for Ivan as well. Eduard Wasiolek argues that the place-name Chermashnia evokes the semantically laden root *chern*, or "black"—which, by translation into the Turkish root *kara*, brings us back to the name Karamazov and the family's dark essence. "Chermashnya is a 'dark wood'" in which greed, murderous sexual desire, and patricidal rage dwell.[3] When, on his way out of the house, Ivan tells Smerdiakov that he is going to Chermashnia after all, the latter understands this as tacit permission to carry out the murder. It is easy to see from here how Chermashnia fits into the novel's larger patterns. The novel's epigraph, taken from the Gospel according to John, introduces the theme of planted seeds.[4] Chermashnia extends this vegetal metaphor: in the dark wood of Chermashnia, the evil seed that Ivan has planted in Smerdiakov's mind and the hereditary corruption of the Karamazov essence both bear fruit. That said, Chermashnia is not just a metaphor. It is also a place, as real as any place in this novel can be. The woodlot is a parcel of forested land and Fyodor Pavlovich's property. By considering it in this concrete sense and by noticing all the things that *do not* happen to Chermashnia, we can gain insight into the economic workings of the world of *The Brothers Karamazov* and, ultimately, how this economic imaginary folds into the novel's big questions.

The second time that Chermashnia comes up is on the other side of Alesha's mystical transport in "Cana of Galilee." Immediately following that chapter, in book 8, Mitia attempts to sell the woodlot twice—first to the merchant Samsonov (who turns out to be too shrewd to accept the dubious offer) and then to the peasant timber dealer Liagavy (who is too drunk)— and to offer it as collateral on a loan from the noblewoman Khokhlakova (who refuses, but is happy to offer Mitia other suggestions for acquiring money, such as mining for gold in Siberia). During the preliminary investigation following his arrest, Mitia reveals that he also tried to sell the deed to the woodlot to Mussialovich, Grushenka's Polish suitor, in order to buy him off. Both father and son are desperate to turn this grove of trees, which neither of them appears to care much about, into cash, which both of them care about quite deeply. To be sure, their motivations are not identical. Mitia is not a profiteer; he mostly wants 3,000, regardless of what the woodlot is really worth, while his father wants to sell it for as much as he can. As it turns out, all attempts to sell the woodlot fail, since Mitia ends up accused of Fyodor Pavlovich's murder. After this, Chermashnia will come up as a point of evidence in Mitia's trial and in Ivan's conversations with Smerdiakov, but as a physical space, it will no longer play a part in the novel. The woodlot goes from being an object of business negotiations to a piece of evidence and a code word authorizing murder. In every case, it is a tool serving someone's purpose. On the level of narrative, too, it is a tool: a potential narrative motivation to get Ivan out of Fyodor Pavlovich's house and leave the old man isolated. As we will see, it is the failure of the woodlot to serve most of these ends that becomes particularly significant in the larger scheme of this novel's rejection of transactional logic.

First, however, it is important to note that there is nothing surprising about the appearance of negotiations over the sale of a woodlot in a Russian realist novel. The condition of Russia's heavily exploited forests was a major topic of public discourse in the second half of the nineteenth century.[5] Articles about the "forest question" appeared both in specialized publications and in major periodicals, including Dostoevsky's own *Diary of a Writer*.[6] The forest question was also discussed on the pages of the *Russian Herald*, where *The Brothers Karamazov* was serialized from 1879 to 1880, as *Anna Karenina* and *The Idiot* had been before it. Among the many important topics connected to the forest question was the economic and social position of Russia's major landowners, the nobility. Ekaterina Pravilova has shown that the forest question was a focal point for discussions about noble property rights and the very notion of the public and its interests in the postemancipation years.[7] Works of literature likewise responded to the forest question and its implications for the future of the noble estate. Aside from *The Brothers Karamazov*, one of the most notable examples of this kind of scene occurs in

Anna Karenina, where Levin chastises Stiva Oblonsky for selling his forest far too cheaply to a merchant.[8]

The woodlot at Chermashnia is a problem to be solved: for both of the interested Karamazovs, it is money in a form that cannot be put to use, an unexploited resource. Even Smerdiakov thinks of his murderous scheme involving Chermashnia as an investment. During his second meeting with Ivan in book 11, he explains that with Mitia out of the picture, Fyodor Pavlovich's inheritance would go to Ivan and Alesha. And Ivan, whether as a gesture of gratitude or as a bribe, might then give part of his portion to Smerdiakov—a sum potentially much larger than the 3,000 he will steal from Fyodor Pavlovich (BKF 615/D 15:52–53). Stiva Oblonsky is also quite badly in need of money, but the meaning of his forest, and his decision to sell it, extends beyond its monetary value. In Tolstoy's version, Levin's conversation with Stiva about the pending sale of the forest to the merchant Riabinin touches on both Stiva's particular failure to value his own property accurately and on the Russian nobility's imperiled position in the face of new social and economic conditions. Levin observes that Stiva has not counted his trees, whereas the merchant has certainly done so, which means that Stiva cannot really know how much his forest is worth and therefore cannot possibly be getting a good deal. That Levin regards it as reasonable for a landowner to pay such close attention to his forest indicates that Stiva's forest matters to him as a landlord's domain, that is, not only as wealth (and a kind of wealth whose quantifiable, monetary value was difficult to establish)[9] but also as a material anchor for an ancient way of life that is emphatically not driven by the profit motive. Later, Levin expresses his views to a sympathetic landowner who has deliberately foregone the most profitable uses of his lands: "We live without calculation, just as if we were tasked, like the ancient vestals, to watch over some fire" (AKP 657/AKN 552).[10] Levin's words imply that there is something absurd about the very notion that any amount of money could measure the noble's relationship to his or her estate. The sale of Stiva's forest to Riabinin requires the quantification of an incalculable value and the reduction of a whole tradition to a one-time monetary transaction.

The conversation about the forest takes place during Levin's visit to Stiva's estate, where the two go hunting for woodcocks in one of the novel's most vividly descriptive scenes. There are no descriptions in *The Brothers Karamazov* or in any of Dostoevsky's other works that match Levin's extraordinary attention to the minute movements of nature:

> From a thicket in which there was still snow came the barely audible sound of water trickling in narrow, meandering streams. Small birds chirped and occasionally flew from tree to tree.

In intervals of complete silence one could hear the rustling of last year's leaves, stirred by the thawing ground and the growing grass.

"Imagine! You can hear and see the grass grow!" Levin said to himself, noticing the movement of a wet, slate-colored aspen leaf beside a spear of young grass. (AKP 163/AKN 141)

Anna Karenina repeatedly suggests a connection between economic conditions and representational possibilities. As we have seen, in the mowing scene, the rhythm of the labor, its location, and the social relations it temporarily secures all create the ground for the scene's poetics. Likewise, in the hunting scene, Levin's ability to watch Stiva's grass grow is based in his relationship to the land as landowner and steward. Riabinin, we can be sure, will not dwell on this natural beauty, and no perspective of his could yield this kind of description. Under the merchant's ownership, the forest will be stripped of its resources while its beauty goes unobserved and unrecorded. It follows, therefore, that it is not just some trees that Stiva is selling, but the very condition of this kind of literary technique. Once the noble landowner surrenders his domains, novels like *Anna Karenina* will not be possible.

Fyodor Pavlovich is craftier than Stiva. He does not want to sell the plot cheaply to the local monopolists, and when competition arrives from out of town, he sees the opportunity to earn a substantial surplus. Monetary transactions play a comparatively minor role in *Anna Karenina*, and the novel tends to emphasize that debt is not only a burden on nobles but also, in a sense, a measure of their social power. For example, Vronsky can keep accruing debts because his aristocratic title gives him ample social capital.[11] The episode with the sale of Stiva's land demonstrates his family's increasingly desperate financial situation—a situation that finally forces him to go to work for the United Agency railroad-bank. His desire to convert his landed property into money is therefore a sign of his increasingly precarious position—and, in the longer term, that of the nobility as a whole.

Several key differences in how these two novels treat the sales of their respective forests highlight how differently they imagine Russia's economic life. It will not come as a surprise that the money economy reaches further in Dostoevsky's novel than in Tolstoy's, since it already did so in *The Idiot*. Indeed, the enormous thematic and narrative significance of money in Dostoevsky's fictions is hard to overstate and has attracted the attention of a large number of readers. As we will see, there are also important ways in which *The Brothers Karamazov* differs from *The Idiot* in how it imagines its Russian economy. The bifurcation in *The Idiot* between merchants' illiquid money, which powers the novel's most explosive scandal scene, and the capitalists' invisible money, which ultimately escapes beyond the bounds of narratability, is absent in *The Brothers Karamazov*. In this respect, *The Idiot* is more similar to *Anna Karenina*, which, as we have seen, also imagines Russia in a state of economic contradiction, albeit in different terms and with different consequences. Money in *The Brothers Karamazov* is not divided into two irreconcilably different kinds. Rather, all the money in play in the novel's plot undergoes a consistent phase change before it can become narratively usable. Peripheral characters belonging to the nobility supply the money, which is either given to or expropriated by the novel's major characters. Within the circumscribed zone of the plot, this money coalesces into regular quantities—most notably, the much-commented 3,000 rubles. By a kind of metaphysical algebra, the sum of 3,000 becomes the potential equivalent of a range of totally disparate things, relations, and even people. The figure of the 3,000 makes these putative equivalences particularly clear because, instead of just rendering everything quantifiable and comparable in the abstract through the medium of money, this stable figure posits the identity of totally disparate things by means of an economic syllogism: if the woodlot in Chermashnia is equal to 3,000 rubles, and 3,000 rubles is equal to Grushenka's love, then it follows that the woodlot in Chermashnia is equal to Grushenka's love. However, over the course of the book it turns out that 3,000 is an accurate valuation for almost nothing, and almost none of the deals in which it is involved go through.[12] The novel sets up these posited equivalences only to refute them by showing that each transaction fails and that the 3,000 rubles itself has an indeterminate, individually variable value. In the process, the plot of *The Brothers Karamazov* reduces this hypertrophied but malfunctioning economy to absurdity and undermines its underlying principle of quantifiability in order to open the way for an alternative human economy founded on mutual indebtedness and responsibility.

THE LANDOWNER AS INVESTOR

I think it is reasonable to speculate that in *The Brothers Karamazov*, Fyodor Pavlovich would be more likely to count the trees and Mitia more likely to admire them in a state of rapture. However, in the novel we have, the woodlot matters for the six failed attempts (if we count Fyodor Pavlovich's negotiations with the Maslovs and Liagavy) to turn it into money. There is also another sense in which Fyodor Pavlovich's land in Chermashnia matters: it constitutes most of the evidence that this "landowner" (*pomeshchik*), as the narrator calls him three times on the first page of chapter 1, owns any land besides what is beneath his house in the town of Skotoprigonevsk (there is also a parenthetical reference to an estate never mentioned again). There is reason to think the instances of *pomeshchik* on the first page of the novel proper are especially significant because it is not otherwise a common word in *The Brothers Karamazov*. While there are a few other landowners, including Miusov and Khokhlakova, the other character who is referred to as a landowner frequently—indeed, epithetically—is *"pomeshchik* Maksimov," a landless individual who, as Greta Matzner-Gore has pointed out, serves as Fyodor Pavlovich's marginal double.[13] In other words, the characters whom the narrator chooses to call landowners have somewhat dubious claims to that status. In the broader context of Dostoevsky's writings, "landowner" is a marked category. As we have seen, in *The Idiot*, wealthy landowners tend to be parvenus of questionable nobility, while legitimate nobles tend to be impoverished and economically dependent on new financial and commercial elites. In an 1871 letter to Nikolai Strakhov, Dostoevsky famously contrasted his work to the "landowner's literature" of writers like Tolstoy and Turgenev, which had defined Russian literature but which, argued Dostoevsky, had lost touch with Russia's social tumult and fragmentation (D 29.1:216).[14]

It is therefore significant that the patriarch of the Karamazovs is a *pomeshchik*. However, never in the course of this novel do we find Fyodor Pavlovich worrying about his lands or negotiating with peasant workers, and he certainly does not mow his own fields like Levin. In fact, it soon turns out that Fyodor Pavlovich is an entirely different sort of *pomeshchik*. In chapter 3, the narrator explains that he "never paused in the investment [*pomeshche-niem*] of his capital and always arranged his little deals successfully" (BKF 13/D 14:12). This pun shifts the meaning of Fyodor Pavlovich's social identity away from the landowner's estate (*pomest'e*) and into a world of capital, investments, and, as the narrator adds, financial dealings with Jews.[15] It is by means of these "little deals" that Fyodor Pavlovich has managed to build his first wife's dowry into a fortune of "up to one hundred thousand rubles in cash," which is the first sum of money we learn about in this novel teeming with such sums (BKF 7/D 14:7). For this kind of *pomeshchik*, the landowner as investor, the sale of a woodlot indicates not decline but a continuation of business as usual: he needs to liquidate one asset to acquire capital to purchase another.

The word *pomeshchik* is not the only fixture of the old noble life that is reappropriated to different ends in *The Brothers Karamazov*. As Carol Apollonio has observed, Fyodor Pavlovich's "first marriage establishes the primary tension of *The Brothers Karamazov*. Adelaida Ivanovna brings money into Fedor Pavlovich's life—something that was absent before."[16] This initial money, "filched" from his wife and built up through his business dealings, powers the plot of the novel (BKF 8/D 14:6). If he had not acquired this noblewoman's wealth, there would be no reason for Grushenka to consider marrying Fyodor Pavlovich, since 3,000 rubles, as the contemporary reviewer V. K. Petersen noted, would have meant little to this wealthy woman.[17] As we read the biographies of all the Karamazovs in the first chapters, it turns out that other nobles have also contributed to the family's finances. Fyodor Pavlovich's second wife, Sofia Ivanovna, grows up a poor charge of the wealthy widow of a certain General Vorokhov. After Sofia's death, this widow returns, takes Ivan and Alesha, pays for their education, and provides 1,000 rubles each for their futures, which grows, with interest, into 2,000 (BKF 13–15/D 14:12–15). Even though the narrator observes that Alesha "seemed not to know the value of money at all," he, like Myshkin before him, needs money to play a role in his novel (such as when he helps pay for Mitia's lawyer), and this money has to come from somewhere: in this case, a rich widow (BKF 21/D 14:20).

Rich nobles fund two of the novel's major plotlines. When Katerina Ivanovna comes to Mitia in desperate financial need, he offers her a 5,000-ruble banknote (BKF 114/D 14:106). Since Mitia had long been borrowing money from his father, this money, too, ultimately comes from Adelaida Ivanovna's dowry. The aristocratic Katerina Ivanovna is saved by another aristocratic woman's wealth. Later, after Katerina Ivanovna pays back the government funds embezzled by her father, she goes to Moscow, where she meets a rich old relative, another general's widow. Here a string of convenient deaths reminiscent of the ill-fated Papushin clan in *The Idiot* takes place: the old woman loses both of her daughters to smallpox, names Katerina Ivanovna the beneficiary of her will, and gives her 80,000 rubles for her dowry (BKF 116/D 14:107). Now Katerina Ivanovna can not only repay Mitia most of the money he lent her but can also request that he mail another 3,000 rubles to her sister in Moscow on her behalf.[18] This, of course, he does not do. Having already fallen for Grushenka (to whom he is in debt because Fyodor Pavlovich sold Mitia's promissory notes to her), Mitia spends the money—or half, as we learn eventually—on carousing in the village of Mokroe. The other half, worn in the pouch on his chest to which he obscurely gestures, becomes one of the novel's most consequential material objects. This money, the ostensible proof of Mitia's honor and a painful reminder that he has failed Katerina Ivanovna's test, also comes from a distant noblewoman whose only narrative purpose is to launch money into circulation.

It is true, as Valentina Tvardovskaia writes, that "not one member of the landowning gentry who appears or is mentioned in the novel is attaining economic success under the new conditions or has made himself over into an entrepreneur," so long as we regard Fyodor Pavlovich as a less than totally legitimate member of the gentry.[19] However, a number of noble families have succeeded in retaining considerable wealth and have not fallen into a condition of economic dependency on the new businessmen and entrepreneurs, as they had in *The Idiot*. In some cases in *The Brothers Karamazov*, nobles continue to defend their financial interests with a measure of success. The rich nobleman Miusov, Adelaida Ivanovna's cousin, even becomes Mitia's joint guardian and helps administer the property left him by his mother. More-over, while Fyodor Pavlovich manages to appropriate his first wife's money, he cannot gain control of the property that came with her dowry, which she continued to control under Russian law.[20] By retaining the property, the Miusov family keeps it out of the plot. Indeed, in the process of set-ting up the wealth that will power the novel, the property of these noble funders passes through a kind of filter: the immovable property is filtered out, while the cash enters the narrative of *The Brothers Karamazov*. Then, severed from its origins in the agricultural estates and the labor of peasant workers (and, before them, serfs), the money undergoes transformations in the hands of the Karamazovs. Whatever particular contexts—fields, forests, pastures, workshops—this money ultimately came from, no traces of its origins remain once it has entered the ostensibly homogeneous monetary flows that crisscross Dostoevsky's novel. To build on Dostoevsky's concept of "landowner's literature," it would seem that *Anna Karenina* foregrounds the representational potential of the noble landowner's special relationship to his (or her) property. In *The Brothers Karamazov*, the *pomeshchiki* have a very different role. On the margins of the narrative, they supply money to power the plot without contributing their estate's distinctive poetics. On the other hand, Fyodor Pavlovich, the nobleman who stands at the center of the novel's events, is a nobleman of a new type: a *pomeshchik-pomestitel'*, or landowner-investor.

With this variant of the Dostoevskian capitalist type at its center, the economic imaginary of *The Brothers Karamazov* differs in significant ways from that of *The Idiot*. As the preceding chapter argued, *The Idiot* trans-formed discourses about financial crisis and gentry decline into literary form by pitting two forms of money with radically different representational possi-bilities against each other. *The Brothers Karamazov* also makes extensive use of the poetics of money, but to different effect. This novel exploits the poten-tial of capital to make for interesting fiction by making the very possibility of universal fungibility its central problematic—one that extends well beyond the sphere of strictly monetary values. Meanwhile, Fyodor Pavlovich consti-tutes a new form of the capitalist type: less businesslike, fonder of scandal and confrontation, and therefore far more capable of holding narrative atten-tion. We learn even less about his business activities than about Totsky's or Epanchin's. The important thing is that he is capable of transforming money and property into narratively usable objects like the bundle of banknotes he wraps up in a package tied with a bow for Grushenka. Thanks to Fyodor Pav-lovich, *The Brothers Karamazov* starts where *The Idiot* posited the limits of realist representation: at least in the delimited space in which the Karamazov family lives out its story, money is abundant, mobile, and apparently pow-erful. On the smaller scale of the provincial town, *The Brothers Karamazov* then carries out a kind of narrative inquiry into the consequences of universal monetization.

CAPITALISM IN THE PROVINCES

The prominence of the woodlot in the business dealings of *The Brothers Karamazov* is one of several indications that this setting of the novel shapes the articulation of its economic imaginary. The novel's major events take place in a provincial town and its adjoining monastery, rather than hypermodern Saint Petersburg. The novel's setting in time suggests that the events of *The Brothers Karamazov* occur roughly simultaneously with those of *The Idiot*. The latter novel begins on November 27, 1867: its plot is synchronized with newspaper coverage of the sensational case of the real-life murderer V. F. Mazurin (D 9:391). Determining the precise temporal setting of *The Brothers Karamazov* has proven more challenging. The preface claims that the novel we have is preliminary to the story of Alesha's maturity, which will be the subjectof the second part of the novel. The narrator explains that the events of *The Brothers Karamazov* therefore take place thirteen years before the "present moment," that is, presumably, thirteen years before January 1879, the date of the preface's publication (BKF 3/D 14:6). However, attempts to establish the novel's precise chronology have led to the discovery of various inconsistencies, so that the events of *The Brothers Karamazov* take place, alternatively, in 1866, 1869, or 1871, depending on which set of past events or which character's biography one uses to construct the timeline.[21] Moreover, some of the historical context and topical concerns brought up in the novel refer to events that happened closer to the date of the novel's publication. For example, Mitia's dream of the "wee one" seems to recall the Samara famine of 1873. Likewise, Ivan appears to describe atrocities committed by the Turks in Bulgaria, more consistent with the events of 1875–76 than with an earlier period.[22] Indeed, Charles Moser argues that "chronology is so telescoped and intermixed in the novel that we simply cannot hold the author to any significant chronological accountability."[23] Recently, Jillian Porter has added another important data point to the discussion of the novel's chronology: the rainbow-colored hundred-ruble bills that are the standard unit of currency in *The Brothers Karamazov* are never described as bearing the portrait of Catherine the Great. This is significant because in one passage in the notebooks, banknotes are referred to as "Catherines" (15:304). Since the new series of bills bearing the portrait of Catherine only entered circulation in 1869, Dostoevsky's decision to remove this reference in the final version of the novel suggests that he took special care, at least where the history of money was concerned, to set the novel before 1869.[24] While

Dostoevsky's references to events in the news nudge the novel toward his and his readers' present, the history of money pulls it back toward the 1860s, in accordance with the narrator's claims in the preface.

There is good reason to pay attention to money's rigorous chronometry: it exercises enormous power in the circumscribed space of Skotoprigonevsk. The prominence of money in this relatively sleepy provincial town may seem counterintuitive. Much of the local economy is based on the surrounding natural resources, rather than real estate deals and the operation of joint-stock companies. In addition to the negotiations over Chermashnia by various Karamazovs, Miusov is engaged in a lengthy lawsuit with the monastery over fishing and logging rights on their adjoining lands. Although the provinces were home to some of the most intensively developed industrial sites in Russia, there are apparently no factories in or around Skotoprigonevsk.[25] The character of daily life is also different in this town, as compared to the metropolitan city: "Roots are deeper, housing is safer, and dwellings are not (for most of the characters at least) single *kamorki* or corners closed off by screens, nor are changes of residence or insecure jobs at all common."[26] In *The Idiot*, the narrator expresses surprise at the Rogozhin family home's apparent longevity amid the constantly changing Saint Petersburg cityscape. In Skotoprigonevsk, it would seem more noteworthy if a new one were to appear. In all of these ways, the setting of Dostoevsky's final novel exemplifies the social, spatial, and material divide that has long separated the two capitals from "the provinces" in Russian literature and culture.[27]

Given the provincial setting of Skotoprigonevsk, we can reasonably expect that the historical forces so prominent in *The Idiot* are likely to lag somewhat in *The Brothers Karamazov*. Since social categories and traditional ways of life have not yet undergone the same degree of destabilization as in the city (whose population was growing rapidly thanks to the migration of peasants from the countryside), it would be reasonable to expect that monetary relations would play a less significant role as replacements for older social forms. Processes already far advanced in the capital appear in earlier stages in the town, and, notably, not only there—some of the novel's money, such as Katerina Ivanovna's, comes from wealthy nobles residing in Moscow, where the nobility has apparently managed to retain its autonomy. That said, Skotoprigonevsk is clearly not a refuge from what is taking place in Saint Petersburg. Georgy Fridlender makes the important point that Dostoevsky's use of the provincial setting differed from that of writers like Leskov and Melnikov-Pechersky. While they tended to see the provinces as a haven for traditional ways of life that were threatened with dissolution in the deracinated cosmopolitanism of the large cities, "Dostoevsky transfers the setting from Petersburg into the provinces for the exact opposite reason, to show that the painful social-psychological processes that he described in his novels of the 1860s had ceased to be the 'privilege' of Saint Petersburg, that they had grown stronger and had encompassed, to a greater or lesser degree, the entire country."[28] In Dostoevsky's fictions, there is no longer any place that could remain sequestered from the changes that originated in Saint Petersburg. Among a range of new ideas and practices, capitalism has arrived in the provinces.

Nevertheless, the move to the provinces brings with it a change in the form of the local economy. The elites operate at a smaller scale in the provincial town. The sums of money involved are not as great—3,000 instead of 100,000, for instance—and distinctions between different types of money are not so acute. Instead of the extremes of *The Idiot*, in which capitalists' wealth moved so quickly that it resisted direct observation and merchants' hoards avoided participation in any kind of economic activity, sums of money in *The Brothers Karamazov* circulate more freely among characters. Merchants are still associated with immobile wealth, but their refusal of circulation is not as consequential. The main merchant, Kuzma Kuzmich Samsonov, rules over his children in an old and gloomy house. The children inhabit the lower floor, while he remains upstairs, isolated and immobile in a corner of this mostly empty space. "The old man could barely walk because of his swollen legs and only rarely rose from his leather armchair" (BKF 369/D 14:333). He had been important in the past as Grushenka's patron but is currently much less important for the plot of *The Brothers Karamazov* than Rogozhin was for *The Idiot*. When Mitia comes to Kuzma Kuzmich in search of money, he resorts to flattery, calling the old man the only "capitalist in this little town" (BKF 371/D 14:335). In reality, he is nothing of the sort, and both Grushenka, who had formerly depended on his patronage but has become a successful businesswoman in her own right, and Fyodor Pavlovich are both more consistent with Dostoevsky's capitalist types. However, Grushenka exceeds her role as a capitalist, both as the object of men's desire and as an active participant in the novel's central drama. Fyodor Pavlovich, for his part, certainly does not fear scandal and controversy like Totsky. The divide between capitalists and merchants is thus not as clearly drawn nor as consequential in this novel. As a result of these softened economic extremes, money is able to move more freely through the space of the narrative.

At the same time, the space in which money can maneuver in this novel is relatively circumscribed. Although, as we have seen, important financial contributions come from Moscow, relatively little money leaves the town and, indeed, connections to the outside world are less robust than in a major city. In order for Ivan to get to the railroad to go to Moscow, he has to traverse a distance of eighty versts, or about fifty-three miles (BKF 277/D 14:252). But, as we will see, this novel compensates in a remarkable way for money's spatial confinement: instead of tracing the spread of money horizontally, to unseen factories and far-off trading partners, *The Brothers Karamazov* emphasizes the vertical extension of monetary logic into morality and theology. The meaning of that metaphysical money will become clearer when considered in the broader context of the novel's preoccupation with monetary relations.

THE MEANING OF 3,000

Money saturates the world of Dostoevsky's works. It has been called the "fifth element," the "ruling power," and a "connective tissue" in his fictional universe.[29] Scholars have examined money as a metaphor for power relations in his works, as a structuring motif, and as a point of contact between the content of the novels and Dostoevsky's own tenuous status as a professional writer in an institutionally weak literary field.[30] Dostoevsky's misers and spendthrifts are obsessed with it (as in "Mr. Prokharchin") and go mad over it (as in *The Double*).[31] His characters get rid of it as a means of purification and sometimes try to destroy it physically, although with some hesitation—as Viktor Shklovsky puts it, "Dostoevsky's characters despise money meekly and unsuccessfully."[32] Jacques Catteau observes that the indestructibility of money is linked to its circulatory function in Dostoevsky's works: "Dostoevsky's world is like a huge system of circulation, where a diseased and mad blood, money, runs through the individual cells, starving some and stuffing others, and goes on its disorderly wanderings without ever being destroyed."[33] Sometimes Dostoevsky's characters are preoccupied with precise and tiny sums, other times with symbolically round figures. Scholars have tended to emphasize the abnormality of monetary transactions in Dostoevsky's fiction. For instance, Guido Carpi characterizes money in Dostoevsky's works as follows: "In Dostoevsky, the accumulation of wealth is usually linked to gambling, crime (theft, murder, fraud), prostitution, speculation or with unexpected inheritance."[34] It is, in the view of most commentators, an "unpredictable, elusive element" in his works, shifting constantly between social, moral, and even metaphysical registers.[35] Much of the time, Dostoevsky's money refuses to remain confined to a narrow sphere of commercial transactions. As the writer Tatiana Tolstaia observes, one is not likely to learn much about day-to-day business practices in nineteenth-century Russia from reading his works.[36]

George Steiner provides a particularly vivid account of Dostoevksy's strange money in his classic *Tolstoy or Dostoevsky*:

> Raskolnikov desperately needs a certain number of rubles, as does Dimitri Karamazov; and it is perfectly true that Rogojin's fortune plays a vital role in

The Idiot. But the money is never earned in any clearly definable manner; it does not entail the attenuating routine of a profession or the disciplines of usury upon which Balzac's financiers expend their powers. Dostoevsky's characters—even the neediest among them—always have leisure for chaos or an unpremeditated total involvement. They are available day and night; no one need go and ferret them out of a factory or an established business. Above all, their use of money is strangely symbolic and oblique—like that of kings. They burn it or wear it over their hearts.[37]

It is undoubtedly true that Dostoevsky places far less emphasis on the origins of his most spectacular sums of money than on the power they exert over people. As the previous chapter argued, money has to be removed from circulation and exchange in order to become the centerpiece of a scene like Nastasia Filippovna's name day party. On the other hand, those other, far less interesting fortunes, like General Epanchin's, continue to do their invisible work behind the backs of the novel's protagonists.

Even by the standards of Dostoevsky's other works, money is especially prevalent in *The Brothers Karamazov*: within his whole money-saturated oeuvre, Dostoevsky's final novel contains the second-highest concentration of lexemes related to money (ceding first place to *The Gambler*).[38] Among the numerous sums of money that characters talk about and obsess over in *The Brothers Karamazov*, 3,000 is by far the most significant. Others are certainly important, such as the 4,500 that Katerina Ivanovna borrows from Mitia and the 1,500 that he wears on his chest, but 3,000 plays a larger role than any other. *Tri tisiachi*—"three thousand"—appears 185 times in the novel in all its declined forms, and always in reference to the fateful sum(s) of money. Given that the novel occupies 697 pages across volumes 14 and 15 of the *Complete Collected Works*, this comes to approximately one mention for every 3.8 pages in that edition. If we consider that it takes some time before this fateful sum even enters the plot—doing so for the first time on page 112 of volume 14, then, in the remaining 586 pages, it occurs once for every 3.2 pages.

Of course, even after the 3,000 rubles enter the novel, their appearances are not evenly distributed throughout the text. Carpi's statistical analysis demonstrates that lexemes related to money—his focus is on all references to money, and not just the 3,000—figure especially prominently in the three chapters featuring Mitia's "confession" to Alesha (book 3, chaps. 3–5) and in the courtroom scene in book 12, while appearing with lesser frequency in the monastery scenes and most rarely in the novel's epilogue.[39] These findings suggest the outlines of an ideological structure where certain narrative zones in the novel privilege nonpecuniary values. However, besides the lexemes that Carpi examines to chart the novel's "economic semantic field," the text also contains numerous metaphorical expressions related to buying and selling.[40] As we will see later in this chapter, these metaphors of purchasing and acquisition are prominent in Zosima's speech, so that, at least in figurative guises, economic operations do enter the world of the monastery, from which Carpi suggests they are largely excluded. These figurative extensions of money are especially significant because they extend its homogenizing reach. Before examining this metaphorical dimension of money in the novel, however, it is necessary to consider the meanings that accrue to the figure of 3,000 in particular.

As a number of readers have noted, the very roundness of the sum suggests that it has symbolic dimensions, and scholars have often read the 3,000 in terms of a broader interest in the symbolic order of Dostoevsky's novels as evidenced by his use, for instance, of colors, spaces, and names.[41] In this sense, the sum of 3,000 rubles fits neatly into the novel's pattern of symbolic numbers, which is apparent even from the table of contents. The novel is divided into four parts, twelve books, each containing between three and fourteen chapters, plus an epilogue, consisting of an additional three chapters. This initial map of the novel's structure gives evidence of an intricate textual organization, of which the reader finds ample evidence when reading this book, which critics have generally judged to be Dostoevsky's most deliberately and complexly structured: Miller has called *The Brothers Karamazov* "a novel of rhymes" in which "characters, fragments of plot, fragments of time—all echo and reverberate in unexpected ways and places."[42] The repetition of certain numbers—most notably, three, four, and twelve—have symbolic resonances with both Russian folklore and Christian tradition.[43] Given the novel's numerous triads—three brothers (with Smerdiakov as problematic remainder), Ivan's three meetings with Smerdiakov, Mitia's three confessions to Alesha and three torments, the three chapters of "lacerations" (*nadryvy*)—the sum of 3,000 seems to fit squarely into these broader patterns structuring the novel. Furthermore, it seems like an ideal compromise between the demands of plausibility (the sum has to be meaningfully large) and this symbolic patterning. This is, indeed, how Valentina Vetlovskaia reads the 3,000. In her view, "the number three . . . is only an indication of the symbolic meaning of these thousands. It approximates the meaning of the words 'in general': some kind of inheritance in general. It is the equivalent of any number, and in itself does not mean anything: so apparent is its arbitrariness. What is important is the inheritance as such, i.e., the material side of the matter."[44] In this sense, three hundred would be too insignificant a sum to motivate the murder of Fyodor Pavlovich, a trifling sum pointing to the humiliating position of Smerdiakov, who earns Fyodor Pavlovich's trust by retrieving three one-hundred-ruble notes that the latter loses in a moment of drunkenness (BKF 126/D 14:116), while 30,000 would be too much—a prize appropriate, perhaps, to the urban millionaires of *The Idiot*, but not to a provincial setting in which a merchant monopolist can be famous for having 100,000.

A number of readers have turned to Dostoevsky's biography to make sense of his repeated use of certain sums of money in his fiction. Elena Shtakhenshneider, a family friend of the Dostoevskys who described her long friendship with Fyodor Pavlovich in her memoirs, paid special attention to the sociological dimension of money in Dostoevsky's works. She connects the content of the novels to the author's biography by observing that Dostoevsky himself was a *meshchanin*, a petty bourgeois. Shtakhenshneider claims that Dostoevsky's class identity affected the plots of his novels. Just as Dostoevsky fails at—or, more often, simply avoids—creating compelling characters from high society, she argues, his status as a *meshchanin* shines through in the fact that "for the representation of large capital, six thousand rubles will always be a huge number for him."[45] Shtakhenshneider juxtaposes this sum, evidently inadequate in her eyes for the representation of truly significant money, to Stavrogin's mother, a general's widow in *Demons*, who apparently marks Dostoevsky's furthest foray into the world of the *bol'shoi svet*, the beau monde. But this failure of verisimilitude is evidently an important socioeconomic symptom, which shows through in Dostoevsky's writings. Try as he might to motivate his plots with what seem to him like large sums of money, Dostoevsky's limited, class-bounded monetary imagination will limit him to expressing the modest fantasies of the *meshchanin*.

For other readers, it was precisely 3,000 that came to demarcate the scope of Dostoevsky's own economic imagination. Viktor Shklovsky amends Shtakhenshneider's observation: it was actually half that—the sum of 3,000 appears in Dostoevsky's works over and over again.[46] Shklovsky cites examples from various works to substantiate his correction, but he does not take issue with Shtakhenshneider's basic point: that a representative sum, not very large, stands for significant money in Dostoevsky's works and thereby reveals his own class status. A few decades after Shklovsky, Joseph Brodsky would respond to the same observation by Shtakhenshneider. In an essay that considers money as the fifth element in the universe of Dostoevsky's fiction, Brodsky returns to the 6,000 as an amount of money that "could buy a year of decent living at the time." Thus the importance of this sum of money for Brodsky is that "six thousand rubles is the monetary expression of a moderate normal existence, and if it takes a petit bourgeois to comprehend this fact, hail to the petit bourgeois."[47] Together, these three readers of Dostoevsky come to a crucial point: whatever the specifics of this sum, its meaning for Dostoevsky extends beyond its exchange value. Three thousand rubles (or six) can serve as a metaphor for the condition of not being poor. More generally, as a relatively arbitrary sum, 3,000 becomes a kind of empty signifier, capable of meaning many different things within Dostoevsky's works.

Some critics have interpreted the 3,000 as a link between Dostoevsky's position as a professional writer and the content of the works he was attempting to sell. Catteau points out that it was precisely 3,000 rubles that Dostoevsky borrowed from the predatory publisher Fyodor Stellovsky on dreadful terms: if Dostoevsky failed to deliver *The Gambler*, he would forfeit to Stellovsky all royalties from his already published works for a term of nine years.[48] It makes sense that sums of money would have an outsized importance in Dostoevsky's works because, as a struggling professional writer and journalist, he was unusual in a literary field composed of wealthy nobles like Tolstoy and Turgenev or government employees like Goncharov and Saltykov-Shchedrin.[49]

Dostoevsky thus faced special pressure to sell his novels, and, as Jonathan Paine has convincingly argued, these commercial considerations shaped the structure of Dostoevsky's works. Paine argues that the 3,000 aids Dostoevsky's commercial venture as a genre signal evoking "easily recognized commercial fiction based on the representation of sexual and financial greed."[50] By virtue of its repetitiousness, this sum also supports one of the novel's primary modes of fictional discourse, which Paine terms "iteration." This mode, which consists of "the retelling of similar narratives in different styles or from different points of view," wagers that the "iteration of similar narratives can change the cumulative perception of their worth."[51] As a stable measure of value, the 3,000 can make the novel's dozens of interpolated retellings of the central crime comparable—a process that reaches its metafictional apogee in book 12, where, together with Mitia, the genre of the novel itself is put on trial for its capacity to reveal the truth.[52]

However, Paine suggests that the instability of the 3,000 is just as significant for the novel as its capacity to make different episodes comparable. Indeed, the more often 3,000 recurs, attached to different tangible objects and intangible values, the more dubious its capacity to signify value becomes.[53] In addition to the multiple efforts by both Fyodor Pavlovich and Mitia to extract 3,000 from the woodlot discussed above, a dizzying array of transactions in the novel involve precisely this amount. Mitia stands accused of murdering his father over 3,000, while the lawyer Fetiukovich defends his client for the same amount. Augmenting the strangeness of this coincidence is Alesha's remark that the famous attorney has agreed to this unusually low fee because of the case's promise of publicity (BKF 568/D 15:10). Otherwise, he could have charged considerably more. Alesha specifies that he, Ivan, and Katerina Ivanovna are all helping pay the lawyer's fees. This means, to return to the discussion of the initial accumulation of money in this novel, that the lawyer's payment comes from two generals' widows: the one who takes care of the young Alesha and Ivan and the other one who gives 80,000 to Katerina Ivanovna.

During the trial, the seemingly most damning evidence against Mitia is that he ran around the whole town in a series of desperate attempts to acquire 3,000, and only hours later he appeared in Morkoe with a great deal of cash. Crucial here is the novel's central monetary dynamic: there are two sums of 3,000 with different provenances and different meanings. Mitia claims that the money he spent at Morkoe came from the pouch he had been wearing around his neck—a pouch containing half the money he had failed to send on Katerina Ivanovna's behalf. But once he spends this money during his second trip to Mokroe, it enters into circulation and becomes indistinguishable from any other money. While it remains unused, the 1,500 sewn up in Mitia's purse resembles Rogozhin's unexchangeable bundle of cash from *The Idiot* in that it is invested with incalculable personal meaning. But the link between money and meaning vanishes as soon as it is spent— and being spent is precisely what Rogozhin's money refuses to do.

Complicating matters is the inability of witnesses to establish how much money Mitia had with him at Mokroe. Mitia is captured with a precise sum: 836 rubles and 40 kopecks. He explains to the investigators that he spent approximately 530 rubles, so that the total he had with him during and immediately before the scene in Morkoe was about 1,500 (BKF 481/D 14:433). However, when the investigator interviews Maksimov, he confidently testifies that Mitia had 20,000 rubles in cash. Asked whether he had ever seen that much money before, Maksimov affirms that he has: "Of course I have, sir, . . . only it wasn't twenty thousand, it was seven, sir" (BKF 504/D 14:453). It is even more difficult to know the truth about money in this novel because it exhibits an extraordinary capacity to generate exaggerations and lies. Mitia's 1,500, perhaps reasonably mistaken for 3,000, metamorphoses in the testimony of witnesses into even larger sums. The prosecutor's allegation that Mitia had 3,000 with him in Morkoe also generates a spectral 1,500 that must be hidden somewhere at the inn where the scandalous party took place. In the novel's epilogue, the innkeeper Trifon Borisych is still desperately looking for this money that Mitia is supposed to have concealed there (BKF 762/D 15:184).

The real murderer, Smerdiakov, initially absconds with the other 3,000, the money prepared by Fyodor Pavlovich in a packet wrapped with ribbon. Smerdiakov explains to Ivan that he planned to use this money as start-up capital to finance his "café-restaurant" on Petrovka Street in Moscow (BKF 225/D 14:205). Ultimately Smerdiakov changes his mind and gives the money to Ivan, who presents it to the shocked courtroom as a demonstration of Smerdiakov's guilt and Mitia's innocence. Once again, the fungibility of money presents an insurmountable obstacle. In response to Ivan's demonstration of the evidence, the prosecutor Ippolit Kirillovich makes an aphoristic pronouncement that could serve as a key to the novel's economics: "Money alone is no proof" (BKF 713/D 15:141). These could be *any* 3,000, the prosecutor alleges, whereas only the specific 3,000 that were present in Fyodor Pavlovich's room at the time of his murder would count as evidence. This tension between two poles of money—the fungibility of money as a medium of exchange versus the haecceity, the *this*-ness, of some particular, physical money, money that has become linked to a particular experience—reaches an extreme in this scene. The familiar distinction from *The Idiot*, between merchants' cash and capitalists' capital, resurfaces to derail the truth-finding procedure of the trial.

Ivan cannot prove that the 3,000 he presents are the same bills that Fyodor Pavlovich had packaged and stashed away for Grushenka. Likewise, Mitia cannot prove that the money he spent in Morkoe originated in a *different* 3,000 than the one stolen from Fyodor Pavlovich. For money to function as a medium of exchange, it must be homogeneous: each ruble must be functionally identical to all the others. On the other hand, the plot of the novel is built on the difference and incommensurability of different monies. As an unproblematic quantifier of value, money makes things comparable. That homogenizing potential of money is most fully realized in the figure of the 3,000, which suggests the possibility that Fetiukovich's legal fee equals a woodlot in Chermashnia equals Mitia's honor equals Grushenka's consent equals Smerdiakov's café-restaurant on Petrovka Street. However, this theoretical equivalence does not hold, and the circulation of the 3,000 is interrupted at crucial moments. While Fetiukovich does get paid, the woodlot does not get sold, and Katerina Ivanovna's sister does not get the 3,000 that Mitia promised to send. Instead, half of the money meant for her ends up sewn into a pouch. Fyodor Pavlovich's 3,000 make a journey from a packet under his pillow to a tree hollow, then into Smerdiakov's sock, then to Ivan's pocket, and finally into the hands of the judge presiding over the trial. Grushenka refuses both offers of 3,000. Smerdiakov never buys his café-restaurant. If these transactions had succeeded, the 3,000 rubles, functioning as a universal equivalent, would have swept up all these events, relationships, things, and people. Going beyond the power of money to quantify and thus render commodities comparable, the 3,000 would have established that all the objects of its transactions were of equal value. But this is precisely what does not happen as the plot unfolds. The dense network of equivalences falls apart. Grushenka is not equal to a woodlot, and all these disparate kinds of value are not quantifiable. What half of the unsent money means to Mitia, sewn up inside the pouch on his chest, is not comparable to half the profit from the sale of the woodlot or half of the lawyer's fees. The plot of the novel reveals that, in fact, 3,000 does not equal 3,000. Money is not all the same.[54] It is with the ultimate collapse of financial transactions in this novel in mind that we can now turn to the metaphorical extension of money into the novel's central theodical debate.

THE PRICE OF REDEMPTION

The first time that the verb "buy" appears in *The Brothers Karamazov*, its object is—perhaps appropriately for this novel—"everything" (BKF 52/D 14:48). The person who utters it is, perhaps surprisingly, Zosima, elder of the local monastery. In the same passage, which records the words he speaks to the "believing peasant women" in book 2, "the whole world" also turns out to be something that can be bought. The currency here is, of course, love, not money, and the difference between the two substances is crucial. Nevertheless, the sheer frequency with which several characters, particularly Zosima, employ the language of commerce in reference to the novel's central theological and ethical problems raises questions about the real extent of money's domain in *The Brothers Karamazov*.

In probing the connections between money and theology—connections linked to such notions as guilt, debt, responsibility, and redemption—Dostoevsky takes his place in a discourse that ranges over thousands of years of human history. The connections between commerce, morality, religion, and capitalism have generated an enormous body of interdisciplinary scholarship, and this topic far exceeds what I can touch on in this discussion of *The Brothers Karamazov*.[55] Some scholars, like the anthropologist David Graeber in his *Debt: The First 5,000 Years*, has traced the links between such notions as debt, responsibility, guilt, value, redemption, and a host of related matters across a range of cultures and thousands of years.[56] Devin Singh has examined the extensive early Christian discourse of money as a "critical structuring principle in theological thought" with lasting consequences for the ways we think about money and the economy today.[57] The important question of Dostoevsky's connection to this deep reservoir of economic rhetoric in Christian thought calls for further research. At the very least, when Dostoevsky taps into the conceptual and rhetorical links between religion and money contained, for instance, in the notion of redemption, he is hardly alone. Like its English equivalent, the Russian words for redemption, *iskuplenie* and *vykuplenie*, both reveal etymological links to commerce, in the Russian case, via the root *kup*, which is found in such Dostoevskian words as *kupets* (merchant) and *kupit'* (to purchase).[58] With its insistent focus on the points of contact between theology and money, *The Brothers Karamazov* also makes an important contribution to the work of numerous modern thinkers, including Friedrich Nietzsche, Georg Simmel, Walter Benjamin, Norman O. Brown, Michel Foucault, and Giorgio Agamben, among many others, who have explored, in the sociologist Nigel Dodd's words, "the source of money's value, its relationship with time and space, its role in society and connections with community, its relationship with power and the state, its ancient links with ritual and religion, as well as its deep associations with the unconscious and with culture, self, and identity."[59] Rather than attempting to locate Dostoevsky in this vast body of thought, both ancient and modern, this section will limit itself to examining the meanings that the monetary rhetoric of the philosophical sections of *The Brothers Karamazov* accrues within the broader context of the novel's engagement with money.

The 3,000 rubles do not enter the monastery, but the rhetoric of money certainly does. Economic conflict persists on the monastery's border (the above-mentioned dispute between the monastery and Miusov over access to natural resources). Monetary considerations crop up in Zosima's teaching. In Alesha's transcript, immediately before Zosima's reflections on how a parent's grief for a lost child can be transmuted into quiet joy, the elder criticizes those priests who claim "that it is as if they can no longer teach the Scriptures to the people, for they are poorly paid, and that if Lutherans and heretics come now and begin to tear away the flock, then so be it, they say, for we are poorly paid" (BKF 292/D 14:265). A significant ellipsis separates the two sections of the elder's words. It is difficult to say who is responsible for it. We know that these are the recorded words of a weak and dying man. The narrator cautions us that "there could hardly have been such continuity in the narration" as appears on the printed page, "because the elder sometimes became breathless, lost his voice, and even lay down on his bed to rest" (BKF 286/D 14:260). Moreover, as Robin Feuer Miller reminds us, "the smallest phrase from Zosima's *life* is a polyphonic one, containing at all times the traces of Zosima, Alesha, the narrator-chronicler, and the author."[60] In a way, the very impossibility of assigning responsibility for the ellipsis to any particular contributor to this palimpsest strengthens the sense that an ambient discourse of money permeates all other topics. The juxtaposition of the priests' complaints about their salaries with Zosima's teaching—which can be read as a teaching that joy comes as compensation for sorrow—takes its place in a long series of implicit and explicit associations between theology and money in *The Brothers Karamazov*.

As is often the case in Dostoevsky's works, a matter of vital importance enters the novel through the words of a fool. It is Fyodor Pavlovich who accuses the monks of trying to "buy God with gudgeons" (BKF 74/D 14:69). The novel's most avaricious character first brings religion into the realm of monetary relations, but the polyphonic discourse of numerous characters keeps it there. Several scholars, notably Robert Louis Jackson and Harriet Murav, have observed that Ivan's objection to the idea that children's suffering could be justified teleologically is based in a monetary framework.[61] As Murav puts it, "According to Ivan, the suffering of children enters some sort of economy: a logic of exchange takes over, and the suffering attains value as that by means of which harmony is purchased. The logic of calculation, of damage done and compensated for, the basis for law and civil society, whose inadequacies religion tries to overcome—ends up reappearing within religion."[62] If Ivan and Fyodor Pavlovich interpret the moral order of Christianity through the logic of money, we might reasonably expect Zosima and Alesha to refute them. However, things turn out to be rather more complicated.

One of the most problematic aspects of Zosima's theodicy is, in the eyes of a number of critics, his reading of the book of Job, which, in the words of Susan McReynolds, "boils this complicated text down to . . . the justice of getting new children in exchange for dead ones."[63] McReynolds, the scholar who has examined the relationship of money and theology in Dostoevsky's fiction most thoroughly, argues that the possibility that Christianity is founded on a "salvational economy" haunts his entire oeuvre.[64] "By the time Dostoevsky composes *The Brothers Karamazov*," she argues, "the conception of God as a merchant and of redemption as something purchased with innocent suffering has become so well established in his fictional universe that it is simply assumed by figures as different as Ivan Karamazov and Father Zosima."[65] As a consequence, "the choice between Ivan and Zosima is not between two different conceptions of God and salvation but between acceptance or rejection of God as a merchant and redemption as an item for sale for the right price."[66] A cryptic passage in the notebooks to *The Brothers Karamazov* suggests that Dostoevsky thought about Ivan's rejection of the Christian moral order in explicitly commercial terms: "The Inquisitor: '*God as merchant.* I love humanity more than *you*'" (D 15:230, italics in the original). However, in McReynolds's view, both the Grand Inquisitor, speaking for Ivan, and Zosima believe that the suffering of children occupies the center of this redemptive economy. Ivan rejects the possibility that salvation could be bought with the suffering of a single child. In Zosima's reading of the book of Job, which lies at the heart of his teaching, "Job's first children are reduced to a marker or coin exchanged between Job and God," as a result of which "they suffer what the novel calls the worst fate—being forgotten."[67] Consequently, "money structures Zosima's faith and Ivan's assault on it."[68] Finally, even Alesha joins in this transactional theology. Iliusha's death becomes a real-life instantiation of the debates about children's suffering in the novel. As both Murav and McReynolds observe, in his speech at the stone in the novel's epilogue, Alesha, too, seems to think about Iliusha's death in terms of its exchange-value—its capacity to produce a "healthful" and "useful" memory for the boys (BKF 774/D 15:195).[69]

The presence of this transactional logic in Zosima's ostensible refutation of Ivan's argument lends powerful support to the idea that money has taken over completely in *The Brothers Karamazov*. However, Iliusha's death also contains the possibility of a radically different meaning. As he is dying at the end of book 10, Iliusha tries to offer his father consolation that is redolent of Zosima's teaching: "When I die, you get some nice boy, another one . . . choose from all of them, a nice one, call him Ilyusha, and love him instead of me" (BKF 561/D 14:507; ellipsis in the original). In response, Captain Snegirev exclaims, "I don't want a nice boy! I don't want another boy!" and quotes a passage from Psalm 137: "If I forget thee, O Jerusalem, let my right hand forget *her cunning*. May my tongue cleave to the roof of my mouth" (BKF 562/D 14:507).[70] Alesha explains the meaning of this biblical reference to the boys: "If I forget all that's most precious to me, if I exchange it for anything, may I be struck" (BKF 562/D 14:508). McReynolds concludes, with this passage, *"The Brothers Karamazov* draws our attention to the Biblically-endorsed possibility of rejecting exchange."[71] From here, an alternative to monetary logic comes into view—an alternative that draws on the same rhetoric of buying but with the altogether different currency of love.

When Zosima tells the peasant women that "love is such a priceless treasure that you can buy the whole world with it, and redeem [*vykupish'*] not only your own but other people's sins," he implicitly draws on a long Christian tradition that invokes monetary metaphors and regards "Christ as the currency of God" with which humanity is redeemed (BKF 32/D 14:33).[72] The crucial difference between the currency of love and the money that circulates in the novel is that the former is uncountable and makes calculation impossible. Given the conclusive failure of 3,000 to represent value in the novel's murder plot, this alternative currency leads away from the very notion of calculability and toward Zosima's teaching of incalculable, universal guilt "for all and everything" (BKF 164/D 14:149). In the murder plot, the trial has failed to reveal the truth because it has sought a single guilty person—one transaction in which the punishment would cancel out the crime. As the novel reveals, all four of the Karamazov brothers are to some fractional extent guilty (and, perhaps, even the narrator and the reader of *The Brothers Karamazov*, insofar as all have failed to recognize Smerdiakov as a brother).[73] As an alternative to the trial, then, with its preoccupation with separating the guilty from the innocent, Zosima's teaching offers universal responsibility and mutual, perpetual indebtedness. In that sense, *The Brothers Karamazov* is one of the best literary illustrations of what Graeber calls a "human economy" (as opposed to a money economy). In Graeber's words, human economies are "ones in which what is considered really important about human beings is the fact that they are each a unique nexus of relations with others—therefore, that no one could ever be considered exactly equivalent to anything or anyone else."[74] In human economies, money can only express incalculable and unpayable debts, which are themselves constitutive of communities. Understood in this way, the novel's hypertrophied money economy takes over the delimited space of Skotoprigonevsk only to collapse, opening the way for an alternative. Whether this alternative could be represented in literature must remain unanswered like all other questions about the continuation of *The Brothers Karamazov*, including the very possibility of the second volume hinted at by the narrator.[75] What already becomes clear in the novel we have is that novelistic narrative can rise again from the ruins of the money economy.

The possibility of a second volume also does not cancel the contradictions that scholars have noted in Zosima's views or, by extension, in the novel's theological message. In different ways, and despite their different methods, both McReynolds and Paine observe an antinomy in the novel's exploration of money. The novel's theological discourse is structured by the logic of monetary transaction and proposes a radical alternative to it. In terms of the novel's relationship to the print market, it constitutes Dostoevsky's attempt to articulate an anticapitalist message in a commercial product—in part by exploiting the narrative possibilities generated by capitalism. Both as a marketable commodity and as a theological novel, *The Brothers Karamazov* proves irreducible to a simple pro or contra with respect to the transactional logic of capitalism.

Chekhov and the Naturalization of Capitalism

Net, ne v'iutsia tam pó vetru chuby
Ne pestreiut v stepiakh bunchuki . . .
Tam cherneiut fabrichnye truby,
Tam zavodskie stonut gudki.

Put' stepnoi—bez kontsa, bez iskhoda,
Step', da veter, da veter,—i vdrug
Mnogoiarusnyi korpus zavoda,
Goroda iz rabochikh lachug . . .

No, forelocks do not whirl in the wind there,
No motley banners appear in the steppe . . .
Factory chimneys show darkly there,
Factory whistles moan there.

The way through the steppe, without outcome
    or end,
Only steppe, and wind, and wind—and suddenly
The multitiered factory building,
Cities of workers' shanties . . .
—Aleksandr Blok, "Novaia Amerika" (The New
America)

REFLECTIONS OF A SHATTERED WHOLE

The Cherry Orchard begins with the arrival of the train. In the play's closing scene, the nobles depart, the destruction of the orchard begins so that Lopakhin can clear the space for rental cottages, and the only character who remains on stage is Firs, the eighty-seven-year-old domestic servant, who was supposed to have been sent to the hospital but has been forgotten and left behind. Firs, who remembers when trips to Paris were accomplished by horse and carriage, regards the emancipation as a great calamity. Previously the social world had been static and comprehensible:

Firs: *(Doesn't hear)* That's right. Masters stood by the servants, servants stood by the masters. Nowadays it's all mixed up; you can't tell who's who.[1]

Now, decades after the emancipation, amid the destabilization of the old social hierarchy and the incursion of trains and factories into Russian life as never before, there is a chaos of change, and while Firs and the cherry orchard are already doomed, the nobility's obsolescence cannot be far behind. Like a number of Chekhov's late works, *The Cherry Orchard* examines the period of transition in which elements of the new and the old temporarily coexist and people who are familiar with the old are now confronted with the inevitability of the new. In Stephen Baehr's summary, Chekhov's final play stages "a 'battle' between two master images—those of the garden and the machine—to symbolically represent the transition occurring in his contemporary Russia from the would-be pastoral world of the old nobility to a modern world of business and industry where the ability to change determines power and wealth."[2] As we have seen in the previous chapters, the retrospectively static world of the nobility in Russian literature had already been under threat from ineluctable change for decades. But whereas in the older literature the obsolescing culture of the nobility had occupied the center of narrative attention, with the forces of capitalism on the peripheries of representation, in Chekhov this arrangement changes in significant ways. There is also a sense in which history finally catches up to literature at the turn of the twentieth century.

Chekhov's late works appeared in the midst of accelerating economic development. Russian industrialization underwent a boom in the 1890s.[3] Numerous joint-stock companies were formed to finance the new industrial enterprises, and as a wider segment of the Russian public became investors, stock market news and investment advice became increasingly common in the media.[4] The railway network had grown more than twentyfold between 1860 and 1895, and the number of workers employed in manufacturing now numbered well over 1.5 million.[5] Modern communications and transport networks stretched across the empire as thousands of telegraph offices were opened, and the volume of rail and waterborne freight increased.[6] The major cities of the empire, especially Moscow, Saint Petersburg, and Warsaw, swelled as hundreds of thousands of migrants from the countryside arrived in search of work. Regional industries like coal mining and metallurgy in the Donbass region and oil production in the Baku Guberniya—thanks to which the Russian Empire was, for a few years at the beginning of the twentieth century, the world's leading oil producer—developed rapidly.[7]

Commercial growth affected Russian print culture as dramatically as it did other sectors of economic and cultural life. Newspapers in particular expanded rapidly: between 1860 and 1891, the number of weekly newspapers grew from 98 to 226, and daily newspapers expanded tenfold, from 7 to 70.[8] This period saw the rise of new literary entrepreneurs, like Aleksei Suvorin, Chekhov's longtime publisher and owner of the popular daily newspaper *New Times*. Expanding literacy led to the diversification of reading habits and the emergence of unprecedentedly popular middlebrow publications. A. F. Marks, publisher of Chekhov's works after 1899 (at which point Chekhov declared, "I am now a 'Marxist'"), became one of the leading publishers in Russia with his illustrated weekly *The Cornfield* (Niva).[9] Founded in 1869, *The Cornfield* attained an extraordinary circulation of 120,000 in 1890 and also became a major vehicle for the distribution of the realist classics when it began to issue free editions of collected works to its subscribers, beginning with Dostoevsky in 1895.[10] As scholars of late imperial print culture have shown, during the final fifty years of the Russian Empire a popular literature emerged along with a large new audience of middlebrow readers interested in works that were less engaged in ideological debates and philosophical searching.[11] Contemporary critics attempted to make sense of Chekhov's radically new poetics in light of these changes in the conditions of literary production and consumption. Meanwhile, Chekhov responded to the increasing visibility of capitalism by making factories and businesses the setting of several of his works of the 1890s.

The late 1880s and 1890s saw the publication of a large number of fictional works about capitalism and capitalists. These included novels by the prolific and long-lived Boborykin, which featured socially conscious entrepreneurs, such as *Vasilii Terkin* (1892) and *The Mountain Pass* (Pereval, 1894). Mamin-Sibiriak contributed novels about the mining and banking industries in *Gold* (1892) and *Bread* (1895). Vladimir Nemirovich-Danchenko, a widely read reporter, novelist, and brother of the now better-known theater director Vasily, published his novel *Tsars of the Stock Exchange* in 1884 (for comparison, Zola's stock market novel, *Money*, came out in 1895). Maksim Gorky's first novel-length work, *Foma Gordeev* (1899), told the story of two generations of a prosperous merchant family: the superhuman patriarch Ignat, who builds the family fortune, and the tortured Foma, who, in D. S. Mirsky's view, represents a new kind of superfluous man.[12] Tolstoy contributed to this literature with his "Master and Worker" (1895), which transformed Hegel's social allegory of the master and the slave into a story about a merchant and a peasant laborer in Russia at the turn of the twentieth century.[13] The young Aleksandr Kuprin, as examined in chapter 1, published his novella about Russian industrialization in 1896. Aleksandr Serafimovich, who would go on to write the socialist realist classic *The Iron Flood*, wrote a series of sketches and stories of factory life in the late 1890s. In contrast to most of the work examined in chapter 1, the factories in these sketches are the solid ground on which the narratives are built; a typical sketch begins with the factory's ordinariness: "As always, the chimneys smoke, while the factory buildings vibrate and hum."[14] In the final years of the nineteenth century, industrial capitalism was entering the literary mainstream.

Several of Chekhov's late works fit this thematic focus, including "A Woman's Kingdom" (1894), *Three Years* (1895), "A Case History" (1898), "In the Ravine" (1900), and *The Cherry Orchard* (1903). In the works of some writers in these years, including those by Boborykin, Gorky, and Chekhov, merchants and capitalists left the literary periphery and assumed central importance as protagonists. Indeed, in the case of Chekhov and Gorky, whom Beth Holmgren has called the "articulate sons" of the Russian merchantry, writers with biographical connections to business owners and traders began to write literature about them.[15] The increasing centrality of capitalists, rather than their victims or opponents, had profound consequences for the representation of economic forces in Russian literature. In the novels of Dostoevsky and Tolstoy from the late 1860s and '70s, capitalists and capitalism had emerged as a source of threats to narrative, such as the danger of endless seriality, incomprehensible terror, and the commodification of the realist novel. In Chekhov, the capitalists themselves, now endowed with the inner complexity of protagonists, must take their turn in confronting the strange new world they have created.

The first performance of *The Cherry Orchard* in January 1904 marks the end of Chekhov's literary career (he died the following July). That career, in turn—depending on the way one periodizes Russian literary history—demarcates either the end of Russia's short literary nineteenth century and the tradition of realism or, on the contrary, the beginning of the long twentieth century of modernism. The beginning of the 1880s, the years when Chekhov began his literary career, famously marks a break, both in political and in literary history. The assassination of Alexander II in 1881 ushered in the regime of Alexander III, exemplified by the passage of the anti-Jewish May Laws of 1882, the collapse of Mikhail Loris-Melikov's constitutional reform program, and the rise of Konstantin Pobedonostsev, the arch-reactionary procurator of the Holy Synod. In literature, the key representatives of the realist generation died (Dostoevsky and Pisemsky in 1881, Turgenev in 1883) or remained absent from literature (Tolstoy had renounced fiction after *Anna Karenina* and only returned to it in 1886 with the publication of "Strider" (Kholstomer) and "The Death of Ivan Ilych"). The following years saw the continued extinction of the old generation, with the deaths of Ostrovsky in 1886, Saltykov-Shchedrin and Chernyshevsky in 1889, and Goncharov in 1890. In 1884, *Notes of the Fatherland* was shut down by the censor, and the *Russian Herald* declined into reactionary obscurity after the death of its longtime editor, Mikhail Katkov, in 1887.[16] Various writers and critics issued complaints about the state of Russian literature in the wake of these losses. It seemed to many that the hopes and commitments that had animated literature for decades had waned. A key term of the period was *bezvremen'e*, a word that literally means "timelessness," which designated this period as one of political and cultural stagnation and hopelessness.[17] In retrospect, the early 1890s have come to mark the commencement of Russian Symbolism, which is sometimes conventionally dated to Dmitry Merezhkovsky's programmatic essay of 1893, "On the Causes of the Decline of Contemporary Russian Literature," together with his collection of poetry of that year, *Symbols*.[18] However, for many commentators interested in the realist tradition, the emphasis was decidedly on the contemporary decline, rather than the rise of something new; these were years of listlessness, of exhaustion after the disappointed reformist and revolutionary hopes of the 1860s and '70s.

The eminent nineteenth-century literary historian Semyon Vengerov described the "Chekhovian period" in Russian literature as one of "despair and hopeless sadness" stemming from the intelligentsia's concession that its reformist hopes had been dashed by an age in which "the people remained in the stone age, the middle classes had not yet left the 'dark wood,'" while the program of Pobedonostsev "unfolded in all its horror."[19] In the literature of the *bezvremen'e*, the tormented and searching protagonists of Tolstoy, Turgenev, and Dostoevsky were replaced by types such as the titular hero of Ignaty Potapenko's *Not a Hero* (1891).[20] In place of the radical social change advocated by the *narodniki* in the 1870s, the new "theory of small deeds," popularized by the journalist and critic Iakov Abramov, advocated incremental change.[21] A new kind of character, the "average person" (*srednii chelovek*), emerged as a distinctive feature of this period, in the work of both Chekhov and many of his contemporaries. The "average person," as Vladimir Kataev clarifies, was not like the "little person" (*malen'kii chelovek*) of the literature of the Natural School. Fiction featuring the "little person" tended to evince a concern for social justice or an interest in revealing a little-known side of social life. On the other hand, "this 'average' person is understood in the works of the 1880s as a representative of the new masses, as any person," not a phenomenon to be brought to the public's attention by literature, but a manifestation of the ubiquity of *byt*, the category of the everyday.[22]

Nor was the "average person" like the concept of the character type that lay at the center of the theory of midcentury realism. The theory of type was complex and even contradictory—particularly with respect to the tension between universal types and types characteristic of a particular moment in national history.[23] Nevertheless, what the narrator of *The Idiot* says at the beginning of part 4 summarizes one of the key features of this theory. Literary types, the narrator claims, are not to be found in real life. They can be "exaggerated," even "almost more real than reality itself." Having read a work of literature, we begin to recognize types in our everyday acquaintances, but these real-life approximations appear "in a somewhat diluted condition" (IPV 462/D 8:353).[24] The older realist strategy of typification yielded characters like Oblomov, Bazarov, Raskolnikov, and many other protagonists of the literature of the 1840s–60s who came to name and exemplify emergent dispositions, forces, or pathologies in Russian society. By contrast, the "average person" of the *bezvremen'e* resembled what Lukács, in his discussion of Zola, calls the "gray, statistical averages" of naturalist characters.[25] A telling example of the new kind of characterization is Tolstoy's Ivan Ilych (the emphasis on the first name and patronymic over the individuating surname is telling). Ivan Ilych does not name a type in the older sense; instead of exemplifying his historical moment, he, like his furniture, remains indistinguishable from everyone else of his class, and the only thing that is truly his own is also, paradoxically, the thing that restores to him a measure of the concentrated meaning of the realist type—his death.

Even those Chekhovian characters who are anything but ordinary in their social position—like the rich capitalists Glagoleva, Lialikova, and Laptev—do not rise to the level of types. Rather than colliding with the constraints of *byt*, they live within it while expressing occasional—and mostly inarticulate—frustration. Neither they nor *byt* experiences significant change or loss. In general, the details of the lives of Chekhov's characters, that is, the content of their stories, tended to appear arbitrary to contemporary critics. Chekhov's preference for shorter forms, which could not provide the encyclopedic surveys and detailed descriptions of longer works, departed from the novel-centered tradition of Russian prose literature in the second half of the nineteenth century, but even within the genre of the short story, his work departed from established practice in symptomatic ways. The literary historian Konstantin Golovin attempted to articulate the peculiar experience of reading Chekhov's stories by contrasting them with what he regarded as the classic short stories of Turgenev:

> Turgenev created the form of the short story among us. But what an immeasurable difference there is between even the most minor of his scenes and those indifferent anecdotes with which contemporary belletrists regale us! The reader trustingly follows Turgenev wherever he goes, knowing in advance that the great artist is not leading him in vain into a peasant hut, into a forest, or a field—that there is nothing accidental [*sluchainogo*] in the encounters awaiting him there. It is not just any everyday scene or landscape that will attract Turgenev's attention. The only things he appropriates from nature and from man are those that contain in themselves characteristics of the typical—in which, consequently, the soul or the idea dwells.[26]

By contrast, contemporary writers, among whom Golovin singles out Chekhov as the "star," seem indifferent to their subject matter, so that despite their technical excellence, "the reader is puzzled why so much talent is wasted on representations that are so paltry" (463). The paltriness and seeming arbitrariness of the contemporary writer's choice of what to represent led to a breakdown of trust between the reader and writer. Turgenev's choice to represent some aspect of the world or to include a particular scene, whether it was set in a peasant hut, a forest, or a field, was always imbued with cognitive and moral value. The fiction of the 1880s and 1890s, on the other hand, was "indifferent" to its choice of subject matter. With Turgenev, the reader would have been assured of the capacity of any detail to refer to a broader or deeper truth, but no such certainty was available to the reader of Chekhov. In the view of Golovin and other critics, his works were inefficient; they did not provide the greatest possible amount of meaning or knowledge relative to their size.

Golovin associated the changes in literary form and technique with changing social conditions at the end of the century. One explanation he offered for the decline in contemporary literature was the rise in influence of a less cultured class of readers and their "bourgeois" individualism, for which no fact or point of view was more important or authoritative than any other, and the pursuit of individual success mattered more than the improvement of social conditions (420). Golovin concludes that Chekhov is a symptom of a broader phenomenon in contemporary literature: the ascendancy of a new reading public with middlebrow tastes: "What characterizes the contemporary direction in literature, as in the whole life of society, is nothing other than the striving to satisfy the tastes of the middle layer, which has managed to rise to such an extent that it already presents art with its demands." Furthermore, this "middle layer" demands that art conform to its standards—and here Golovin borrows the title of a satire by Saltykov-Shchedrin—of "moderation and tidiness" (*umerennosti i akkuratnosti*) (480). The increasing power of the "middle layer" augmented the effects of broader changes in society, which extended to the experience of time. As a result, writers were now being forced to publish stories that were "hurriedly thrown together so as not to waste the hurried reader's time" (462). What is more, the organic form of the great realists was being replaced by a seemingly random organization in the newer work, so that longer pieces consisted "merely of a series of minor sketches mechanically thrown or strung together on a common thread." So pronounced was this serial structure, so absent the inner unity of the work, that "it would be possible to set aside any given part of the work and release it as a separate story" (463). In other words, modern manufacturing techniques were beginning to have an effect on literature, as writers churned out modular pieces that they combined together "mechanically" in whatever configuration would be most profitable.

Another of the major critical voices of the period, Nikolai Mikhailovsky, assessed Chekhov's stories in terms of a broader tendency in contemporary literature to offer readers mere mechanical reproductions of reality, which were indifferent to issues of selection or interpretation. In a review of Chekhov's 1890 collection *Gloomy People*, Mikhailovsky observes, "Mr. Chekhov's choice of subject strikes one with its accidentalness."[27] He goes on to condemn the writer's apparent indifference to his subject matter:

> [Chekhov's] imagination draws bulls being transported on the railroad, then a thirteen-year-old girl killing an infant, then a mail coach traveling from one station to another, then a merchant drinking, eating a chaser, and signing who knows what, then a student's suicide, and so on. . . . Mr. Chekhov is not a writer independently navigating his material and sorting it from the point of view of some general idea, but some kind of almost mechanical apparatus. . . . Mr. Chekhov is not the only one in such a situation. Such are the general conditions in which literature now finds itself. And not only literature: such is "reality," which one is forced to acknowledge as fact.[28]

From Mikhailovsky's perspective, Chekhov is almost not even a writer at all, insofar as a writer must organize his or her material in accordance with the "point of view of some general idea."[29] Yet, he adds, this mechanical indifference of Chekhov's fictions does not originate in some peculiarity of the author's method; rather, he produces these indifferent works, despite his very evident talent, because of the abiding "pantheism" of the times, as Mikhailovsky elsewhere termed the contemporary attitude toward reality. Over the course of the following decade, Mikhailovsky would refine his analysis of Chekhov's works in their social context. In an essay from 1899, he elaborates the notion of contemporary literature's relationship to society:

> There is no basis for the evaluation of life events in order of their significance, for they all flow from a single source and all the same merit artistic reproduction. This theory, strictly speaking, has elevated the naked fact to a principle. Our *belles lettres* as a whole has for a long time constituted a multitude of shards from a broken mirror from each of which—sometimes truly and accurately, sometimes with distortion and murkily—some corner of life is reflected, but without any connection to the whole.[30]

Part of the problem for Mikhalovsky is that contemporary writers, in their pursuit of aesthetic experience, are indifferent to what they represent. However, the critic also posits that there is a homologous relationship between the form of contemporary literature and the form—or, more accurately, the formlessness—of contemporary life. Taking the commonplace of nineteenth-century literary theory, that the novel, as Stendhal wrote, is "a mirror going along a main road," reflecting whatever light reaches it, Mikhailovsky proposes that contemporary literature no longer provides a reflection of the whole.[31] Indeed, as he makes clear in another essay, such an image of the whole is no longer available, and writers like Chekhov can only express "a feeling of vexation at the incongruousness of life in which there is 'neither morality nor logic.'"[32]

THE ACCIDENTAL CAPITALIST

It was not only Chekhov's readers who found themselves adrift in a fragmented and incomprehensible world. Among the numerous cases of illusory certainty and inarticulate communication in Chekhov's works, those characters who attempt to navigate Russian capitalism also find themselves lost in confusion and indecisiveness. In contrast to the canonical literature of the mid-nineteenth century, in which labor and industry were relatively peripheral, Chekhov brings factories, capitalists, and on occasion even workers to the forefront. The owners of these enterprises tend to be capitalists of the second generation, who have inherited their property and have little enthusiasm for it. They are not possessed by the same spirit of relentless accumulation that had defined the marginal businessmen of Dostoevsky back in the 1860s. Nor are they the monstrous, all-devouring capitalists that one finds in the works of Boborykin and Kuprin. In Chekhov's stories, unlike in much of the earlier literature, the "intelligibility of the merchant's intellect and soul" is fully on display.[33] These people struggle with the consequences of their rapid upward mobility in a social system where, it seems, wealth has come increasingly to define one's position. But it is not only a sense of guilt that they experience. They are afraid of their own factories and dread going to work, yet they feel that they cannot give up their companies and sell their properties.

In contrast to the works of Tolstoy, Dostoevsky, and Boborykin, capitalism in Chekhov's stories does not appear as a sudden irruption of radically new socioeconomic conditions into traditional Russian society. Rather, characters in his stories confront elements of Russian capitalism as burdensome and inescapable facts of contemporary life. In place of the "some sort of" factory on the periphery of the realist novel, Chekhov's factories are central to the plot of his industrial stories and to the lives of their characters. But this does not make them more accessible. Instead, their meaning dissolves into the epistemic fog that pervades the world of Chekhov's fictions in general.

Traces of capitalism appear in Chekhov's stories in a world composed of overlapping and only partially integrated historical layers. The same landscapes contain traces of the deep past as well as the most modern infrastructure. Factories, railways, and telegraph wires often flit by, barely noticed by the characters whose experience structures many descriptive scenes. In some of the stories, characters traverse landscapes in which nature, artifacts of preindustrial culture, and industrial infrastructure succeed each other in a continuous flow of objects glimpsed on the horizon. For example, the young Egorushka, traveling in a cart in "The Steppe" (1888), sees that "behind the prison could be glimpsed the sooty smithies, behind them the cozy, green cemetery, which was surrounded by a stone fence; from behind the fence, white crosses, hiding in the greenery of cherry trees, peeked cheerfully. . . . Behind the cemetery, the brick factories smoked. Thick, black smoke rose in big coils from beneath the long reed roofs" (Ch 7:15–16). The cart's motion produces a parallax in which each object moves aside, revealing something else behind it. In the process, factories emerge, wedged between various features of small-town life. Industry does not appear, as it did in the works examined in chapter 1, as a striking intrusion that disrupts a familiar and established way of life. For Egorushka, the factories are part of the familiar scene he is leaving behind.

The layering of old and new is particularly evident in the conclusion to "The Peasants" (1897), where Olga, the widow of a man who had returned from Moscow to his native village, and her daughter, Sasha, leave the village in search of some means of subsistence. As in the landscape glimpsed by Egorushka in "The Steppe," the emotional tone of the scene in "The Peasants," with its seemingly arbitrary succession of objects, depends on the inner experience of individual characters, with no discernible judgment passed by a narratorial voice:

> The sun rose high, and it became hot. Zhukovo was left far behind. The walk was easy, and Olga and Sasha soon forgot about the village and about Maria; they were happy, and everything amused them. Now a burial mound, now a row of telegraph poles, which follow one another who knows where, disappearing on the horizon, and the wires hum mysteriously; now a little farm in the distance, all in green, exuding a hint of humidity and hemp, and it seemed, for some reason, that happy people live there, now the skeleton of a horse, bleaching alone in the field. (Ch 9:312)

I have tried to preserve the tenses and syntax in this passage, where, as soon as Olga and Sasha leave the village, the tense shifts, and the objects they see as they walk are described with a series of present-tense perfective verbs. As a result, the succession of objects they see—the ancient burial mound, modern telegraph wires, farm, and horse skeleton—breaks down into a series of discontinuous moments, each preceded only by the conjunction *to*. As Olga and Sasha walk in their perpetual present, the wires of the telegraph hum "mysteriously." This marker of modern technology has no discernible effect on the rural landscape that Olga and Sasha inhabit, and the message being transmitted between two distant points passes them by, leaving them on a dusty road with ancient graves and bleaching bones. Like the factories glimpsed by Egorushka, the telegraph wires are a reminder that this landscape has been irrevocably transformed by modern technology, but this apparatus of industrial civilization appears to the characters as so much additional scenery.

In the late story "In the Ravine" (1900), the industrial village of Ukleevo appears to be mired in immemorial squalor. From the road, a passerby sees the tower of the local church and factory smokestacks, but these are not symbols of a struggle between some older and putatively more authentic spiritual Russia and the new world of capitalism. Instead, we learn immediately that the only sense the locals have of the town's past is that once upon a time, a local deacon devoured a colossal amount of caviar (Ch 10:144). Meaningless, mindless consumption and waste define both the local church and the town's business elite. In this case, rather than historicizing the excesses of industrialization, the story associates the behavior of the local capitalists with primordial animality. In contrast to the conscious and reluctant capitalists of the other works examined in this chapter, Aksinia, who has no compunction about committing infanticide to take over the Tsybukin family business, is likened to a snake, and her naive smile and unblinking eyes suggest a total lack of interiority. At no point does anyone in the story offer an explanation for why things are the way they are that extends beyond platitude, like when Lipa asks an old man why her son had to suffer, and he replies, "Who knows? . . . You can't know everything" (Ch 10:175). The brutally exploitative society of "In the Ravine" appears to be a terrible tautology.

In general, Chekhov's later and longer stories express a conception of history in which clear logical or causal connections between events have become obscured. Industrial capitalism asserts a presence in towns and villages that is both powerfully material and, from the point of view of capitalists and skeptical observers alike, striking in its meaninglessness. The narrative perspective in many of these stories is linked to characters who express confusion and uncertainty when they confront the physical manifestations of economic change. As a result, the stories neither purport to objectively chronicle the transformation of social and economic conditions, like the novels of Boborykin, nor propose alternative forms of social life, like the novels of Tolstoy and Dostoevsky. Characters confront the manifestations of industrial capitalism like the massive factories in "A Woman's Kingdom" and "A Case History" with a sense of disorientation at these seemingly necessary yet arbitrary institutions.

THE CLOSED LOOP OF CIRCULATION IN "A WOMAN'S KINGDOM"

Most of Chekhov's works about the lives of industrialists and entrepreneurs present Russian capitalism as an unexplained state of affairs. Giant factories emerge out of an epistemic murk as an objective fact that allows little room for agency, irrespective of one's place in the economic hierarchy. Chekhov's capitalists find themselves in this world not of their own making as if they have been suddenly thrown into it. They are often presented with a task or an obligation that they struggle to understand and can neither fulfill nor refuse. The situations they face are not totally unprecedented in Russian literature. They struggle with the injustice of their privilege and try to understand their place in the world. Although the contemporary critical reception regarded Chekhov as an indifferent reproducer of reality, in the late works his depiction of Russia's economic life is often dense with moral meaning. But characters' awareness of this meaning, much less their ability to act in accordance with it, is severely constrained. More often than not, questions remain unposed and action untaken in these stories, and capitalism appears as a huge but indefinite presence, dimly perceived somewhere in the background of people's lives.

The protagonist of the 1894 story "A Woman's Kingdom" (Bab'e tsarstvo) tries to figure out what to do with a sum of money that resists leaving its customary circuit. The first words of the story underscore an abiding confusion about the meaning of this money and its sources: "Here [is] a thick packet of money." The first word, "here" (*vot*), can indicate the presence of the money ("A packet of money is here"), or it can be an imperative ("Here, take this packet of money"). The money is not simply introduced as an object within the purview of Anna Akimovna, the factory heiress; rather, it is thrust into view as if suddenly sprung on reader and protagonist alike. For a few moments, neither we nor she can understand where this money comes from or what it means. The next sentence offers an explanation, of sorts, for the money's sudden arrival: "This [is] from the forest *dacha*, from the assistant." Here the outlines of a narrative start to form, but in the original text only the third sentence includes a verb and thus offers any possibility of fitting the money into a causal chain: "He writes that he is sending fifteen hundred rubles, which he won in a lawsuit against someone, having won the case on appeal" (Ch 8:258). The characteristic indefiniteness of the "someone" the assistant has sued demonstrates Anna Akimovna's relationship to her own success, which comes to seem unmotivated and inexplicable.

This rigorously structured story is punctuated at regular intervals by further instances of *vot*: "Here, lying to the side, is a packet of letters, already read" (Ch 8:258); "Here is the railroad crossing and gate" (Ch 8:262); "Here, finally, is the broad street, on which the famous Gushchin house stands" (Ch 8:262). Like the click of a slide projector, each *vot* reveals a new scene. These are presented like a series of snapshots, discrete pieces of the world with the intervening links removed. At other moments, *vot* announces Anna Akimovna's impulsive resolution to take a course of action ("Here [*vot*], I'll just give [the money] to Chalikov" [Ch 8:260]; "I'll just go and get married!" [*Vot voz'mu i vyidu zamuzh*; Ch 8:282]). But these sudden bursts of resolve lead nowhere, as Anna Akimovna's decisions to change her life peter out in the conventions, almost palpable in their density, that structure her life. The frequent appearances of *vot* mark the lack of causal consistency on the level of the paragraph. On a larger scale, an analogous sense of discontinuity shapes Anna Akimovna's life. She has somehow ended up enormously rich, but also indifferent and unhappy in her status as a factory owner.

A moment after the introduction of the money whose movement will form a ring enclosing the action of the story, she reflects that "justice is necessary" but that, "for some reason," she feels guilty whenever her representatives win their frequent lawsuits. From this pang of conscience, one might conjecture that Anna Akimovna is a repentant property owner like Privalov in the novel of Mamin-Sibiriak and that she will use her wealth to try to ameliorate the plight of her workers. But Anna Akimovna is not that kind of protagonist, and Chekhov is not that kind of writer. In "A Woman's Kingdom," as well as in several other works examined in this chapter, business owners feel frightened and helpless in the presence of their own property. Their vaguely sensed guilt metamorphoses into something else—embarrassment, inarticulate anxiety, a dimly sensed frustration. Their attempts to change things melt away among daily cares, routines, and conventions. They continue to dread their factories and warehouses but cannot sever their connection to their property. In "A Woman's Kingdom," despite Anna Akimovna's occasional commentary on the social debts and responsibilities of a factory owner, the plot of the story develops around a much more limited question: she feels the urge to get rid of the money she has for some reason been awarded. Several times an option for doing this presents itself, but each time she finds herself frustrated by a sudden change of mood and decides to keep the money.

A number of scholars have observed that moods and impressions exert a greater force on characters in Chekhov's works than ideas or convictions do. Indeed, as Charles May puts it, one of the great innovations of Chekhov's prose is the "conception of the short story as a lyrically charged fragment in which characters are less fully rounded realistic figures than they are embodiments of mood."[34] Aleksandr Chudakov has discussed the conditioning of ideas by "the fortuitousness of everyday material life, of those particular circumstances by which [the idea] is accompanied in real existence" in Chekhov's works.[35] That is to say, a character's thoughts, feelings, convictions, and epiphanies are conditioned by chance occurrences and shifts in his or her physiological and psychic states. Indeed, whereas writers of the realist generation tended to focus on a key idea with which a character was preoccupied, Chekhov's stories instead take the chain of events that cause the idea as their primary object of representation. The unfreedom of a typical Chekhovian character's thought process is captured, as Kataev has observed, by a common rhetorical formula: *kazalos'—okazalos'*; at first things *seem* to be one way, but then they *turn out* to be otherwise. The emphasis here is less on the truth of a character's ideas than on the circumstances under which the ideas arise, the ways in which they are conditioned or determined. This "epistemological" theme in Chekhov's works, which Kataev identifies in the stories of the 1880s, develops in the industrial stories of the 1890s and is particularly apparent in "A Woman's Kingdom."[36]

The scene in which Anna Akimovna dines with the lawyer Lysevich and the government official Krylin is exemplary in this regard. Lysevich, a fashionable decadent, insists on the beauty of an epicurean lifestyle. In response, Anna Akimovna launches into a monologue that could have found a place in a hypothetical industrial novel by Turgenev, Tolstoy, or Dostoevsky.[37] She speaks of the moral torments she endures at the thought that her factory exploits workers and that she will have to answer to God for her life. But the fact that these remarks appear in a work by Chekhov, rather than these other writers, changes everything. At this dinner, moral torments become sources of aesthetic experience not just for the reader but also for the characters experiencing them. Lysevich responds to this speech with a purely aesthetic evaluation of Anna Akimovna: "How beautiful she is!" (Ch 8:282). Anna Akimovna does not find his remark patronizing. Rather than deciding that Lysevich has trivialized her words, she evaluates her own performance in similar terms. Chekhov's narrator ruthlessly analyzes how she delights at the realization that she had spoken well and that she "thinks so honorably and beautifully." She now imagines, in what might be taken as a moment of enlightened condescension, that it would look similarly beautiful if she were to marry Pimenov, a skilled worker from her factory. This same feeling of self-admiration returns a bit later, while she is listening to Lysevich praise Maupassant. Anna Akimovna, like Anna Karenina before her, is a narcissistic reader.[38] As she recalls the plot of the French novel, she thinks about herself. She concludes that "one cannot live like this, that there is no need to live badly when one can live beautifully," but this is no Tolstoyan realization that she must really change her life. Instead, she recalls her own beautiful speech from earlier that evening and thinks about Pimenov again (Ch 8:286). Later, after the pretentious servant Mishenka laughs at the ridiculous idea of a millionaire factory owner marrying a worker, all of her previous dreams start to seem embarrassing.[39] She realizes how laughable Pimenov would look in the company of Lysevich and Krylin and imagines that he does not even know how to hold a fork. She despairs at the thought that the only people who pay attention to her are the needy poor, and the idea of becoming their benefactor loses its aesthetic appeal just as much as the idea of marrying a simple worker does.

The thought of marrying Pimenov comes to Anna Akimovna by accident, a consequence of her attempts to get rid of the 1,500 rubles she won in the lawsuit. At first she decides to give it all to a poor civil servant with a large family, but finds the bizarre, Dostoevskian excess of his self-abnegation repellant. As she is about to leave their apartment, she meets their lodger, who turns out to be this Pimenov who works at her factory, and she contemplates giving the money to him instead. Again, she changes her mind and, afraid of offending the skilled worker's dignity, returns with the money still in her purse. While the options Anna Akimovna considers for getting rid of the money introduce potential turning points both in the plot of the story and in her life, considerations of taste and decorum prevent her from making these choices. Instead, she eventually decides simply to give the money to Lysevich after he asks why he has not received his customary holiday bonus. As a result, the money won for her by the assistant and facilitated by the legal system is fed back into that system via her lawyer. As the money disappears into Lysevich's pocket, she feels that she has finally found an application for the cash that feels "somehow cordial and natural" (Ch 8:287). Now the only question that troubles her is whether Krylin deserves a bonus as well, which she resolves by slipping him three hundred rubles.

This packet of money that so suddenly appears before the reader and turns out to be so hard to spend bears some resemblance to Rogozhin's shocking presentation of a huge packet of money to Nastasia Filippovna in *The Idiot*. However, the difference in what happens to these respective sums is what most effectively illustrates the difference between *The Idiot*, with its parallel economies, and the stability of the unavoidable yet incomprehensible infrastructure of capitalism in "A Woman's Kingdom." Whereas that scene in *The Idiot* emphasizes the contrast between the money of the merchants, which cannot be spent, and the money of the capitalists, which cannot be seen, there is only one kind of money in "A Woman's Kingdom," and this can only move in one direction. The profits from the factory and the winnings from lawsuits accumulate in the hands of Anna Akimovna and her associated accomplices and allies in the civil service and the legal system, and she is frustrated in all her attempts to move her money against this unidirectional flow. Whereas Rogozhin's money keeps circulating outside commodity exchange, Anna Akimovna's money refuses to leave the hands of the wealthy. Instead of illustrating a Russian dual economy with its emergent and residual elites, the money in "A Woman's Kingdom" traces the economic flows that continuously enrich people like Anna Akimovna, even if those people have no particular desire to get richer.

The rare feeling of naturalness and ease that Anna Akimovna experiences when she gets rid of the 1,500 rubles by giving them to Lysevich stands out against her sense that her position as the owner of a factory is arbitrary. Anna Akimovna is clearly uncomfortable in her role as an industrialist. Having grown up in peasant poverty, she inherited a giant factory from her father, who also experienced an extraordinary change of fortune.[40] Although she reassures herself when she receives the money that "justice is necessary" and her money has thus been legitimately acquired, the juridical and economic order seems to be an accident whose only justification is that it exists. Anna Akimovna is uninterested in her factory and tends to avoid it. She recalls with dread the one occasion when she toured its interior. What she remembers is a chaos of incomprehensible and unconnected objects:

> High ceilings with iron beams, a multitude of enormous, rapidly turning wheels, belts, and levers, the piercing hiss, the screeching of steel, the clatter of carts, the harsh puffing of steam, the faces, pale or red or blackened from coal dust, the shirts soaked with sweat, the glint of steel, copper, and fire, the smell of oil and coal, and the wind, now very hot, now cold, produced on her an impression of hell. (Ch 8:260)

In a description that is already familiar from similar episodes in Grigorovich, Reshetnikov, and Mamin-Sibiriak, Anna Akimovna's visit is dominated by her confusion and fright at the surroundings. Instead of a coherent scene, the reader is presented with a list of pieces. There are numerous adjectives and participles, but no verbs organizing the sequence of images. Both the machines and the workers' bodies are fragmented, broken up into parts linked syntactically but not narratively. Each of Anna Akimovna's senses responds separately, and when a verb finally comes at the end of the long sequence, linking all the preceding elements together, it is "produced"—a striking transformation of this enormous mill employing thousands of workers in the manufacture of metal into a factory of impressions on Anna Akimovna. Like the larger economic system, the mill remains opaque, both in terms of what it does and, perhaps more importantly, why it does it.

160

Anna Akimovna does not return to the mill, and most of the action moves between the upper and lower floors of her "woman's kingdom," the house with its almost exclusively female population of relatives and staff. As Holmgren observes, Chekhov offers "no positive alternative" in this spatially and socially bifurcated house, where the bottom floor is devoted to card games, eating, and gossip, while the richly decorated rooms of the upper floor host people like Krylin and Lysevich.[41] The story ends with Anna Akimovna and her servant Mashen'ka crying, both unable to find love.[42] As with a number of Chekhov's other works, contemporary readers thought that this was the beginning of a novel, but the completed work ends with Anna Akimovna in the middle of her personal predicament.[43] She feels trapped in her role as a capitalist. As Robert Louis Jackson puts it, "She nominally rules a kingdom of which she is in reality a dependent."[44] But there is one important narrative resolution: she has managed to get rid of the money.[45]

"A CASE HISTORY": THE FACTORY AS NERVOUS ILLNESS

The sense that the massive apparatus of industrial production has been created for no clear reason and to no one's particular benefit defines the mood of the central passage in "A Case History" (Sluchai iz praktiki, 1898). As in "A Woman's Kingdom," a sense of pointlessness abounds in the world of the factory, its owners, and all of their affairs. The pervading sense of accident is apparent even in the story's title: this is merely a case (*sluchai*) in the medical assistant Korolev's professional career. Furthermore, even Korolev's participation in the story is an accident. The first sentences are full of equivocation: a telegram arrives asking a professor of medicine to come to the Lialikovs' home to treat their daughter, but the telegram is long and poorly written, and the professor seems to have little interest in undertaking the time-consuming journey to treat a factory owner's daughter (ChN 379/ Ch 10:75). So the narrator laconically informs the reader that the professor does not go himself to check on Liza but sends Korolev, his assistant.

Early in the story, the narrator reveals that Korolev comes from Moscow and has scant personal familiarity with either the countryside or factories. What little he knows comes from reading or from a few visits to the homes of factory owners. On seeing a factory, "he always thought about how everything was so quiet and calm on the outside, while inside, probably, there was the impenetrable ignorance and stupid egoism of the owners, the dull, unhealthy labor of the workers, fights, vodka, and insects" (ChN 379/ Ch 10:75). The perspective on the factory in this story will thus be of an outsider, and explicitly one whose perceptions have been colored by reading contemporary discussions of industrial working conditions. In the course of his visit, Korolev observes the factory several times and attempts to make sense of this phenomenon, which evidently demands explanation.

Looking at the buildings of the factory, Korolev reflects on the poor sanitary conditions. He first likens it to the chronic health conditions that afflict the workers inside. Like those conditions, the factory itself is a "misunderstanding, the cause of which was also unclear and ineradicable." In the next paragraph, this misunderstanding acquires a different shade of meaning. The factory now seems to Korolev less like a disease and more like a particularly senseless kind of exploitation:

> There has been a misunderstanding here, of course, . . . he thought, looking at the crimson windows. Fifteen hundred or two thousand people working without rest, in an unhealthy environment, making bad quality chintz, half starving and only occasionally sobering up from this nightmare in taverns; . . . and only two or three, the so-called owners, receive any profit from it, although they do not work and despise poorly made chintz. But what benefit is there, what use do they make of it? (ChN 384/Ch 80–81)

Even those who profit from the labor of these 1,500 or 2,000 people employed in making low-quality goods, Lialikova and her daughter, "are miserable, they are a sorry sight, only Khristina Dmitrievna, that middle-aged, slightly stupid old maid in a pince-nez receives any pleasure from it. So it means that these five buildings sell bad quality chintz on the eastern markets simply so that Khristina Dmitrievna may eat sterlet and drink Madera" (ChN 384/Ch 10:80). It seems to him that the entire industrial economy, with its purported benefits—the efficient production of large quantities of affordable goods that a modern transportation network can distribute to distant consumers—and its deleterious effects is converted into a mechanism inadvertently serving the Lialikovs' aging governess. The Lialikovs themselves seem not to benefit from the business at all; they merely perpetuate it because it is already there, despite their contempt for the bad chintz that they manufacture and sell. Meanwhile, the workers, contrary to the claims of the governess, live poorly and suffer from the unhealthy conditions of their work.

This idea that the factory was a colossal investment in the production of useless things had already found expression in "The Kreutzer Sonata," as discussed in chapter 2. However, the causal chain of injustice in Tolstoy's work (women forced to commodify themselves in the sexual economy adorn themselves with luxury goods whose manufacture necessitates the enslavement of millions in factories) is replaced, in "A Case History," by "misunderstanding." And although this factory, like the steel mill in "A Woman's Kingdom," is owned by a woman, she too suffers because of her ownership and feels oppressed by it. Why, then, is there an enormous factory whose sole real beneficiary is Khristina Dmitrievna, a "slightly stupid old maid in a pince-nez"?

Korolev's thoughts about the factory continue to change, but their evolution is not the gradual development of an idea. Rather, the accidental intrusions of the outside world constantly modify his impressions, with the link between event and reaction established by impersonal expressions such as "and it appeared that . . ." He wanders through the still spring night, listening to the sounds of the natural world. As he looks at the only two windows that remain lit in the entire complex, he imagines that these are the eyes of a monster. As he watches, he hears the disturbing sound of the night watchmen announcing the time by beating sheets of metal, and the factory acquires a demonic aspect in Korolev's imagination. "It seemed as if, in the night's stillness, these sounds were coming from the red-eyed monster itself, the devil himself, who here owns both the owners and the workers and is deceiving them all" (ChN 384/Ch 81). Suddenly Korolev sees the factory not as a disease but as some kind of demonic creature, doing the will of the devil. Then he decides that it only "seems" that the factory works for Khristina Dmitrievna, when it is really controlled by this evil force.

But even this is not the end of his thought process. In the eerie stillness of the early morning, Korolev finds himself under the sway of thoughts that pull him out of his reflections on social injustice and metaphysical evil. Instead, his imagination turns to more distant comparisons to make sense of the factory: "Set against the gray dawn, when there was not a soul around, the five factory buildings with their chimneys had a particular appearance, different from that of the daytime; he forgot completely that inside there were steam engines, electricity, telephones, and his thoughts turned to stilt houses, the stone age, and he felt the presence of a crude, unconscious power" (ChN 385/Ch 10:82). Following this description, the language of the story acquires a decidedly gothic coloration. "'Terribly unpleasant,' thought Korolev. . . . And it seemed again as if all around everything had died out" (ChN 385/Ch 10:82). Nighttime, strange light conditions, disturbing sounds, and the proximity of death transport Korolev into a fantastical world in which the factory is not the product of consummately modern technological and economic conditions, but an immemorial monster and a primitive, inhuman power.

Korolev is not alone in his fear of the monstrous factory. As he talks to Liza, the night watchmen again beat out the hour on their sheets of metal, and she winces. In explaining her physical reaction to Korolev, she resists the medicalization of her condition: "It seems to me that I do not have an illness, but that I worry and am afraid because that is how it must be and cannot be otherwise. Even the healthiest person cannot but worry if a criminal is walking around under his window" (ChN 386/Ch 10:83). Like a kind of successor to Anna Karenina, Liza has little direct contact with industry (it seems unlikely that she has ever gone into the factory), but she finds herself oppressed and frightened by sensory traces of it, like the sound of metal being beaten and the exterior of the factory buildings. Both she and Anna feel a resultant psychological distress that becomes especially intense at night, whether as Anna's nightmares or Liza's heart palpitations and insomnia. In both cases, the feelings that these women experience—feelings provoked by the disturbing industrial infrastructure—become the main objects of representation. In "A Case History," so many metaphors develop around the factory—an incurable disease, the devil, a Paleolithic world, a criminal—that the factory itself is obscured. Two years before Chekhov's story, the protagonist of *Moloch* had looked out his window at the fiery steel mill at night and thought about an ancient anthropophagic god. But for the engineer Bobrov, this metaphor captured something specific about the place of the workers in the factory system. "There he is—Moloch, demanding warm human blood!"[46] Bobrov's guilt eventually drives him to attempt to destroy the steel mill and kill himself in the process, and although he fails to take this last step, the novella ends with him seeking escape from his sense of guilt in morphine. Korolev is clearly much less invested in his ideas about the Lialikov factory. Nor is there anything like the implied author's pointed criticism of industrialization in Chekhov's story.

Korolev speaks to Liza in the tone of an educated man who appreciates a liberal heiress's feelings of guilt. When she shudders at the sound of the night watchman's signal and complains of her anxiety symptoms, he responds with approval: "You have an honorable kind of insomnia. In any event, it is a good sign" (ChN 387/Ch 10:84). He then launches into a monologue that echoes that of several of Chekhov's idealistic, forward-looking characters. He notes that his and Liza's generation sleeps worse than their parents, torments itself with questions, and that their children or grandchildren will know the answers. "Life will be good in fifty years or so. It's just a pity that we will not live to see it" (ChN 387/Ch 10:85).[47] But, as Kataev cautions, Korolev's words should not be taken as authorially sanctioned statements.[48] Indeed, the story's structure, with its constantly shifting metaphors of the factory, undermines the authority of any such statement purporting to assess the present or prognosticate about the future.[49]

In its final pages, the story retreats from its depiction of the terrifying factory. Korolev's focus shifts from thoughts of a future society to considerations of his own personal happiness after a pleasant talk with an intelligent young woman. By the end of the story, Korolev is in good spirits, and the formerly frightening windows of the factory reflect the cheerful light of morning. "Korolev no longer remembered the workers, or the structures on stilts, or the devil, and instead thought about the time, perhaps already near, when life would be just as bright and joyous as this quiet Sunday morning; he thought how pleasant it is on a morning like this, in spring, to ride with a troika, in a good carriage, and feel the warmth of the sun" (ChN 388/Ch 10:85). It seems unclear at first whether Korolev is still fantasizing about a bright future for humanity, as when he tells Liza that in fifty years life will be better, or if it is now a merely personal dream of future happiness. However, a subtle verbal hint suggests a radical miniaturization of the world of his thoughts. Korolev reflects on how pleasant it is to feel the warmth of the sun, and the story ends with the diminutive *na solnyshke*: his troubled thoughts about the deep past and the distant future, about the inexplicable plight of the workers and the evil that controls the world, have given way to the banal satisfaction of the moment.

Even as Korolev forgets about his disturbing impressions of the factory, the story preserves a record of the factory's capacity to disturb him and Liza on a visceral level, not as an abstractly considered social problem but as part of the material world that imposes itself on them. Consequently, the story's final refusal to maintain focus on the factory does not seem to suggest the existence of a real alternative to a world dominated by industry. The works of Tolstoy and Dostoevsky had, in their distinct ways, asserted the foreignness of capitalism and industry as against some more authentic Christian or agrarian Russian tradition. On the other hand, the factory in "A Case History" is as much a part of the Russian landscape as the telegraph wires in "The Peasants" and the distant factories and forges in "The Steppe." While Chekhov's stories posit the persistence of preindustrial forms of culture in the mannerisms and customs of peasant workers, they also portray capitalism as a long-standing, multigenerational social order. Sometimes this reality comes into a character's focus; at other times it slips out of view. But whether anyone pays attention to it or not, it remains out there, making money. Anna Akimovna and Liza do not take an active part in the operation of their factories, but they do not have to: the factories are perfectly capable of managing themselves.

THREE YEARS: CAPITALISM AS SECOND NATURE

Three Years is Chekhov's most extended examination of the accidental capitalist and the inexplicable, almost ontological mystery of the business. To a greater extent than the shorter "A Woman's Kingdom" and "A Case History," the plot of *Three Years* unfolds far from the world of manufacturing and commerce. In the space of about a hundred pages, this novella tells the story of Aleksei Laptev, a thirty-something merchant and heir to a successful (as far as anyone can tell) hat-making business in Moscow. We learn about his unhappy marriage to a provincial noblewoman named Yulia Mikhailovna, as well as his unhappy childhood, which he spent, together with his tormented siblings, in fear of their tyrannically traditionalist father, an opaque and ambitious merchant. Laptev meets Yulia Mikhailovna in the provincial town where she is helping to care for his dying sister. After a brief period of courtship and a few trips to this unspecified place, Laptev proposes, and Yulia Mikhailovna, after initially refusing, accepts, thinking more about the prospect of living in the big city than about marriage with Laptev. The couple then moves to Moscow, where, contrary to Yulia Mikhailovna's hopes, they begin to lead a life of stultifying banality. They have boring conversations, go to performances they do not enjoy, and raise the orphaned children of Aleksei's sister. Time passes. The narrative ends with the kind of nonconclusion that bewildered Chekhov's critics. Laptev embraces the two daughters he adopted after his sister died, looks at his wife and their mutual friend, who is obviously in love with her, thinks that he still has many years left to live, and says to himself, "Time will tell" (*Pozhivem—uvidem*; Ch 9:91).

In the early 1890s, Chekhov had planned to write a long novel about Moscow life. However, as in his other attempts at writing novels, the work shrank as it developed, and in this case, *Three Years*—subtitled a "story" when it was first published in the journal *Russian Thought* in 1895—featured fewer characters and fewer scenes in the same three-year time span, as compared to the earlier plans.[50] When it was published, even this shorter work was criticized by reviewers for being unnecessarily distended.[51] Indeed, very little takes place in these three years and over these one hundred pages. In "A Woman's Kingdom," Anna Akimovna had confronted the impasse of her life over the course of an evening and a day. Laptev and Yulia Mikhailovna endure their confinement in a meaningless life over a much longer period. More than anything, we read about the listlessness and boredom of these characters, who have to face the relentless seriality of their daily lives. Curiously, this interminable repetition and the dread it induces, particularly in Laptev, finds suitable formal expression in the novella's relative brevity. At one point we read: "Life flowed on as usual from day to day, promising nothing special" (ChV 402/Ch 9:66). If this were a long novel, it would have to be full of *something*—day after day, or at least moment after moment, of narratively meaningful content. Even Oblomov's famous refusal to get out of bed only occupies the first quarter of his story and is enlivened by a series of meetings with visitors. A novel endlessly affirming over several hundred pages that "life flowed on as usual from day to day" would be more akin, perhaps, to the narration of distended boredom in a work like Thomas Mann's *The Magic Mountain* (1924) than a work of nineteenth-century literature. But the short form, with just a few episodes, turns out to be especially well suited to this compressed representation of eventlessness. These few pages suggest a whole, empty, repetitive life.[52] However, this is not exactly the hypothetical sequel to *The Idiot* in which the Totsky and Epanchin families go about their lives, in which disruptive events no longer interfere with business. Neither Aleksei nor Yulia Mikhailovna is happy, and their incongruity with the life they lead provides the material for a few events.

When events do take place in *Three Years*, however, they have little effect on the development of the narrative. Like Anna Akimovna's opportunities to get rid of the money, they turn out to be mostly dead ends, abandoned avenues into other kinds of plots. Some of these foregone alternatives recall the classic Russian novels of previous decades, but in *Three Years*, they do not form the same kinds of thematic and narrative patterns as in the literature of the previous period. In one of the most striking episodes in the novella, Laptev and Yulia Mikhailovna go to an art gallery, but compared to characters' confrontation with paintings in *The Idiot* or *Anna Karenina*, their experience of art is inarticulate, muted, and unsatisfying for the visitors.[53] Toward the end of their visit, after several hours of boredom, something suddenly changes for Yulia Mikhailovna when she looks at a small landscape painting:

> Yulia imagined herself walking across the little bridge, then down the path farther and farther, and it is quiet all around, drowsy corncrakes cry, the fire flickers far ahead. And for some reason, it suddenly started to seem to her that she had seen those same clouds that stretched across the red part of the sky, and the forest, and the fields long ago and many times; she felt lonely, and she wanted to walk, walk, walk down the path; and where the sunset's glow was, there rested the reflection of something unearthly, eternal. (ChV 401/ Ch 9:66)

Afterward she tries unsuccessfully to explain this experience to her husband and their mutual friend. She becomes frustrated with the art that hangs in their house, which now seems to her banal, and she feels particularly irritated when Laptev engages in conversations about art. This experience with the painting is a kind of epiphany for Yulia, but it is a reduced epiphany. Its effect on her is not of the same magnitude as what Myshkin experiences when he contemplates Holbein's *The Body of the Dead Christ in the Tomb*. Her experience with the painting and the limited access to meaning that it provides only further underscores the absence of meaning in her everyday experience.

Perhaps more significant than the content of this experience is its narrative motivation. In the middle of this scene there comes a quintessentially

Chekhovian phrase: "And for some reason, it suddenly started to seem to her . . ." As Petr Bitsilli has observed, indefinite and impersonal locutions, such as "it seemed [*kazalos'*]," "something [*chto-to*]," and "as if [*kak bud-to*]," distinguish the perspectival constraint of Chekhov's narration, in contrast to those realist writers who wrote—at least at times—"from *no particular* viewpoint."[54] In *Three Years*, the narrator offers no insight into the origin of Yulia's impression or its meaning. Some mysterious, inarticulable feeling breaks through the sense of arbitrariness that pervades this work and then withdraws again. Immediately after this moment, when we read about Yulia Mikhailovna's frustration with Laptev's comments on art, time reasserts itself. On the next line we read, "Life flowed on as usual from day to day" (ChV 402/Ch 9:66).

The narrative then switches to another pseudo-event. Laptev and Yulia Mikhailovna go to a court hearing and witness a scene where the defense attorney delivers his speech with indifference and, for some reason, expresses anger toward the jurors. In the end, the jury arrives at a verdict that reveals their total garbling of the defense attorney's argument: they conclude that there was a break-in but no theft, or perhaps there was a theft, but if so, then there was no break-in. This is a far cry from the courtroom drama of *The Brothers Karamazov*. In the world of *Three Years* it seems that all the institutions of progress and high culture, from the arts to the judicial system, must dissolve under the corrosive effect of all-consuming banality. This banality is particularly evident in the form of time in this novella. The courtroom scene is swept up in a flow of meaningless, increasingly empty units of time. Immediately following that scene is a two-sentence paragraph that concludes the chapter: "In May the Laptevs moved to their summer house in Sokolniki. By then Yulia Mikhailovna was already pregnant" (ChV 403/Ch 9:67). The abrupt transition from "one morning," which begins the courtroom scene, to "in May" is then followed in the beginning of the next chapter by an even more dramatic acceleration: "More than a year went by" (ChV 403/Ch 9:67). Time speeds up, becoming ever poorer in content. The few episodes that punctuate it only reinforce the sense that nothing important is really happening.

In the story's present—that is, more than a year after the announcement of Yulia Mikhailovna's pregnancy in May—even the train fails to bring change. This terrible harbinger of modernity in Tolstoy, Dostoevsky, Nekrasov, and, indeed, in other works by Chekhov is reduced and trivialized here. Whereas in *The Cherry Orchard*, Lopakhin's very first words ("The train has arrived, thank God" [Ch 13:197]) link this self-made capitalist and the arrival of the train to the decline and supersession of the nobility, the scheduled passing of the train by the Lopakhins' summer house signals simply that it is time for tea.

In this environment even language itself seems threatened with destruction. *Three Years* is particularly dense with Chekhov's characteristic nonsignifying speech. Laptev's father-in-law keeps singing the same meaningless syllables, "ru-ru-ru." At the Laptevs' warehouse, the salesclerks' speech is degraded in various ways. One of them, losing his mind, once attempted to articulate his objection to the tyrannical elder Laptev but managed only to call the owners "plantation owners" (*plantatory*) instead of "exploiters" (*ekspluatatory* [ChV 364/Ch 9:34]). No one understands this half-conscious insinuation of the workers' enslavement, and the other employees laugh at the clerk's inarticulacy. Meanwhile, the senior salesclerk speaks in pseudo-profundities, such as "'Nature exceeding its usual activity. . . . Where it goes in is where it comes out'" (ChV 362/Ch 9:33; ellipsis in the original). At other times, even if people attempt to exchange meaningful words, communication proves impossible. After Yulia attends a church service, the salesclerks congratulate her, "but the choir sang so loudly that it was impossible to hear anything" (ChV 369/Ch 9:38). People talk continuously in this novella, but most of what they say seems not to matter—sometimes it makes no sense; at other times it is drowned out by noise. The overall effect of this indefiniteness and boredom, of language losing its referentiality, is a sense that meaning is withdrawing out of reach. But in the midst of this meaninglessness, the material basis of Laptev's life looms increasingly large: his business fortune—or, as one critic put it, his status as a "fake capitalist,"[55] a rich man who does not understand how or why he is rich.

It has been argued that one of the distinctive features of Chekhov's work is that in his stories and novellas, Russian merchants and entrepreneurs become subjects and protagonists.[56] In place of the caricatures of suspicious bearded men with names like Kuzma Kuzmich and Semyon Semyonovich that we find in much of nineteenth-century Russian literature, Chekhov's merchants are complex and conflicted selves—individuals who exist separately from their hereditary estates and their business activities. But it would seem that this entry of the merchant into literature comes at a price: people like Laptev—or like the Lialikov family in "A Case History" and Anna Akimovna in "A Woman's Kingdom"—cannot bring their increasingly large businesses with them into the realm of intelligibility. Indeed, in these works of Chekhov, most incomprehensible of all, it seems, are the very businesses and factories that these people own. In *Three Years*, Laptev derives his great wealth and his idleness from a hat business, but he avoids going to work in the warehouse as much as possible. Even when we accompany him inside, we get rather little insight into its operations. It seems that Laptev does not take much interest in his warehouse either. And since in Chekhov the reader's perspective is so closely linked to that of particular characters, we are unable to get any more information than Laptev provides us. When he does finally go to the warehouse, we see bits of rag, hear clerks communicating in strange, undeciphered codes, and it turns out that Laptev is as lost in his own family's warehouse as the reader is likely to be. But he was raised to work here, and whether he wants it to or not, his whole life revolves around this business.

Eventually the elder Laptev becomes too blind to work, and his other son, Fyodor, who unlike Aleksei had continued to work at the warehouse, stops going there "for some reason" and turns to writing "something" (ChV 416/Ch 9:78). When Fyodor comes to Aleksei to show him this "something," it turns out to be a generic essay about Russia's mission to save Europe. At this point, Aleksei's frustrations about the pointlessness of his existence finally boil over. What had been in the background—the business, the family's merchant identity, their bad education and limited prospects—now comes to the fore. Fyodor insists that the Laptevs' business fortune makes the family distinguished, to which Aleksei responds: "Big deal—a million-ruble business! A man of no special intelligence or ability happens to be-. come a trader, then a rich man, he trades day in and day out with no system or goal, not even a lust for money, he trades mechanically, and money comes to him, not he to it" (ChV 419/Ch 9:81). This is not a story of hard work and inventiveness rewarded; in Aleksei's explanation, this huge business simply crops up, not the result of special talent, or great effort and determination, but just so—in accordance with inexorable and apparently unknown laws. Its origins, Aleksei insists, lie in the trader's desire to dominate his sales-clerks and swindle his customers. And this petty desire comes to ensnare a whole group of people, whole generations of employees and employers alike. Fyodor responds, "Our business is hateful to you, and yet you make use of its income," which only confirms what Aleksei has been saying (ChV 420/Ch 9:81). Finally, Fyodor grows angry at Aleksei's complaints and storms out—only to get lost in the huge house on his way to the exit.

Then, as he is finally leaving, Fyodor suffers a sudden breakdown, and in the following months he goes mad. Aleksei is forced to assume control of the family business, but he understands nothing about it. The chief clerk continues to speak in his oracular quasi-language, concealing things from Laptev and only communicating with the blind, inert father. The whole business strikes Laptev as one big "oddity" (*chudachestvo*) (ChV 426/Ch 9:87). When Laptev finally demands to learn the true state of the finances, and the clerks deliver their report, we might expect that, in the midst of this disorder, the Laptev family fortune has evaporated and the business is deep in debt. Indeed, Chekhov's notes suggest that in his early plans for the novella, the business was to be sold.[57] In the final version, however, things turn out to be much stranger. It seems that no amount of mismanagement can actually harm the business. In the report, Laptev learns that, somehow, its income is increasing by 10 percent annually and that their family fortune amounts to not 1 million, but 6 million. Although it appears that no one is really in charge, they somehow cannot stop making money. And so, a few pages before the end of the novella, one solid and certain thing emerges from the haze of ennui and doubt: the business, apparently untended to, a matter of total indifference to the man nominally in charge, keeps growing inexorably. It does not need this self-conscious merchant—this "Hamlet of Zamoskvorech'e," as one critic derisively called Laptev, referring to the traditional merchant quarter of Moscow (Ch 9:494).

Laptev does not understand what is happening, and, because his concerns are the focal point of the novella, neither do we. The background of his life, this human-made world of business, withdraws from our awareness and assumes an objective character as something indurately mysterious, separate from us, operating according to its own, unknown laws. This is what Lukács, writing twenty years later, would call "second nature," a world of anthropogenic conventions and structures which, "like nature (first nature), . . . is determinable only as the embodiment of recognized but senseless necessities and therefore . . . is incomprehensible, unknowable in its real substance" and is thus experienced by human beings as "a prison instead of as a parental home."[58] Whereas in Romantic poetry the lyric moment could be charged with the "meaningful unity of nature and the soul or their meaningful divorce," no such relationship to second nature is possible, Lukács argues.[59] The decidedly un-Chekhovian philosophical idiom of Lukács's book notwithstanding, the Laptev family business confronts its reluctant owner precisely as a "charnel-house of long-dead interiorities."[60] This warehouse, the family's multigenerational accomplishment, has become, for Laptev, a crushing and unarticulable burden.

The industrialists and millionaires in Chekhov's works do not struggle to shape the recalcitrant material of (first) nature in accordance with their ambitions. They are not the powerful creators of some heroic phase of early Russian capitalism. Their great challenge is not to realize their vision, defeat their competitors, and grow rich, but to make sense of the colossal enterprises that they ostensibly control but that are not objects of their agency. The task of building these business empires is always the work of another generation—one that usually appears in nineteenth-century Russian literature as semilegendary ancestors. Their descendants confront a naturalized capitalism as people bereft of any navigational tools to help them traverse this terrain. With respect to Russia's capitalist realism, Chekhov marks both an end and a beginning. The process that had begun decades earlier with the seemingly sudden appearance of incomprehensible factories in the Russian landscape and illegible capitalists on the margins of fictional narratives has been completed. In the late works of Chekhov we have examined here, these objects and characters no longer threaten to destabilize the narratives into which they intrude; rather, they have become central to literature in their own right. This change, rather than elucidating the cavernous interior of the factory, appears to have plunged the entire world into its ominous gloom. The task of trying to make sense of capitalism from the inside has remained a challenge for literature ever since.

THIS BOOK HAS argued that the experience of capitalism forced Russian writers to confront the limits of literary representation and that some of the greatest works of Russian realist literature incorporated those limits into their structure. These responses to economic and social transformation did not amount to literary reflections of material realities. Russian literature freely imagined what did not yet exist or was just coming into being. It proposed alternatives and prognosticated catastrophes that were informed not only by contemporary economic conditions but also by the world-changing potential of new ways of imagining space and time. The problems that literature faced when attempting to give legible form to economic change were complex and multifaceted. The transformative potential of capitalism seemed to threaten some of the basic conditions of realist representation. In the factory interior, for example, literature encountered a space in which an unprepared observer could make no sense of the tumult and noise and in which it was impossible to speak, hear, see, or even move around without danger. Such an environment nullified almost all of the basic procedures of realist narrative, since observation, communication, and even thought became nearly impossible for the bewildered characters who entered this space.

The factory could at least be avoided by most of the characters who populated Russian novels. Other aspects of the capitalist transformation intruded directly into the functioning of novelistic narrative. In *Anna Karenina*, capitalism threatened not only the physical survival of the nobility but also the extraordinary descriptive richness of "landowner's literature." Levin's mowing scene revealed how the careful balance of description and narration depended on a system of social estates and property relations with the landowning nobility at the center. Once that painstaking synchronization was disturbed, whether by the violent intrusion of the train or by the grotesque distension of the consumer economy, disaster was sure to ensue.

The Idiot dramatized the distinction between money as an object of the plot—a bundle of cash capable of accumulating enormous emotional energy and incalculable personal value—and an ungraspable, perpetually mobile type of money that resisted entanglement in scandal and, by extension, in the events of narrative. The struggle between the novel's capitalists and merchants—each faction an extension of its characteristic form of money—came to an end with the victory of the capitalists, and the bleak consequences of this victory soon came into view. The triumph of faceless, risk-averse capitalists endangered the novel's ability to represent subjectivity and narrate noteworthy events, both of which were lost along with the capitalists' vanquished opponents. In general, the capitalists of nineteenth-century Russian literature are not larger-than-life adventurers and seekers of fortune like Zola's Saccard, hero of *The Kill* (La Curée) and *Money*. Instead of producing spectacular failures, they accumulate relentless success. Rather than displacing sensitive nobles and impassioned merchants as the protagonists of novels, these capitalists threaten the category of the protagonist as such.

The Brothers Karamazov took the proliferation of the money economy even further than *The Idiot* to show how relations mediated by money could flatten values and homogenize relationships between people and things. Like *Anna Karenina*, Dostoevsky's final novel enacted the recuperation of the Russian novel's representational richness in the face of encroaching capitalism. In the end, the money economy collapses into meaninglessness due to its paradoxical ability to accrue incommensurable values. In place of the simplified valuations and transactional relationships imposed by money, *The Brothers Karamazov* posits an intricate system of infinite, unpayable debts, which the novel can account for much better than financial transactions or Western jurisprudence can.

Finally, Chekhov's stories suggest that the progress of capitalism threatened the intelligibility of the world. In the works of the earlier novelists, capitalists had been congruent with their opaque and ungraspable money. Now, in these stories, it turns out that the capitalists themselves do not understand how their factories function or, more importantly, why. In the late stories of Chekhov, capitalism appears as an incomprehensible given. His characters often see it not as a historical development but as some monstrous atavism—before losing sight of it altogether. Tellable events, complex protagonists, meaningful values and knowledge—all this appeared to be under threat. The coming of capitalism seemed to herald social and literary catastrophe.

In the following years, new developments in both literature and politics charged some aspects of the capitalist world, particularly the factory, with new meaning. The emergence of a new way of representing the factory through the eyes of a character who was supposed to be there, as in the work of Kuprin, made it possible to gain some analytical purchase on the infrastructure of capitalism. With the appearance of literature informed by Marxist politics and structured around the perspectives of workers, like Gorky's *Mother* (1906), the factory became a space of political struggle, rather than the negation of communicability. The early twentieth century gradually saw

174

the emergence of a literature by and about members of the industrial work-ing class, as evidenced, for example, by the first *Proletarian Writers' Collec-tion*, published in 1914. In his preface, Gorky addressed a proletarian reader-ship with the promise that this book might be seen by future generations as "one of the Russian proletariat's first steps to the creation of its own litera-ture."[1] As in that collection, some of the most notable responses to industri-alization during this period appeared in poetry rather than prose. That same year, Aleksei Gastev, an avant-garde poet who after the revolution would go on to pioneer research into scientific management, wrote a poem called "We Grow out of Iron." The lyric persona declares: "I myself grow steel shoulders and immeasurably powerful arms. I have merged with the iron structure. / I have risen. / With my shoulders I force up the rafters, the upper beams, the roof."[2] No trace of the old poetics of the factory remains here. Its illeg-ibility had been linked to a sense of its arbitrariness: there seemed to be no good reason for these massive and terrifying constructions in the middle of the Russian landscape. In Gastev's poem, the association of the factory with an invasive, inarticulable force is gone, replaced by the figure of a worker and the factory fusing into a superhuman iron being. From here, the way lay open to the aestheticization of the industrial site in the Soviet production novel and the emergence of what Nicholas Kupensky has called the Soviet industrial sublime.[3] Of course, this transformation of the poetics of the fac-tory depended on the reimagining of the factory as an extension of the work-ers' agency and of industrialization as part of a meaningful historical pro-cess. Gastev's poem is not socialist realism, but it is imbued with the sense that the workers have decoupled the factory from capitalism and made it their own.

A more optimistic interpretation of Russia's industrial revolution was also possible without the clear disavowal of capitalism. "The New America," the 1913 poem by Aleksandr Blok which provides the epigraph to chapter 5, imagines an industrial future for Russia on the other side of a rupture with the past. At first the poem's lyric persona concentrates on the enumer-ation of losses: the past, once immediately available, is now out of reach. When he smells smoke and hears distant drones, he first wonders if these are the signs of a battle between the warriors of medieval Rus' and the Po-lovtsians. No: Slavic warriors are not dipping their helmets into the Don River, as they did in the *Tale of Igor's Campaign*. Industry has appeared where the ancient battles once raged, and the steppe can no longer serve as a bridge to the Russian Middle Ages. Its spatial and temporal expanses are suddenly interrupted by the sight of a giant factory, and its flatness is broken by mines bringing up minerals from the depths of the earth. At first it seems that this severing of historical continuity must be the devastating herald of Russia's assimilation into the flat and dismal universality of a new, American age. But this is not Dostoevsky's America, which always serves as a metaphor for soulless materialism and spiritual death. Blok's America represents the promise of something absolutely new. In the last lines, the poem makes a remarkable turn:

> Black coal—subterranean Messiah,
> Black coal is here king and betrothed,
> But the sound of your stony songs,
> Russia, bride, brings no fear!
>
> Coal groans and salt appears white,
> And iron ore howls . . .
> Above the empty steppe
> the star of new America shines for me![4]

The star of new America that shines over the marriage of Russia and the carbon Messiah signals both the regeneration of Russia and the domestication of industry. Less than four years after the publication of Blok's poem, the October Revolution changes everything.

There remains one more point to consider: What does it mean to speak of Russia's nineteenth-century capitalist realism, particularly today? This book has described a group of anomalously realist novels and stories about an anomalous capitalism. In the conceptual background of its argument, one question in particular has stood out: How should we think about capitalism and the novel in Russia when both of these appear as "national malformations" by analogy with Western economic and literary history?[5] Among the globally famous nineteenth-century realisms, the Russian variant exhibits the most tenuous, least self-evident connection to capitalism. On the other hand, in the case of Western literatures, the thesis that the realist novel is firmly rooted in social and economic modernity is central to the historiography. "Etymologically," writes Harry Levin, "realism is thing-ism. The adjective 'real' derives from the Latin *res*, and finds an appropriate context in 'real estate.'" And this etymology points toward the common history of realist literature and modern capitalism: "While fiction moves from Balzac to Proust, things are in the saddle, riding mankind at a swifter and swifter pace."[6] To be sure, Russian realism, as well as Russian life, differed in crucial ways. In terms of economic realities, Russia had fewer things—fewer manufactured goods, fewer factories, fewer units of currency. In terms of Russian literature's economic imaginary, perhaps those commodities, factories, and rubles acquired a more threatening, more palpably alien aspect than they did in the realisms of France and Britain. If so, then the very strangeness of these things in the works of Dostoevsky, Tolstoy, and Chekhov gives special meaning to Russia's capitalist realism.

A few more words remain to be said about terminology. The concept of capitalist realism entered widespread circulation in twenty-first-century discourse with the publication of Mark Fisher's *Capitalist Realism* in 2009. For Fisher, capitalist realism describes the capitulation of the contemporary social, political, and economic imagination to tautology: it is a realism of the kind that explains that things are the way they are because that is how they are. It is the characteristic form of social thought of an age when "capitalism seamlessly occupies the horizons of the thinkable."[7] Rather than a term of aesthetics, this kind of realism finds its clearest articulation in the phrase "Be realistic," meaning don't hope for too much.

A recent volume edited by Alison Shonkwiler and Leigh Claire La Berge takes up Fisher's term and applies it to the analysis of both social and literary forms. In their introduction, Shonkwiler and La Berge argue for the historical specificity of a late twentieth-century concept of capitalist realism against the assumption that "all realism is already capitalist."[8] In modern Russian literary scholarship, that assumption can hardly be taken as a given. It has been the goal of this book to clarify the relationship of these two terms in nineteenth-century Russia, not with the aim of establishing that Russian realism too was always already capitalist, but to illuminate some of the ways that Russian realism confronted capitalism as a problem—of social thought, of historical imagination, and of aesthetic representation. This book has traced Russian literature's engagement with capitalism on various levels, from the formal impasses generated by the endless, iterative temporality of business to the representational challenge posed by the factory interior and by the alternating concretion and abstraction of money. It has sought to demonstrate that for Russian literature, the relationship between capitalism and the historical experience that realism tried to capture was a matter of profound concern and one of the sources of this tradition's remarkable creativity. Now, on the other side of the Soviet century, realism remains a vital literary mode and capitalism is running up against the ecological limits of the earth. It is possible that the rich store of ideas Russian realism developed in its experience of historical change in the nineteenth century might prove illuminating for the twenty-first. However, that is the beginning of another discussion, and, as Dostoevsky would say, the present one is over.

Notes

INTRODUCTION

1. On the ideas "racing about in the air" of St. Petersburg, see Dostoevskii to M. N. Katkov, Wiesbaden, September 19 (22)–15 (27), 1865, in D 28.2:136. The quotation about trembling creatures comes from D 6:212. On the role of the contemporary media context in shaping Dostoevsky's composition of *Crime and Punishment*, see Klioutchkine, "The Rise of *Crime and Punishment* from the Air of the Media." On the evolution of Raskolnikov's own understanding of his motive, see Frank, *Dostoevsky: The Miraculous Years*, 86–88, 107–22.

2. On the role of the police in recovering debts in Imperial Russia, see Antonov, *Bankrupts and Usurers*, 195–205.

3. English translation from Dostoevsky, *Crime and Punishment*, 98. Russian original in D 6:77. Ellipsis in the original. Subsequent references to *Crime and Punishment* will cite this edition, followed by the corresponding passage in D. I have occasionally modified the translation.

4. On Dostoevsky's novelized polemic against the atomizing effects of a commercialized *Gesellschaft*, see Guski, "'Geld ist geprägte Freiheit.'" For a study that emphasizes mutual responsibility and indebtedness in Dostoevsky's fictions, see Rowan Williams, *Dostoevsky*.

5. Valentino observes that a promissory note serves as a "catalyst" for the action of both *Crime and Punishment* and *The Brothers Karamazov*. See *The Woman in the Window*, 30. Valentino's observation is also taken up by Porter. See *Economies of Feeling*, 104.

6. Dostoevsky, *Crime and Punishment*, 97/D 6:76; ellipsis in the original.

7. Dostoevsky, *Crime and Punishment*, 546/D 6:418.

8. Dostoevsky, *Crime and Punishment*, 62/D 6:52.

9. See, for example, Courtemanche, *The "Invisible Hand" and British Fiction*; and Andriopoulos, "The Invisible Hand," as well as the discussion of *Anna Karenina* and the gothic in chapter 2.

10. Some contemporary critics assigned more weight to the economic motive for Raskolnikov's crime than most modern interpretations would allow. See Pisarev, "Bor'ba za zhizn" (1867), in *PSS*, 9:118–71.

11. I borrow the evocative formulation "fan of possibilities" from Anderson, "One Exceptional Figure Stood Out."

12. Kliger, *The Narrative Shape of Truth*, 119.

13. For an overview of urban retail in late Imperial Russia, see Hilton, *Selling to the Masses*, 14–109.

14. Gertsen, *SS*, 12:94.

15. This significantly reworked version of Gogol's text was marketed as a reliable guide to the British public's enemy in the ongoing Crimean War (1854–56), ostensibly written in English by "a Russian noble." See R. May, *The Translator in the Text*, 15–17.

16. De Vogüé, *The Russian Novel*, 273.

17. Woolf, "The Russian Point of View," 250.

18. Woolf, "The Russian Point of View," 251.

19. Raymond Williams, "Base and Superstructure in Marxist Cultural Theory."

20. Tooze, "Imagining National Economies," 213–14.

21. Polanyi, *The Great Transformation*, 147.

22. Buck-Morss, "Envisioning Capital," 440.

23. Poovey, *Genres of the Credit Economy*, 415.

24. See, respectively, Tooze, "Imagining National Economies"; and Mitchell, "Rethinking Economy."

25. Gorlov, *Nachala politicheskoi ekonomii*, 1:i.

26. Gorlov, *Nachala politicheskoi ekonomii*, 1:358. Smith writes: "When the division of labour has been once thoroughly established . . . every man . . . lives by exchanging, or becomes in some measure a merchant, and the society itself grows to be what is properly a commercial society." *Wealth of Nations*, 1:26. I thank an anonymous reviewer of an earlier version of this introduction for pointing out Gorlov's unreferenced paraphrase of Smith.

27. Dal', *Tolkovyi slovar'*, 4:663, 4:557. The posthumous third edition of the Dal' dictionary, significantly expanded by Jan Baudouin de Courtenay and published 1903–9, does not make any substantial changes to these definitions.

28. Mikhel'son, *Ob"iasnitel'nyi slovar'*, 735.

29. *Entsiklopedicheskii slovar' Brokgauza i Efrona*, vol. 20a (1897), 590.

30. Kotsonis, *States of Obligation*, 32–33.

31. Kotsonis, *States of Obligation*, 80, 79.

32. Von Laue, "A Secret Memorandum," 64–65.

33. K. Marx, *Selected Writings*, 161.

34. For a concise overview of different views on when—and where—capitalism began, see Kocka, *Capitalism*.

35. Braudel, *Civilization and Capitalism*, 232–34.

36. Hobsbawm, *The Age of Capital*, 1.

37. Sheffle, *Kapitalizm i sotsializm*.

38. Raymond Williams, *Keywords*, 51.

39. *Marx/Engels Gesamtausgabe*, 2:5:17; Marks, *Kapital*, 1. The Russian translation of the first volume of *Capital* was begun by Mikhail Bakunin, who soon abandoned the work. German Lopatin completed a large portion, but ceased working on the translation in November 1870 when he embarked on an attempt to rescue Chernyshevskii from Siberian exile. The translation was completed by Nikolai Daniel'son and Nikolai Liubavin, and the radical publisher Nikolai Poliakov undertook publication. The book was deemed too complex to be dangerous by the censor and was printed by the press of the Ministry of Railways. This was the first translation of *Capital* into any foreign language, preceding both the French (1872) and English (1887) translations. On the book's translation, see White, *Marx and Russia*, 13–15. On its reception, see Fedyashin, *Liberals under Autocracy*, 133–37. For a detailed account of the translation project and its participants, see Resis, "*Das Kapital* Comes to Russia."

40. Ziber, "Ekonomicheskaia teoriia Marksa," 198. This work was published in the following journal installments: *Znanie* nos. 10 and 12 (October and December 1876) and no. 2 (February 1877); *Slovo*, nos. 1, 3, 9, 12 (January, March, September, December 1878).

41. Ziber, "Ekonomicheskaia teoriia Marksa," 177.

42. That said, "the West" certainly exhibited heterogeneity in its economic development. For instance, a far larger proportion of the French labor force continued to work in agriculture through the end of the nineteenth century than in Great Britain or Germany.

43. On some indicators of Russia's economic lag, including extent of railways, exports of manufactured goods, and urban population over the course of the later nineteenth century, see Spulber, *Russia's Economic Transitions*, 138–52.

44. In the European context, the various possible constituents of a Russian middle class or bourgeoisie, from professionals to merchants, generally failed to coalesce into a Western-style civil society. See Clowes, Kassow, and West, *Between Tsar and People*; and Balzer, *Russia's Missing Middle Class*.

45. See Antonov, *Bankrupts and Usurers*, 3–4.

46. Pravilova, *A Public Empire*, 3.

47. Gregory, *Before Command*, 31.

48. Gatrell, *The Tsarist Economy*, 231.

49. Bakić-Hayden has described backwardness as "a constitutive metaphor in the social-scientific language of influential philosophers and writers" commenting on Russia since the eighteenth century. See "Nesting Orientalisms," 917–18. According to Wolff, "Eastern Europe in the eighteenth century provided Western Europe with its first model of underdevelopment." *Inventing Eastern Europe*, 9.

50. Gerschenkron, "Economic Backwardness in Historical Perspective."

51. Chaadaev, *PSS*, 1:527.

52. See Walicki, *The Controversy over Capitalism*, 107–31.

53. Quoted in Polunov, *Russia in the Nineteenth Century*, 100. On Russia's enlightened bureaucrats in the age of Alexander II, see Lincoln, *In the Vanguard of Reform*.

54. Fedyashin, *Liberals under Autocracy*, 132.

55. On the history of this word in nineteenth-century literary and journalistic discourse, see Kataev, "Boborykin i Chekhov."

56. Boborykin, "Pis'ma o Moskve," 261.

57. On the economic and social thinkers who clustered around the *Vestnik Evropy*, see Fedyashin, *Liberals under Autocracy*.

58. See Kingston-Mann, *In Search of the True West*, 93–111.

59. Wortman, *The Crisis of Russian Populism*, 10.

60. For an overview of the place of Tuhan-Baranovsky in prerevolutionary Russian economics and his relationship to legal Marxism, see Barnett, "Tugan-Baranovsky and *The Russian Factory*."

61. See Tugan-Baranovsky, *The Russian Factory*, 419–45.

62. McCloskey, *The Rhetoric of Economics*.

63. On Schäffle, whose ideas Chicherin somewhat inaccurately labels "socialist," see Hodgson, "Albert Schäffle's Critique of Socialism." For an overview of Spencer's significance in the intellectual history of the nineteenth century, see Francis, *Herbert Spencer*.

64. Chicherin, *Sobstvennost' i gosudarstvo*, 339.

65. Belinskii, "Mysli i zametki o russkoi literature" (1846), in *PSS*, 9:432. English version from Belinsky, "Thoughts and Notes on Russian Literature," 5–6. Translation modified.

66. For the most comprehensive account of early Russian railroad financing and construction, see Haywood, *Russia Enters the Railway Age*.

67. For an overview of the meanings that accrued to the railway in Russian literature, see Baehr, "The Troika and the Train." On "railway mania," see Gatrell, *The Tsarist Economy*, 151.

68. As Frank notes, "D. I. Pisarev, while still remaining a political radical, was nonetheless a partisan of exactly such rapid capitalist development and large-scale industrialization." Frank, *Dostoevsky: The Stir of Liberation*, 364.

69. Pisarev, "Realisty" (1864), in *PSS*, 6:225–26.

70. Pisarev, "Realisty," 333.

71. Shell, *The Economy of Literature*, 11–62.

72. For an overview of this subfield, see Woodmansee and Osteen, *The New Economic Criticism*.

73. Goes locates the origin of Russian literature's interest in contemporaneous economic life to the anonymous "Povest' o Karpe Sutulove," which tells the story of a traveling merchant. See Goes, "'Tolles Geld,'" 226–33. One could, perhaps, trace this interest even earlier, to the mid-fifteenth-century merchant Afanasii Nikitin's *Khozhenie za tri moria*. However, this text is highly unusual in its

context. "Its subject, for the most part, is outside the community's socio-cultural canon, and that canon is unable to integrate it within any existing category." See Lenhoff and Martin, "The Commercial and Cultural Context," 339.

74. On the place of critiques of greed and miserliness in Russian classicism, see Goes, "'Tolles Geld,'" 225–26; and Porter, *Economies of Feeling*, 115–18.

75. See Kliuchkin, "Sentimental'naia kommertsiia."

76. Baratynskii, *Polnoe sobranie stikhotvorenii*, 137–40.

77. Porter, *Economies of Feeling*, 3–19, 93–97.

78. O'Driscoll, "Invisible Forces," 142.

79. Gerschenkron, "Time Horizon in Russian Literature," 703, quoted in O'Driscoll, "Invisible Forces," 171.

80. Valentino, *The Woman in the Window*, 61. On the theory of the passions and the interests, the notion of economic self-interest as a "calm passion," and early arguments in favor of capitalism, see Hirschman, *The Passions and the Interests*.

81. Gukovskii, *Pushkin*, 366.

82. Kliger, *The Narrative Shape of Truth*, 1–42.

83. Lotman, "Theme and Plot," 461–67; quotation at 467.

84. See Wachtel, "Rereading 'The Queen of Spades.'"

85. For an account of degeneration and grotesque aesthetics in Shchedrin, see Kokobobo, *Russian Grotesque Realism*, 78–97. On Boborykin and naturalism, see Kuleshov, "O russkom naturalizme."

86. Pushkin, *SS*, 5:234.

87. As Rosenshield puts it, if Germann had won with his last card and become instantly wealthy, this would have meant the "continuation of death-in-life," which he only leaves behind in the daring of his gamble. See *Challenging the Bard*, 123. It is this moment of life-affirming risk that generates the story.

88. Pushkin, *SS*, 5:233. "Tak, v nenastnye dni, / Zanimalis' oni / Delom".(So in nasty weather / they would get down to / business).

89. See Gerschenkron, "Time Horizon in Russian Literature."

90. "The crucial achievement of the two revolutions [the French Revolution of 1789 and the roughly concurrent industrial revolution in Great Britain] was thus that they opened careers to talent, or at any rate to energy, shrewdness, hard work and greed." Hobsbawm, *The Age of Revolution*, 232.

91. Balzac, "Gobseck," in *The Human Comedy*, 241.

92. Kliger, "Shapes of History," 237.

93. Buryshkin, *Moskva kupecheskaia*, 5.

94. Lounsbery, "The World on the Back of a Fish," 64.

95. Goncharov, *PSS*, 4:162.

96. Dostoevskii to A. N. Maikov, Dresden, March 25 (April 6), 1870, in D 29.1:118.

97. Kostanzhoglo is the positive model of a successful landowner and entrepreneur from the unfinished second volume of Nikolai Gogol's *Dead Souls*. Lopukhov and Rakhmetov are two exemplary men from Nikolai Chernyshevskii's *What Is to Be Done?*

98. Dobroliubov, "Chto takoe oblomovshchina?," 157–59.

99. Moretti, *The Way of the World*, 26.

100. Boborykin, *Kitai-Gorod*, 372.

101. See MacNair, "'Zolaizm' in Russia."

102. Originally published in 1790, this work incurred the outrage of Catherine II, who ordered all copies seized. It was only made widely available to the Russian reading public in 1905.

103. Saltykov-Shchedrin, *SS*, 15.1:199.

104. I discuss this scene, and the increasingly important role Totskii plays, despite his distance from the main events, over the course of *The Idiot*, in chapter 3.

105. Much of the relevant scholarship in Russian literary studies is cited throughout the book where relevant. However, a number of studies, particularly those concerned with the economics of writing and publishing in Imperial Russia, have also informed my argument in ways that are harder to convey in particular footnotes. These include Frazier, *Romantic Encounters*; Guski and Schmid, *Literatur und Kommerz im Russland*; Lounsbery, *Thin Culture, High Art*; Makeev, *Nekrasov*; Neuhäuser, *F.M. Dostojevskij*, chap. 3; Ollivier, "Argent et révolution"; Anikin, "Money and the Russian Classics"; Reitblat, *Ot Bovy k Bal'montu*; Todd, *Fiction and Society*; and Valentino, "What's a Person Worth?" Two recent works take a distinctive approach—considering literature as a source of insights for reforming the discipline of economics or understanding the ideological foundations of the 2008 financial crisis. See, respectively, Morson and Schapiro, *Cents and Sensibility*; and Weiner, *How Bad Writing Destroyed the World*.

106. Here, the work of Holland, Kliger, and Lounsbery, cited throughout this book, has been most important in shaping my approach.

107. See Bojanowska, *A World of Empires*; Grigoryan, *Noble Subjects*, 99–122; and Lounsbery, "The World on the Back of a Fish." See also the earlier economic criticism of Goncharov in O'Driscoll, "Invisible Forces," 203–38.

108. Paine, *Selling the Story*, 107–12.

CHAPTER ONE

1. Blagoveshchenskii, *Semidesiatye gody*, 5. Originally published as N. A. Blagoveshchenskii, "Na liteinom zaovde (Iz ocherkov russkogo chernorabochego truda)," *Otechestvennye zapiski*, no. 4 (April 1873): 464–90. Blagoveschenskii is best known as the editor of *Russkoe slovo* from 1864 until its closing in 1866.

2. I have found it useful throughout this chapter to borrow Gérard Genette's terminology of narrative focalization, rather than the more common narratological concept of point of view. Genette's emphasis on the distinction between "the character whose point of view orients the narrative perspective" and the narrator, that is, the one "who speaks," is particularly useful in these scenes because they are almost all internally focalized episodes—that is, the experience in question is communicated to us as it was experienced by a particular character—within larger third-person narratives that are not focalized through the same character. See Genette, *Narrative Discourse*, 185–94; quotations on 186.

3. Scarry, *Resisting Representation*, 3.

4. Denning, *Culture in the Age of Three Worlds*, 91–92.

5. Quoted in Culler, *Structuralist Poetics*, 167.

6. Wasiolek, "Design in the Russian Novel," 51.

7. Woloch, *The One vs. the Many*, 27.

8. Chernyshevskii, *PSS*, 11:127. Translation from Chernyshevsky, *What Is to Be Done?*, 190.

9. Pisarev, "Mysliashchii tip" (1865), in *PSS*, 8:224.

10. Chernyshevskii, *PSS*, 11:130; *What Is to Be Done?*, 193.

11. Chernyshevskii, *PSS*, 11:126, 126, 131; *What Is to Be Done?*, 188, 189, 195.

12. Orwell, "Charles Dickens," 3.

13. Lesjak, *Working Fictions*, 2.

14. Lesjak, *Working Fictions*, 15.

15. Raymond Williams, *Culture and Society*, 118.

16. Scarry, *Resisting Representation*, 65.

17. Scarry, *Resisting Representation*, 65–66.

18. Although France's industrial lag became exceedingly apparent in the overwhelming defeat of the French military in the Franco-Prussian War (1870–71), it is in French literature, and in the *Rougon-Macquart* (1871–93) in particular, that the farthest-reaching literary examination of a society transformed by capitalism is to be found. As in the case of Russia, the relative underdevelopment of France may have encouraged an intensified literary interest in capitalism. I thank Richard Riddick for pointing out the possible parallel to me. On the geopolitical consequences of German industrialization and France's lag, see Hobsbawm, *The Age of Capital*, 41.

19. P. Brooks, *Realist Vision*, 113–14.

20. Zola, *Germinal*, 27.

21. I write here of imaginary topographies to emphasize that certain locations, such as St. Petersburg and Moscow, the authentic village, and the cultured noble estate, accrued far more meaning and descriptive detail in the Russian literary tradition than the vast provinces and their largely fungible settlements and landscapes. See Lounsbery, "Provinces, Regions, Circles, Grids."

22. Buckler, *Mapping St. Petersburg*, 179–94.

23. Buckler, *Mapping St. Petersburg*, 194.

24. See Polunov, *Russia in the Nineteenth Century*, 98–100.

25. See Burds, *Peasant Dreams and Market Politics*, 21–27.

26. See Gatrell, *The Tsarist Economy*, 84–86. According to the census of 1897, out of a wage labor force of approximately 9 million, 3.2 million were employed in "mining, manufacturing, transport, trade, and construction." In terms of factory workers and miners in particular, there were officially 1.65 million in the 1880s and 1.85 million in 1900. Gatrell notes that these numbers are low "because peasants concealed the extent of their non-agricultural earnings" (86).

27. This was the evaluation of Vladislav Zhukovskii, an entrepreneur and legislator who delivered a memorial speech for the recently deceased Witte in 1915. Quoted in Anan'ich and Ganelin, *Sergei Iul'evich Vitte*, 396. Anan'ich and Ganelin note that Witte's views "underwent a surprising evolution" from a "committed slavophile" to one of the architects of Russia's industrialization (394).

28. Vitte, "Manufakturnoe krepostnichestvo," 18, 19.

29. V. V., *Sud'by kapitalizma v Rossii*, 73; quoted in Buryshkin, *Moskva kupecheskaia*, 67.

30. *Ukazatel' russkogo otdela*.

31. Kolyshko, *Ocherki sovremennoi Rossii*, 16.

32. V—n, "Novye knigi," 35.

33. Gogol, *Dead Souls*, 137; Gogol, *SS*, 5:146–47.

34. See Bowers, "Through the Opaque Veil," 161–64.

35. See Ivanits, "Three Instances," 60–64.

36. See Vdovin, "'Nevedomyi mir.'"

37. See the overview of this problem in Vdovin, "'Nevedomyi mir.'"

38. Lounsbery, "On Cultivating One's Own Garden," 270. Emphasis in the original.

39. Matzner-Gore, "Dmitry Grigorovich and the Limits of Empiricism," 372.

40. Matzner-Gore, "Dmitry Grigorovich and the Limits of Empiricism," 370.

41. Grigorovich, *Rybaki*, 285–86.

42. Brunson, *Russian Realisms*, 27.

43. Brunson, *Russian Realisms*, 38.

44. See Brunson's discussion of the descriptive technique in Grigorovich's sketch in Brunson, *Russian Realisms*, 33–34.

45. Grigorovich, *Rybaki*, 286.

46. Melville, "The Paradise of Bachelors and the Tartarus of Maids," 1265–66.

47. Leo Marx identifies this moment when the whistle of a factory or a train pierces the stillness of nature as a characteristic device of American writing about industrialization. See L. Marx, *The Machine in the Garden*, 11–33.

48. For an examination of both "The Paradise of Bachelors and the Tartarus of Maids" and *Moby-Dick*, which were published four years apart, in terms of

Melville's response to the factory system of Lowell, Massachusetts, and an emergent global division of intellectual and manual labor, see Evans, "'That Great Leviathan.'"

49. Originally published in *The Contemporary* in 1864, Reshetnikov's work bore the generic designation "etnograficheskii ocherk."

50. Reshetnikov, *Gde luchshe?*, in *Izbrannye proizvedeniia*, 2:245.

51. Reshetnikov, *Gde luchshe?*, in *Izbrannye proizvedeniia*, 2:473–86.

52. Glickman, "Industrialization and the Factory Worker in Russian Literature," 651. See also Zelnik, *Labor and Society in Tsarist Russia*, 227–28, 347n.

53. *Sankt-Peterburgskie vedomosti*, no. 303, November 5, 1868; quoted in Saltykov-Shchedrin, *SS*, 9:562.

54. Dostoevskii to N. N. Strakhov, Dresden, May 18 (30), 1871, in D 29.1:216.

55. Saltykov-Shchedrin, *SS*, 9:322.

56. Saltykov-Shchedrin, *SS*, 9:323.

57. L. Lotman, *Realizm russkoi literatury*, 161.

58. Turgenev, "Vospominaniia o Belinskom" (1869), in T 11:51.

59. A. Shenshin [Afanasii Fet] to L. N. Tolstoi, Moscow-Kursk Railway, Eropkino Station, March 26, 1876, in Tolstoi, *Perepiska*, 1:445.

60. Mikhailovskii, "O Reshetnikove" (1880), in *Literaturnaia kritika*, 172.

61. Reshetnikov, *Gde luchshe?*, in *Izbrannye proizvedeniia*, 2:594. Reshetnikov was also personally familiar with factory labor. In a letter to Blagoveshchenskii, he recounts his own time at a foundry in Perm' *guberniia*. See F. M. Reshetnikov to N. A. Blagoveshchenskii, Perm', July 10, 1865, in Veksler, *Iz literaturnogo naslediia*, 341.

62. Reshetnikov, *Gde luchshe?*, in *Izbrannye proizvedeniia*, 2:594.

63. Reshetnikov, *Gde luchshe?*, in *Izbrannye proizvedeniia*, 2:291.

64. Glickman, "Industrialization and the Factory Worker in Russian Literature," 635.

65. For example, "Nowhere does Turgenev disappoint more conspicuously than in his final novel." Allen, *Beyond Realism*, 212.

66. However, the novel is set in the late 1860s, which makes the plot slightly anachronistic.

67. See Turgenev's 1870 note in T 9:399.

68. Nezhdanov's name combines the negative particle *ne* with the root of the verb *zhdat'*, "to wait."

69. On Solomin's Finnish or Swedish appearance, see T 9:223. Paklin suggests that Solomin resembles certain "heroes of labor." This refers to *Geroi truda: Istoriia chetyrekh angliiskikh rabotnikov*, the title of an 1870 translation of Smiles. The *narodnik* critic Petr Tkachev would also discern Solomin's resemblance to "entrepreneurial Americans." See T 9:558–59.

70. Turgenev to M. E. Saltykov-Shchedrin, Bougival, October 31 (November 12), 1882, in Turgenev, *Perepiska*, 2:306.

71. L. N. Tolstoi to L. L. and D. F. Tolstoi, Moscow, January 20?, 1898, in LNT 71:260.

72. Linin, *K istorii burzhuaznogo stilia*, 61.

73. P. D. Boborykin to A. N. Pynin, quoted in S. Chuprinin, "Moskva i moskvichi v tvorchestve Petra Dmitrievicha Boborykina," introduction to Boborykin, *Kitai-Gorod*, 5.

74. Boborykin, *Kitai-Gorod*, 372.

75. Boborykin, *Kitai-Gorod*, 336.

76. Mamin-Sibiriak, *Privalovskie milliony*, in *SS*, 2:240.

77. Mamin-Sibiriak, *Privalovskie milliony*, in *SS*, 2:239–40. I have picked contemporaneous translations of the industrial terminology used in this scene from Andreev, *Tekhnicheskii russko-frantsuzko-nemetsko-angliiskii slovar'*.

78. On the ramifications of Russia's defeat, see Lincoln, *The Great Reforms*, 36–60.

79. Benjamin, "The Storyteller."

80. Andrea Zink makes the significant observation that Russian society in this story is internally divided, unlike the English. The Russian authorities' failure to learn anything from the English, unlike Lefty, exposes the disastrous consequences of Russian authoritarianism. See Zink, "Nikolai Leskov's Natural Economies," 208.

81. Leskov, "Skaz o tul'skom kosom levshe i o stal'noi blokhe," in *SS*, 7:58. Translation from *Satirical Stories*, 52.

82. Leskov, *SS*, 7:26; *Satirical Stories*, 47.

83. Leskov, *SS*, 7:59; *Satirical Stories*, 52–53; translation modified.

84. We will see another association of preindustrial labor and poetry in Tolstoy's later writings in the following chapter.

85. Leskov, *SS*, 7:499.

86. See Hicks, *Mikhail Zoshchenko and the Poetics of* Skaz, 60–77. "*Skaz* appears to represent an alternative current of narrative form to the Realist novel," in which the narrator's language becomes the primary object of representation, rather than a (relatively) transparent medium for the conveyance of the theme and plot (60).

87. Kuprin, *Molokh*, in *SS*, 2:73.

88. Kuprin, *Molokh*, in *SS*, 2:73.

89. Kuprin, "Iuzovskii zavod" (1896), in *SS*, 9:64–78.

90. See, for example, the industrial memoirs of Pavlov, *Za desiat' let praktiki*.

91. I am referring to such works as Serafimovich's *Na zavode* (1898) and Gor'kii's *Mother* (1906). On the emergence of the factory as an aesthetic space in the production novels of the 1920s, for which the work of Serafimovich, Gorky, and Kuprin served as a foundation, see McCauley, "Production Literature and the Industrial Imagination."

CHAPTER TWO

1. On the quasi-familial relations of lord and peasant in Tolstoy's fiction and thought, see Hruska, "Love and Slavery," 627–46. Anna Berman has written extensively on the importance of siblinghood and its implications for Tolstoy's vision of the social whole. See *Siblings in Tolstoy and Dostoevsky*.

2. On the labor and payments owed by the emancipated peasants to landowners under the terms of the temporary obligations, see Moon, *The Abolition of Serfdom in Russia*, 77–79.

3. Tolstoy and Winters, *Android Karenina*.

4. The prospect of peasant revolution is arguably present in Tolstoy's original as well, encoded into the peasant dreams that I discuss below. Aleksei Remizov observed how these dreams in Tolstoy echo Grinev's nightmare in Pushkin's *The Captain's Daughter* (1836). If this is so, then the nightmare of peasant uprising may still lurk behind the industrial visions of Anna and Vronsky. See Remizov, *Ogon' veshchei: Sny i predson'e* (1954), in *SS*, 7:259.

5. Onion, "Reclaiming the Machine," 139.

6. Bowser and Croxall, "Introduction: Industrial Evolution," 2.

7. Guffey and Lemay, "Retrofuturism and Steampunk," in *The Oxford Handbook of Science Fiction*, 444.

8. Jameson, *Postmodernism*, 38–45; quotation at 44.

9. McNamara, *Urban Verbs*, 212.

10. On neural networks, see Gershgorn, "We Don't Understand How AI Make Most Decisions"; and Knight, "The Dark Secret at the Heart of AI." For a prescient warning about the inability of investment bankers to calculate the risk of complex financial instruments like collateralized debt obligations, see Krugman, "Innovating Our Way to Financial Crisis."

11. For more on the concept of cognitive mapping, see Jameson's seminal article "Cognitive Mapping."

12. On the distinction between the relative successes of capitalism in Russian literature and Russian life, see Kagarlitsky, *Empire of the Periphery*, 208.

13. The felicitous phrase "industrialization of time and space" comes from Schivelbusch, *The Railway Journey*.

14. See Ogle, *The Global Transformation of Time*.

15. See Kern, *The Culture of Time and Space*.

16. On the representational consequences of focusing on the speed of the locomotive vs. the extension of the railway, see Lounsbery, *Life Is Elsewhere*, 201.

17. Leskov reproduces this conversation in the story "Zhemchuznoe ozherel'e" (1885), in *SS*, 7:432. See Lounsbery, *Life Is Elsewhere*, 182. For more on this conversation, which apparently took place sometime in the 1870s, see Moser, *Pisemsky*, 190.

18. Leskov, "Zhemchuznoe ozherel'e" (1885), in *SS*, 7:432.

19. Polonskii's poem appeared in the *Russkii vestnik* in October 1868 and thus offers an interesting commentary on Lebedev's famous apocalyptic interpretation of the railroad, which appeared in chapter 5 of part 3 of *The Idiot*, published in the previous month's issue.

20. Polonskii, *Stikhotvoreniia*, 243–45.

21. De Certeau, *The Practice of Everyday Life*, 112.

22. Dwyer, "Of Hats and Trains." See also Lounsbery, *Life Is Elsewhere*, 181.

23. In an unsent letter to Ivan Turgenev, Tolstoy expressed his personal hatred of rail travel in the following terms: "The railroad is to traveling as a bordello is to love—just as comfortable but just as inhumanly mechanical and murderously monotonous." Tolstoi to I. S. Turgenev, Geneva, March 28 (April 9), 1857, in LNT 60:169–70. See also Al'tman, "Zheleznaia doroga." The link between rail travel, chemical stimulants, and violence is explored in "The Kreutzer Sonata" (1889). For an overview of the railroad in *Anna Karenina*, see Stenbock-Fermor, *The Architecture of "Anna Karenina*," 55–74.

24. For a discussion of the protomodernist problem of the referential adequacy of language in *Anna Karenina*, particularly as this problem concerns Anna, see Weir, *Leo Tolstoy*, 144–46.

25. Batuman, review of *Android Karenina*.

26. Tolstoy to N. N. Strakhov, Iasnaia poliana, April 23, 26, 1876, in LNT 62:269. On the application of the notion of the situation rhyme to the analysis of *Anna Karenina*, see Knapp, *"Anna Karenina" and Others*, 20.

27. For major statements of the opposing views on this issue, see Alexandrov, *Limits to Interpretation*; and Morson, *"Anna Karenina" in Our Time*. Kliger has noted the generic differences between Anna's and Levin's plotlines, associating the tight plotting of the former with the novel of adultery. See *The Narrative Shape of Truth*, 154.

28. Babaev, *"Anna Karenina*," 51.

29. Meerson, *Dostoevsky's Taboos*.

30. On the relationship of rails and rules in the novel, see Pickford, *Thinking with Tolstoy and Wittgenstein*, 31–36.

31. Liza Knapp builds on observations by Osip Mandel'stam, Roman Jakobson, and Richard Gustafson in considering Anna's red bag as a metonym of the peasant's sack. See *"Anna Karenina" and Others*, 48–52.

32. I am grateful to Katherine Bowers for this suggestion.

33. Nabokov, *Lectures on Russian Literature*, 177.

34. Wasiolek, *Tolstoy's Major Fiction*, 153.

35. Browning, *A "Labyrinth of Linkages*," 38. Emphasis in the original.

36. See the review of such interpretations in Browning, "Peasant Dreams in *Anna Karenina*," 525–26. The muzhichok's use of French links him to all the

novel's Francophone falsehoods, as well as to Anna's predecessor, Madame Bovary. See Meyer, *How the Russians Read the French*, 182–85.

37. Nabokov, *Lectures on Russian Literature*, 176.

38. Katz, *Dreams and the Unconscious*, 140.

39. Pavlenko, "Peasant as the Political Unconscious," 20.

40. Newlin, "Peasant Dreams, Peasant Nightmares," 601, 613.

41. Magda, "Anna's Things," 1.

42. On Anna's red bag as a bag of pleasures, see Knapp, *"Anna Karenina" and Others*, 49–50.

43. See Browning, A *"Labyrinth of Linkages,"* 36–38.

44. Sato and Sorokina, "'Malen'kii muzhik,'" 143.

45. Jackson, "Text and Subtext.

46. Goscilo, "Motif-Mesh as Matrix."

47. Gustafson, *Leo Tolstoy: Resident and Stranger*, 212.

48. Mandelker, *Framing "Anna Karenina,"* 58–80; quotation at 67.

49. Sato and Sorokina, "'Malen'kii muzhik,'" 139–53; Peace, "From Pantheon to Pandemonium."

50. For a periodization of the gothic and a discussion of its importance in Russian literature, see Vatsuro, *Goticheskii roman v Rossii*. On the gothic in Turgenev and Chekhov, see Bowers, "Through the Opaque Veil."

51. Bowers, "The Fall of the House," 146.

52. On Dostoevsky's response to Maturin in *The Brothers Karamazov*, see Miller, *Dostoevsky's Unfinished Journey*, 128–39. On the importance of Radcliffe, see Miller, *Dostoevsky and "The Idiot,"* 109–12. See also Bowers, "Shadows of the Gothic," 88–143.

53. Hruska, "Ghosts in the Garden," 1–10.

54. Holquist, "The Supernatural as Social Force," 179–80.

55. Elbert and Ryden, introduction, 1–2.

56. Clemens, *The Return of the Repressed*, 3.

57. Clemens, *The Return of the Repressed*, 3.

58. See the discussion of Lebedev's interpretation in Hollander, "The Apocalyptic Framework"; and Bethea, *The Shape of Apocalypse*, 62–104.

59. Nekrasov, *PSS*, 2:169.

60. On Zhukovskii and the gothic, see Pursglove, "Does Russian Gothic Verse Exist?"

61. On Bervi's critique of profit, see Offord, "The Contribution of V. V. Bervi-Flerovsky," 247.

62. On this and the broader issue of Tolstoy's lifelong interactions and late admiration for Bervi-Flerovskii's ideals, see Eikhenbaum, *Lev Tolstoi*, 9–28.

63. N. Flerovskii, *Polozhenie rabochego klassa v Rossii* (1869), 252–53.

64. Blagoveshchenskii, *Semidesiatye gody*, 10.

65. Nefedov, "Nashi fabriki i zavody," 34.

66. For more on Katkov's reaction to part 8 of the novel, with its expression of opposition to the Russo-Turkish War, see Fusso, *Editing Turgenev, Dostoevsky, and Tolstoy*, 192–203.

67. [Mikhail Katkov], "Chto sluchilos'," 449.

68. The name of this organization appears to refer to the St. Petersburg Mutual Credit Society (Obshchestvo vzaimnogo kredita), which was a major lender during the stock market boom that ended with a crash in 1869. See Lizunov, "Russian Society and the Stock Exchange," 113–14.

69. Kliger, *The Narrative Shape of Truth*, 40.

70. Morson, *"Anna Karenina" in Our Time*, 11.

71. Jameson, *The Antinomies of Realism*, 26.

72. Nabokov, *Lectures on Russian Literature*, 193.

73. Lukács, *The Theory of the Novel*, 151.

74. Lukács, *The Theory of the Novel*, 151.

75. Nabokov, *Lectures on Russian Literature*, 193.

76. See Tapp, "Moving Stories," 350.

77. Alexandrov, *Limits to Interpretation*, 143–44. See also R. F. Christian, "The Passage of Time in *Anna Karenina*"; and Alexandrov, "Relative Time in *Anna Karenina*."

78. Grigoryan, *Noble Subjects*, 143.

79. There is at least one other important metaphor of reconciliation in this scene: Alexander Burry and S. Ceilidh Orr have argued that the arc-like motion of the scythe expresses a particular vision of the Orthodox ideal of *sobornost'*. See "The Railway and the Elemental Force," 77–78.

80. On Tolstoy's encounter with Marx, whom he read no later than 1895, and the relevance of this encounter to this essay, see Paperno, *Who, What Am I?*, 110.

81. Tolstoy's association of agricultural labor with human flourishing in this work marks a significant departure from early fictions like "A Landowner's Morning," where unfree agricultural labor destroys the bodies of serfs. See Lounsbery, "On Cultivating One's Own Garden," 282–83.

82. Gorlov, *Nachala politicheskoi ekonomii*, 1:ii.

83. On this debate, see Kingston-Mann, *In Search of the True West*, 93–131.

84. Tęgoborski, *Commentaries on the Productive Forces of Russia*, 1:451. The original French text is found in *Études sur les forces productives de la Russie*, 2:203.

85. Fet, "Zametki o vol'nonaemnom trude," 92. This essay was originally published in *Russkii vestnik* 38, no. 3 (March 1862): 358–79, and 39, no. 5 (May 1862): 219–73.

86. Fet, "Zametki o vol'nonaemnom trude," 92.

87. For much of the nineteenth century, the word *rabochii* was regarded as

pejorative, referring to marginal individuals who performed work devoid of prestige. Skilled workers preferred more specific designations for their paid labor. See Palat, "Rabochii."

88. Babaev, commentary to *Anna Karenina* in Tolstoi, *Sobranie sochinenii v 22 tomakh*, 9:445.

89. A., "Po povodu novogo romana Gr. Tolstogo," 420.

90. Bakhtin, "Forms of Time," 225.

91. Bakhtin, "Forms of Time," 250. Tolstoy had incorporated idyllic elements into earlier works, particularly his semiautobiographical *Childhood* (1852) and *Family Happiness* (1859). See, respectively, Lounsbery, "On Cultivating One's Own Garden," 286–87; and Hruska,"Love and Slavery," 634.

92. The capacity of the idyll to smooth out the ugly realities of manual labor and social hierarchy had already made it a popular solution to ideological problems in the works of Vasilii Trediakovskii and Andrei Bolotov in the eighteenth century. See Newlin, *The Voice in the Garden*, 104–5.

93. Lounsbery, "On Cultivating One's Own Garden," 283.

94. Tolstoi, "Strashnyi vopros" (1891), in *PSS*, 29:119.

95. See Robbins, *Famine in Russia*, 6–8.

96. The concept of interest draws together aesthetic experience and economic thought. Raymond Williams has shown how "interest" evolved since the Middle Ages to acquire numerous shades of meaning and concludes that "this now central world for attention, attraction and concern is saturated with the experience of a society based on money relationships." *Keywords*, 173. For a discussion of the history of the interesting, see Epstein, *The Transformative Humanities*, chap. 16.

CHAPTER THREE

1. Tugan-Baranovsky, *The Russian Factory*, 350; Anan'ich, "The Russian Economy and Banking System," 416.

2. A good example is the series of articles published by the economist V. P. Bezobrazov under the title "O nekotorykh iavleniiakh denezhnogo obrashcheniia v Rossii," in *Russkii vestnik* 43, no. 1 (January 1863): 155–203; 45, no. 5 (May 1863): 362–84; and 45, no. 6 (June 1863): 637–81.

3. On the banking crisis of 1859 and its consequences for the redemption program, see Hoch, "The Banking Crisis." See the valuable overview of the economic context of Dostoevsky's works over the whole range of his career in Karpi, *Dostoevskii-ekonomist*, 23–119.

4. Mironov, *The Standard of Living and Revolutions in Russia*, 126, 210.

5. Boborykin's *Biblioteka dlia chteniia* shut down soon thereafter, and even *Sovremennik* lost over half its subscribers. See Nechaeva, *Zhurnal M. M. i F. M. Dostoevskikh*, 19–20. Dostoevsky blames the failure of the journal on coinciding

crises in journalism and the financial system. See Dostoevskii to A. E. Vrangel', March 31–April 14, 1865, in D 28.2:119.

6. [D. D. Minaev], "Nota Bene," 221. Carpi also makes note of this critical response, although in support of a different interpretation of money in *The Idiot*. See Karpi, *Dostoevskii-ekonomist*, 71. See also Burenin's observation, from a review in *Sankt-Peterburgskie vedomosti* in 1868, that Dostoevsky has to provide his hero with a most unlikely fortune in order to allow him to play a part in the social life of the "northern Palmyra." Zelinskii, *Kriticheskii komentarii*, 3:10.

7. On the history of the legal and cultural category of the *raznochintsy*, see Wirtschafter, *Structures of Society*.

8. Michael Holquist traces the etymology of "idiot" to its original Greek meaning of "'private,' 'own,' 'peculiar.' Myshkin, then, as idiot, stands in for the isolated individual." *Dostoevsky and the Novel*, 111.

9. Nastasia Filippovna's status as the object of various characters' acquisitive desires does not mean that she remains passive in the novel. On the contrary, Sarah Young has argued that she comes to exert a determining influence on the plot as she "scripts" her own life as a Gothic novel. See *Dostoevsky's "The Idiot."*

10. As David Bethea has pointed out, Nastasia Filippovna's surname—Barashkova—establishes her function in the novel as a sacrificial being. See *The Shape of Apocalypse*, 83–84. Susan McReynolds has examined Dostoevsky's conflicted attitude toward what he saw as the transactional nature of sacrifice (and the Crucifixion in particular). See *Redemption and the Merchant God*.

11. Among the numerous interpretations that emphasize the novel's fragmentation, Holquist reads *The Idiot* in terms of "the failure of *kairos* to effect *chronos*." *Dostoevsky and the Novel*, 122. For Frank, the "tragedy" of the novel lies in its conclusion that Myshkin's Christ-like ideal is "incompatible with the normal demands of ordinary social life" and that any possibility of redemption must be deferred to an otherworldly—and extranovelistic—realm. See *Dostoevsky: The Miraculous Years*, 341. For Viacheslav Ivanov, Myshkin is an "incompletely incarnated soul," fated to remain "a spirit, stranded on Earth, a foreigner, a guest from other lands." See *Dostoevskii* (1932), in *SS*, 4:541–42.

12. Regarding newspapers, Dostoevsky writes: "Read them, for God's sake; one can't do otherwise now, not out of fashion, but because the visible connection between all events, public and private, is becoming ever stronger and clearer." Dostoevskii to S. A. Ivanova, Geneva, September 29 (October 11), 1867, in D 28.2:233.

13. These two narrative impulses certainly do not exhaust the famously polymorphic narrative of *The Idiot*. Studies by Young and Miller have both shown how the multiplicity of voices in the novel—for Young, those of the characters seeking to tell their own stories, for Miller, the multiple voices and tones adopted by the narrator—underscore the ethical and epistemological stakes of reading. See Young, *Dostoevsky's "The Idiot"*; and Miller, *Dostoevsky and "The Idiot."*

14. "Can it be that my fantastic *Idiot* is not reality itself, even the everyday

itself? Yes, especially now there must be such characters among those layers of our society which have been torn away from the land—layers, which are in reality becoming fantastic." Dostoevskii to N. N. Strakhov, Florence, February 26 (March 10), 1869, in D 29.1:19.

15. Numerous works of fiction and journalism from the period examined the rise of merchants to positions of social and cultural prominence. Dostoevsky himself would address this phenomenon in his *Dnevnik pisatelia*. See the issue for October 1876, where Dostoevsky asserts: "Now the former limits of the former merchant have suddenly expanded frightfully. He has been joined by the European-style speculator, previously unknown in Russia, and the stock-exchange gambler. . . . I repeat: we understood the power of the moneybag before as well, but never in Russia until now was the moneybag regarded as the highest thing on earth." *A Writer's Diary*, 1:670; D 23:159.

16. "Imaginaries are semiotic systems that frame individual subjects' lived experience of an inordinately complex world and/or inform collective calculation about that world. . . . Viewed in these terms, an economic imaginary is a semiotic system that gives meaning and shape to the 'economic' field." See Jessop, "Cultural Political Economy," 344.

17. Gorlov, *Nachala politicheskoi ekonomii*, 1:358.

18. Frank observes that *"The Idiot* is filled with all sorts of minor characters who are related to the main plot lines only by the most tenuous of threads and who take over the book on the slightest of pretexts." *Dostoevsky: The Miraculous Years*, 329. Ivanits finds that, unlike Dostoevsky's other novels, the minor characters in *The Idiot* tend not to come from the common people, the *narod*. See Ivanits, *Dostoevsky and the Russian People*, 80–81.

19. [A. S. Ushakov], *Nashe kupechestvo*, 1:2.

20. For an overview of the representation of the merchant in nineteenth-century Russian literature, see Holmgren, *Rewriting Capitalism*, 17–53.

21. For a discussion of the legal and cultural context of moneylending in Imperial Russia, see Antonov, *Bankrupts and Usurers*, 35–73.

22. On the emerging interest in the stock market among the Russian public in the late 1850s, see Lizunov, "Russian Society and the Stock Exchange," 108–10.

23. On the speculative boom of the mid- to late 1860s, see Moshenskii, *Rynok tsennykh bumag*, 51–57. Moshenskii writes that "lottery bonds in particular played the decisive role in the formation of a mass market for obligations" (138). See also 235–36.

24. On lottery bonds in Imperial Russia, see Ukhov, "Financial Innovation and Russian Government Debt."

25. Porter discusses the history of the preceding form of Russian paper money, the *assignatsiia*, and government attempts to combat devaluation and counterfeiting, as well as the effect of the double currency system on the early works of Dostoevsky in *Economies of Feeling*, 89–106.

26. "The ruble should be identical in price to metal coin; ours has long since fallen by 3½ times with respect to silver." Dal', *Tolkovyi slovar'*, 1:23.

27. On Totskii and his capitalist attitude toward money, see below.

28. On the preponderance of credit-based over cash transactions in Imperial Russia, see Antonov, *Bankrupts and Usurers*, 76–78.

29. Hollier, "The Use-Value of the Impossible," 22.

30. Misers appear in Dostoevsky's works as early as "Gospodin Prokharchin" (1846), where a lowly civil servant, having effectively starved himself to death, leaves behind a vast hoard of unspent money. In what is presumably an ironic reference to his failure to do anything with his money, the narrator labels Prokharchin an "unexpected capitalist" (*neoizhidannyi kapitalist*; D 1:261). For more on the evolution of the old miser type in Dostoevsky and the literature of the 1830s–40s, see Porter, *Economies of Feeling*, 109–41.

31. On Russian associations of the Old Believers with economic success, see Rosenthal, "The Search for a Russian Orthodox Work Ethic." Pavel Mel'nikov-Pecherskii provided readers of *Russkii vestnik* with a detailed description of Old Believer religious mores and business practices in his massive multipart epic of Volga merchant life *Na gorakh and V lesakh*, which appeared between 1871 and 1881.

32. Skavronskii, *Ocherki Moskvy*, 1:114–15. The city of Moscow was traditionally associated with the merchantry, and as the nineteenth century progressed, became the center of large commercial enterprises. As the merchants grew in economic power, interest in their lifestyle and mores increased. For a vivid account of the rise of the great Moscow merchant families by an émigré descendant, see Buryshkin, *Moskva kupecheskaia*.

33. This recursive structure can be seen as a variation on the doubling of given name and patronymic in the case of merchant characters in the works of Dostoevsky, for example Kuz'ma Kuz'mich Samsonov (*The Brothers Karamazov*) and Semën Semënovich Shelopaev (*Crime and Punishment*). This onomastic doubling, relatively common in real Russian names, acquires significance in light of Dostoevsky's tendency to choose names for his characters that speak to the personality, destiny, or social position of their bearers, as well as his debt to the naming practices of Nikolai Gogol. See the pioneering study by Bem, "Lichnye imena u Dostoevskogo."

34. Sokolov, "Torgovlia i kredit bez deneg," 29.

35. K. Marx, *Capital*, 231.

36. See also Comer, "Rogozhin and the 'Castrates.'"

37. On the link between the irrational economic processes of the 1830s and the appearance of fantastic forms in literature, see the introduction.

38. See Rieber, *Merchants and Entrepreneurs*, 85. The Third Guild had the lowest capital requirement to enter and was abolished in 1865. The legal system of the postreform period stipulated that guild privileges extended after

the death of the merchant head of household to his daughters, including, in this case, Myshkin's mother, who is the aunt's younger sister.

39. Ivanits, *Dostoevsky and the Russian People*, 89; Miller, *Dostoevsky and "The Idiot,"* 81.

40. For a different reading of this scene in connection to the history of Russian paper currency, see Porter, "Dostoevsky's Narrative Economy," 81.

41. The narrator describes Prince Shch. as "one of those people, one might even say doers [*deiatelei*] of recent times. . . . Together with an engineer acquaintance, he contributed, by gathering information and research, to correcting the planned itinerary of one of the most important railways. . . . The prince, out of some special curiosity, never avoided making the acquaintance of Russia's 'businesspeople' [*delovymi liud'mi*]" (IPV 186/D 8:154–55). As an apparently legitimate nobleman who has adapted himself to modern economic conditions and actively seeks out the acquaintance of capitalists, this other prince is quite exceptional in the novel.

42. Kliger, "Shapes of History," 229.

43. Dal', *Tolkovyi slovar'*, 4:607. Boborykin, ever the linguistic innovator, uses the word in his 1868 novel *Zhertva vecherniaia*, where it illustrates a character's affected style. See Boborykin, *Sochineniia*, 1:217.

44. On the status of soldiers' children, see Wirtschafter, *From Serf to Russian Soldier*, 39–40.

45. Tax farming was the practice of collecting taxes (primarily liquor taxes, which were the single largest source of Russian government revenue in the mid-nineteenth century) by a private business contracted by the government. Tax farming was widely criticized in the Russian press in the years leading up to the Great Reforms for its potential for abuse and was finally abolished in 1863. See D. Christian, "A Neglected Reform."

46. Minaev, "Nota Bene," 221.

47. Although Myshkin's epileptic visions have often been read as glimpses of transcendence into a higher realm, Tat'iana Kasatkina has argued that the world glimpsed in these ecstatic visions is a false promise, a "joy that brings death." See "Rol' khudozhestvennoi detali," 89.

48. Bethea, *The Shape of Apocalypse*, 91.

49. Moretti, *The Bourgeois*, 165.

50. Young attributes great structural significance to this gap, during which the central relationship between Nastasia Filippovna, Myshkin, and Rogozhin develops. "Holbein's *Christ in the Tomb*," 91–93.

51. Lounsbery, "The World on the Back of a Fish," 62–64.

52. Lounsbery, "The World on the Back of a Fish," 64.

53. The classic account of the link between empiricism and the rise of the novel is Watt, *The Rise of the Novel*, 15–24.

54. My reading of the following passage in *Winter Notes on Summer Impressions* is indebted to Kliger's work. See especially *The Narrative Shape of Truth*, 123.

CHAPTER FOUR

1. See the convenient visualization of the novel's publication history in Paine, *Selling the Story*, 255.

2. See Peace, *Dostoyevsky*, 246.

3. Wasiolek, *Dostoevsky*, 173. Arina Petrovna, the wife of Captain Snegirev, reveals the meaning of Karamazov by misspeaking Alesha's surname as "Chernomazov" (D 14:184).

4. Miller, *"The Brothers Karamazov,"* 14, passim.

5. See Costlow, *Heart-Pine Russia*, 81–115.

6. See Costlow's discussion of Dostoevsky's article in *Heart-Pine Russia*, 110–11. The article itself can be found in D 23:38–42.

7. Pravilova, *A Public Empire*, 57–84. In *The Brothers Karamazov*, there is also a reference to the "forest question" in Miusov's ongoing lawsuits against the local monastery over fishing and logging rights on the shared border of their land (BKF 32/D 14:31).

8. Stiva sold his forest on the pages of *Russkii vestnik* in March 1875, about four years before Fedor Pavlovich and Mitia attempted to sell theirs in the same journal in June and October 1879, respectively.

9. See Kotsonis, *States of Obligation*, 89.

10. See Costlow's discussion of this passage in *Heart-Pine Russia*, 106.

11. See Alexandrov, *Limits to Interpretation*, 217. On the relationship between perceived trustworthiness and creditworthiness, see Antonov, *Bankrupts and Usurers*, 138–40.

12. On the failure of most of the novel's transactions, see Paine, *Selling the Story*, 159.

13. Matzner-Gore, "Kicking Maksimov Out of the Carriage," 424–25.

14. See Holland's discussion of Dostoevsky's response to "landowner's literature" in *The Novel in the Age of Disintegration*, 115–23.

15. On the connection of Jews to economic matters in Dostoevsky, see Postoutenko, "Wandering as Circulation."

16. Apollonio, *Dostoevsky's Secrets*, 147.

17. Oniks [V. K. Petersen], "Vstuplenie k romanu angela," *Literaturnaia gazeta* no. 6 (1881), quoted in Zelinskii, *Kriticheskii komentarii*, 4:504. See the discussion of Petersen's reviews of the novel in D 15:506–7.

18. She repays all but two hundred rubles. As Paine notes, she will later give two hundred to Alesha to give to Captain Snegirev, which means that this ill-considered act of charity is paid for by Mitia and, by extension, Adelaida Ivanovna. See Paine, *Selling the Story*, 138.

19. Tvardovskaia, "Postreform Russia's Social Inventory in *The Brothers Karamazov*," 54.

20. Noblewomen in Imperial Russia famously retained control of their property in marriage, including dowries. See Marrese, *A Woman's Kingdom*, 44–70.

21. Meijer, "A Note on Time," 49.

22. In the story "A Little Boy at Christ's Christmas Party," published in the January 1876 issue of *Dnevnik pisatelia*, Dostoevsky describes the scene of children dying "at the shriveled breasts of their mothers (in the time of the Samara Famine)." This language is very similar to what Mitia sees in his dream. Compare D 14:456 and 22:17. See also the commentary in 15:436–37. On the historical referent of Ivan's discussion of Ottoman atrocities, see 15:552.

23. Moser, "*The Brothers Karamazov* as a Novel of the 1860s," 75.

24. Porter, "Dostoevsky's Narrative Economy," 88.

25. Among Russia's far-flung industrial sites, the factories and workshops producing metal instruments in Pavlovo, near Nizhnii Novgorod, were among the most important concentrations of industry in the empire. See Boborykin's reportage on the industrial development and working conditions of Pavlovo in "Russkii Sheffil'd."

26. Piretto, "Staraia Russa and Petersburg," 82.

27. See Lounsbery, "Provinces, Regions, Circles, Grids."

28. Fridlender, *Realizm Dostoevskogo*, 328.

29. Respectively, Brodsky, "The Power of the Elements," 157; Catteau, *Dostoevsky and the Process of Literary Creation*, 135; and Porter, *Economies of Feeling*, 89.

30. Respectively, Lantz, *The Dostoevsky Encyclopedia*, 262; Belknap, *The Structure of "The Brothers Karamazov,"* 67–69; Todd, "The Ruse of the Russian Novel."

31. See Porter, *Economies of Feeling*, chaps. 3–4.

32. See Apollonio, *Dostoevsky's Secrets*, 54–55; and Shklovskii, *Za i protiv*, 128.

33. Catteau, *Dostoevsky and the Process of Literary Creation*, 164.

34. Karpi, *Dostoevskii-ekonomist*, 69.

35. Christa, "Dostoevskii and Money," 104.

36. See Tolstaia's essay on Russian literature's disdain for economic normalcy: "Kuptsy i khudozhniki."

37. Steiner, *Tolstoy or Dostoevsky*, 153–54.

38. Shaikevich, "Prostranstvo semanticheskikh slovarei," 704.

39. Karpi, *Dostoevskii-ekonomist*, 208–11.

40. Carpi acknowledges that the language of the realist novel, with its frequent hints and suggestions, presents difficulties for quantitative analysis of particular "semantic fields." See Karpi, "'Den'gi do zarezu nuzhny,'" 76. This article is an extended version of the chapter on *The Brothers Karamazov* in *Dostoevskii-ekonomist*.

41. The scholarly literature on symbolic meanings in Dostoevsky is vast. For instance, on color, see Johae, "Towards an Iconography of *Crime and Punishment*," 178–84; on space, see Bakhtin, *Problems of Dostoevsky's Poetics*, 149–50. On symbolic names, see Bem, "Lichnye imena u Dostoevskogo."

42. Miller, *"The Brothers Karamazov,"* 13.

43. See Vetlovskaia, *Roman F. M. Dostoevskogo "Brat'ia Karamazovy,"* 239–69.

44. Vetlovskaia, *Roman F. M. Dostoevskogo "Brat'ia Karamazovy,"* 267.

45. Shtakhenshneider, *Dnevnik i zapiski*, 438.

46. Shklovskii, *Za i protiv*, 128.

47. Brodsky, "The Power of the Elements," 158.

48. Catteau, *Dostoevsky and the Process of Literary Creation*, 139.

49. See Todd, "Dostoevskii as a Professional Writer."

50. Paine, *Selling the Story*, 158–59.

51. Paine, *Selling the Story*, 100, 22.

52. On the trial of the novel in *The Brothers Karamazov*, see Holland, "The Legend of the *Ladonka*."

53. Paine, *Selling the Story*, 159–60.

54. This is, of course, a recurrent theme in Dostoevsky. As Nancy Ruttenberg observes, writing about *Notes from the House of the Dead* (1862): "The symbolic value of money as 'coined freedom' as long as it is in circulation may be contrasted with the coin Gorianchikov receives as 'an unfortunate' from the peasant girl and which he is careful to keep for the duration of his sentence." Ruttenberg, *Dostoevsky's Democracy*, 239n112. The reference to money as "coined freedom" is found in D 4:17. What is crucial in *The Brothers Karamazov* is that the heterogeneity of money arrests the process of universal homogenization.

55. For a recent overview of this scholarship, see Singh, *Divine Currency*.

56. Graeber, *Debt*.

57. Singh, *Divine Currency*, 3.

58. McReynolds draws attention to this fact. See "'You Can Buy the Whole World,'" 89.

59. Dodd, *The Social Life of Money*, 4.

60. Miller, *"The Brothers Karamazov,"* 74.

61. See Jackson, "Alyosha's Speech at the Stone," 235.

62. Murav, "From *Skandalon* to Scandal," 767.

63. McReynolds, "'You Can Buy the Whole World,'" 101.

64. McReynolds, *Redemption and the Merchant God*, 31.

65. McReynolds, *Redemption and the Merchant God*, 157.

66. McReynolds, "'You Can Buy the Whole World,'" 95.

67. McReynolds, "'You Can Buy the Whole World,'" 102.

68. McReynolds, "'You Can Buy the Whole World,'" 94.

69. See Murav, "From *Skandalon* to Scandal," 770; and McReynolds, "'You Can Buy the Whole World,'" 107–8.

70. Psalms 137:5–6 KJV. According to the Septuagint numbering used in Eastern Orthodox Bibles, this is Psalm 136.

71. McReynolds, "'You Can Buy the Whole World,'" 108.

72. Singh, *Divine Currency*, 105.

73. See Berman, *Siblings in Tolstoy and Dostoevsky*, 124–28.

74. Graeber, *Debt*, 208.

75. Scholars are divided about whether Dostoevsky seriously planned a second volume. For an overview of the testimony of some of Dostoevsky's acquaintances on this issue, as well as an argument that Alesha was destined to become a regicidal revolutionary, see Volgin, *Poslednii god Dostoevskogo*, 30–49.

CHAPTER FIVE

1. *The Plays of Anton Chekhov*, 356; Chekhov, Ch 15:222.

2. Baehr, "The Machine in Chekhov's Garden," 99.

3. See Anan'ich, "The Russian Economy and Banking System," 408–17.

4. See Lizunov, "Russian Society and the Stock Exchange," 114–22.

5. That is, from 1,626 to 37,058 kilometers. Kahan, *Russian Economic History*, 30. On the number of manufacturing workers, see Gatrell, *The Tsarist Economy*, 86.

6. Kahan, *Russian Economic History*, 32–34.

7. See Friedgut, *Iuzovka and Revolution*, 1:3–68. On Russian oil production, see Anan'ich, "The Russian Economy and Banking System," 415.

8. Karasev, "Obshchii obzor gazetnoi periodiki," in *Ocherki po istorii russkoi zhurnalistiki*, 2:449.

9. Chekhov to L. A. Avilova, Ialta, February 5, 1899, in Ch 26:75.

10. J. Brooks, *When Russia Learned to Read*, 113; Dinershtein, *"Fabrikant" chitatelei*, 38–39.

11. See, for instance, J. Brooks, *When Russia Learned to Read*. On the growth of middlebrow literature in Russia and Poland, see Holmgren, *Rewriting Capitalism*, 93–114.

12. Mirsky, *Contemporary Russian Literature*, 115.

13. For two recent readings that interpret Tolstoy's story as a response to Hegel, see Paperno, *Who, What Am I?*, 117–20; and Juharyan, "Tolstoi's Own Master and Slave Dialectic."

14. Serafimovich, "Istoriia odnoi zabastovki" (1899), in SS 4:246.

15. Holmgren, *Rewriting Capitalism*, 33. Chekhov's father was a serf until his own father bought the family's freedom and went on to become a storeowner in the southern city of Taganrog. Gorky was raised by his modestly prosperous grandparents, who owned a dyeing shop, but was forced by the tyrannical

grandfather to survive by working innumerable odd jobs, as he would later describe in *Childhood* (1912), the first volume of his autobiographical trilogy.

16. On the fate of *Otechestvennye zapiski* and *Russkii vestnik* in the 1880s, see Grossman, "Rise and Decline of the 'Literary' Journal," 171–72.

17. The term became particularly linked to Mikhailovskii following the publication of his article "Geroi bezvremen'ia" in 1891. See Nikolaev, "'Literaturnye portrety bezvremen'ia.'"

18. Scholars have discussed the emergence of Symbolism as a reaction to the threat of industrialization. See, for example, Rosenthal, *Dmitri Sergeevich Merezhkovsky*: "Russian Symbolism was an artistic response to the ideological doldrums of the eighties and the industrialization of the nineties. Its intense mysticism, rarified aestheticism, and extreme subjectivism were evoked by the need for a new ideology to battle both the traditional intelligentsia and the new forces of industrialism" (37).

19. Vengerov, *Ocherki*, 126.

20. On Potapenko as part of the literary context for the works of Chekhov, see Kataev, "Chekhov i ego literaurnoe okruzhenie," 41–47.

21. On the impact of the "theory of small deeds" on the literature of the period, see Boele, "'New Times Require New People.'"

22. Kataev, "Chekhov i ego literaturnoe okruzhenie," 31.

23. On the theory of type in European realism, see Wellek, "The Concept of Realism," 242–47. On Belinsky's influential theory of type, see Terras, *Belinskij*, 117–18, 147–48.

24. One of the fullest discussions of type, with particular emphasis on Dostoevsky's theory and practice, can be found in Jackson, *Dostoevsky's Quest for Form*, 92–123.

25. Lukács, *Balzac*, 95, quoted in Demetz, "Balzac and the Zoologists," 417–18.

26. Golovin, *Russkii roman*, 462.

27. Mikhailovskii, "Ob ottsakh i detiakh i o Chekhove" (1890), in *Literaturno-kriticheskie stat'i*, 600.

28. Mikhailovskii, "Ob ottsakh i detiakh i o Chekhove," 606.

29. Mikhailovskii's description of Chekhov as mechanical apparatus indifferently reproducing whatever it perceives, recalls the technologies that were enabling the cost-effective reproduction of images in journals at the end of the nineteenth century, including those, like *Niva*, that were also major vehicles for Chekhov's commercial success. See Durkin, "Chekhov and the Journals of His Time," 241.

30. Mikhailovskii, "Koe-chto o sovremennoi belletristike: K Pushkinskomu iubileu" (1899), in *Poslednie sochineniia*, 1:35–36.

31. Stendhal, *The Red and the Black*, 371.

32. Mikhailovskii, "Koe-chto o Chekhove" (1900), in *Poslednie sochineniia*, 1:300.

33. Holmgren, *Rewriting Capitalism*, 53.

34. C. E. May, "Chekhov and the Modern Short Story," 201.

35. Chudakov, "The Poetics of Chekhov," 366.

36. Kataev, *Proza Chekhova*, 21–30.

37. Kataev makes a similar point. See *Proza Chekhova*, 147.

38. See Morson, *"Anna Karenina" in Our Time*, 82.

39. For Kataev, the sequence by which Anna Akimovna comes to realize the ridiculousness of her speech reflects Chekhov's interest in the process by which characters grow alienated from their absolute pronouncements in the late stories. See *Proza Chekhova*, 145–49.

40. On the paralyzing self-consciousness of Chekhov's upwardly mobile merchants, see Holmgren, *Rewriting Capitalism*, 44–46.

41. Holmgren, *Rewriting Capitalism*, 46.

42. On Anna Akimovna's suspension between two impossibilities—Lysevich's literary fantasies and the other fantasy of a modest life with Pimenov—see Flath, "Delineating the Territory."

43. See Ch 8:498.

44. Jackson, "Chekhov's 'A Woman's Kingdom,'" 8.

45. Indeed, in Jackson's allegorical reading of this story, Anna Akimovna's decision to give the money to Lysevich means that "she has resolved the crisis of her life" by choosing evil. "Chekhov's 'A Woman's Kingdom,'" 2.

46. Kuprin, *SS*, 2:32.

47. Compare Astrov from *Uncle Vanya*: "Will those who come one or two hundred years after us, and for whose sake we are now laying a path—will they remember us with kind words?" (Ch 13:64).

48. Kataev, *Proza Chekhova*, 271.

49. See Shcherbenok, "'Killing Realism.'" According to Shcherbenok, "Chekhov's is not a world where the epiphany of meaning fails to occur due to people's shortcomings; rather, his is a world where meaning is systematically shown to be governed by metaphoric and metonymic substitutions, deferrals, projections, and disseminations" (313).

50. See Polotskaia, "'Tri goda.'"

51. For several reviews critical of the excessively drawn-out form of *Three Years*, see Ch 9:463.

52. *Three Years* thus explores at greater length Chekhov's distinctive interest in subverting traditional expectations of meaningful events. See Popkin, *The Pragmatics of Insignificance*, 21–51.

53. On the significance of photography, painting, and of Holbein's *The Body of the Dead Christ in the Tomb* in *The Idiot*, see Brunson, *Russian Realisms*, 162–96. So significant is the productive tension between narrative and the photographic and painterly image for that novel that Brunson contends that "it is still fair to say that *The Idiot*, in some fundamental measure, is a novel about the

visual arts" (168). On Anna's portrait in *Anna Karenina*, see Mandelker, *Framing "Anna Karenina,"* 101–21.

54. Bitsilli, *Chekhov's Art*, 53; emphasis in the original.

55. Polotskaia, "'Tri goda,'" 28.

56. Holmgren, *Rewriting Capitalism*, 44.

57. See Polotskaia, "'Tri goda,'" 24–25. The relevant note can be found in Ch 17:19.

58. Lukács, *The Theory of the Novel*, 62, 64.

59. Lukács, *The Theory of the Novel*, 63, 64.

60. Lukács, *The Theory of the Novel*, 64.

CONCLUSION

1. *Sbornik proletarskikh pisatelei*, 6.

2. Gastev, *Poeziia rabochego udara*, 7.

3. Kupensky, "The Soviet Industrial Sublime."

4. Blok, "The New America," in *PSS* 3:182.

5. This is how Moretti terms those peripheral cases, such as Italy and Russia, where bourgeois rationality does not take hold, either in the economy or in literature. See *The Bourgeois*, 145–68.

6. Levin, *The Gates of Horn*, 34, 33.

7. Fisher, *Capitalist Realism*, 8.

8. Shonkwiler and La Berge, "Introduction: A Theory of Capitalist Realism," 1.

Bibliography

A. [Avseenko, V. G.]. "Po povodu novogo romana Gr. Tolstogo." *Russkii vestnik* 117, no. 5 (May 1876): 400–420.

Addison, Joseph. "Adventures of a Shilling." In Joseph Addison and Richard Steele, *Selected Essays from "The Tattler," "The Spectator," and "The Guardian,"* edited by Daniel McDonald, 108–12. Indianapolis: Bobbs-Merill, 1973.

Alexandrov, Vladimir. *Limits to Interpretation: The Meanings of "Anna Karenina."* Madison: University of Wisconsin Press, 2004.

Alexandrov, Vladimir. "Relative Time in *Anna Karenina.*" *Russian Review* 41, no. 2 (April 1982): 159–68.

Allen, Elizabeth Cheresh. *Beyond Realism: Turgenev's Poetics of Secular Salvation.* Stanford, Calif.: Stanford University Press, 1992.

Al'tman, M. S. "Zheleznaia doroga v tvorchestve L. N. Tolstogo." *Tolstovskii sbornik* 5 (1964): 66–71.

Anan'ich, Boris V. "The Russian Economy and Banking System." In *The Cambridge History of Russia*, vol. 2, *Imperial Russia 1689–1917*, edited by Dominic Lieven, 394–426. Cambridge: Cambridge University Press, 2006.

Anan'ich, Boris V., and R. Sh. Ganelin. *Sergei Iul'evich Vitte i ego vremia.* Saint Petersburg: Izdatel'stvo Dmitrii Bulanin, 1999.

Anderson, Perry. "One Exceptional Figure Stood Out." *London Review of Books* 37, no. 15 (July 30, 2015): 19–28.

Andreev, P. P. *Tekhnicheskii russko-frantsuzko-nemetsko-angliiskii slovar', zakliuchaiushchii v sebe slova, upotrebliaemye v promyshlennosti, v prikladnykh naukakh i iskusstvakh.* Saint Petersburg: Tipografiia ekspeditsii zagotovleniia gosudarstvennykh bumag, 1881.

Andriopolous, Stefan. "The Invisible Hand: Supernatural Agency in Political Economy and the Gothic Novel." *ELH* 66, no. 3 (Fall 1999): 739–58.

Anikin, Andrei V. "Money and the Russian Classics." *Diogenes* 162 (Summer 1993): 99–109.

Antonov, Sergei. *Bankrupts and Usurers of Imperial Russia: Debt, Property, and the Law in the Age of Tolstoy and Dostoevsky.* Cambridge, Mass.: Harvard University Press, 2016.

Apollonio, Carol. *Dostoevsky's Secrets: Reading against the Grain*. Evanston, Ill.: Northwestern University Press, 2009.

Babaev, E. *"Anna Karenina" L'va Tolstogo*. Moscow: Khudozhestvennaia literatura, 1978.

Baehr, Stephen L. "The Machine in Chekhov's Garden: Progress and Pastoral in *The Cherry Orchard*." *Slavic and East European Journal* 43, no. 1 (Spring 1999): 99–121.

———. "The Troika and the Train: Dialogues between Tradition and Technology in Nineteenth-Century Russian Literature." In *Issues in Russian Literature before 1917: Selected Papers of the Third World Congress for Soviet and East European Studies*, edited by J. Douglas Clayton, 85–106. Columbus, Ohio: Slavica, 1989.

Bakhtin, Mikhail. "Forms of Time and of the Chronotope in the Novel." In *The Dialogic Imagination*, edited by Michael Holquist, translated by Caryl Emerson and Michael Holquist, 84–258. Austin: University of Texas Press, 1981.

———. *Problems of Dostoevsky's Poetics*. Edited and translated by Caryl Emerson. Minneapolis: University of Minnesota Press, 1984.

Bakić-Hayden, Milica. "Nesting Orientalisms: The Case of Former Yugoslavia." *Slavic Review* 54, no. 4 (Winter 1995): 917–31.

Balzac, Honoré de. *The Human Comedy: Selected Stories*. Translated by Linda Asher, Carol Cosman, and Jordan Stump. New York: New York Review Books, 2014.

Balzer, Harley D., ed. *Russia's Missing Middle Class: The Professions in Russian History*. Armonk, N.Y.: M. E. Sharpe, 1996.

Baratynskii, E. A. *Polnoe sobranie stikhotvorenii*. Edited by V. M. Sergeev. Leningrad: Sovetskii pisatel', 1989.

Barnett, Vincent. "Tugan-Baranovsky and *The Russian Factory*." In *Late Imperial Russia: Problems and Prospects. Essays in Honour of R. B. McKean*, edited by Ian D. Thatcher, 84–100. Manchester: Manchester University Press, 2005.

Barthes, Roland. "The Reality Effect." In *The Rustle of Language*, translated by Richard Howard, 141–48. Berkeley: University of California Press, 1989.

Batuman, Elif. Review of *Android Karenina*, by Leo Tolstoy and Ben H. Winters. *New Yorker*, February 19, 2010. https://www.newyorker.com/books/page-turner/android-karenina.

Belinskii, V. G. *Polnoe sobranie sochinenii*. 13 vols. Moscow: Izdatel'stvo akademii nauk, 1953–59.

Belinsky, V. G. "Thoughts and Notes on Russian Literature." In *Belinsky, Chernyshevsky, Dobrolyubov: Selected Criticism*, edited by Ralph E. Matlaw, 5–6. New York: E. P. Dutton & Co., 1962.

Belknap, Robert L. *The Structure of "The Brothers Karamazov."* The Hague: Mouton, 1967.

Bem, Alfred. "Lichnye imena u Dostoevskogo." In *Sbornik v chest' na Prof. L. Miletich: Za sedemdesetgodishninata ot rozhdenieto mu (1863–1933)*, 409–34. Sofia: Izdanie na Makedonskiia nauchen institut, 1933.

Benjamin, Walter. "The Storyteller: Reflections on the Works of Nikolai Leskov." In *Illuminations: Essays and Reflections*, edited by Hannah Arendt, translated by Harry Zohn, 83–110. New York: Schocken, 1967.

Berman, Anna. *Siblings in Tolstoy and Dostoevsky: The Path to Universal Brotherhood*. Evanston, Ill.: Northwestern University Press, 2015.

Bethea, David. *The Shape of Apocalypse in Modern Russian Fiction*. Princeton, N.J.: Princeton University Press, 1989.

Bezobrazov, V. P. "O nekotorykh iavleniiakh denezhnogo obrashcheniia v Rossii." *Russkii vestnik* 43, no. 1 (January 1863): 155–203; 45, no. 5 (May 1863): 362–84; 45, no. 6 (June 1863): 637–81.

Bitsilli, Peter M. *Chekhov's Art: A Stylistic Analysis*. Translated by Toby W. Clyman and Edwina Jannie Cruise. Ann Arbor, Mich.: Ardis, 1983.

Blagoveshchenskii, N. A. *Semidesiatye gody na fabrikakh i zavodakh*. Moscow: Zemlia i fabrika, 1929.

Blok, A. A. *Polnoe sobranie sochinenii i pisem v dvadtsati tomakh*. 20 vols. Edited by G. P. Berdnikov et al. Moscow: Nauka, 1997–2014.

Boborykin, P. D. *Kitai-Gorod. Proezdom*. Moscow: Pravda, 1988.

———. "Pis'ma o Moskve." In *Moskva—Peterburg: Pro et contra. Dialog kul'tur v istorii natsionsal'nogo samosoznaniia*, 259–85. Saint Petersburg: Izdatel'stvo Russkogo Khristianskogo gumanitarnogo universiteta, 2000.

———. "Russkii Sheffil'd (Ocherk sela Pavlova)." *Otechestvennye zapiski*, no. 1 (January 1877): 77–104; no. 2 (February 1877): 305–46; no. 4 (April 1877): 345–94.

———. *Sochineniia v trekh tomakh*. 3 vols. Moscow: Khudozhestvennaia literatura, 1993.

Boele, Otto. "'New Times Require New People': The Demise of the Epoch-Making Hero in Late Nineteenth-Century Russian Literature." In *Dutch Contributions to the Fourteenth International Congress of Slavists: Ohrid, September 10–16, 2008: Literature*, edited by Sander Brouwer, 133–50. Amsterdam: Rodopi, 2008.

Bojanowska, Edyta M. *A World of Empires: The Russian Voyage of the Frigate Pallada*. Cambridge, Mass.: Harvard University Press, 2018.

Bowers, Katherine. "The Fall of the House: Gothic Narrative and the Decline of the Russian Family." In Bowers and Kokobobo, *Russian Writers and the Fin de Siècle*, 145–61.

———. "Shadows of the Gothic: Adapted Terror in Russian Fiction, 1792–1905." PhD diss., Northwestern University, 2011.

———. "Through the Opaque Veil: The Gothic and Death in Russian Realism." In *The Gothic and Death*, edited by Carol Margaret Davidson, 157–73. Manchester: Manchester University Press, 2017.

———, and Ani Kokobobo, eds. *Russian Writers and the Fin de Siècle: The Twilight of Realism.* Cambridge: Cambridge University Press, 2015.

Bowser, Rachel A., and Brian Croxall. "Introduction: Industrial Evolution." *Neo-Victorian Studies* 3, no. 1 (2010): 1–45.

Braudel, Fernand. *Civilization and Capitalism: 15th–18th Century.* Vol. 2, *The Wheels of Commerce.* Translated by Siân Reynolds. Berkeley: University of California Press, 1992.

Brodsky, Joseph. "The Power of the Elements." In *Less Than One: Selected Essays,* 157–63. New York: Farrar, Straus and Giroux, 1986.

Brooks, Jeffrey. *When Russia Learned to Read: Literacy and Popular Culture, 1861–1917.* Princeton, N.J.: Princeton University Press, 1985.

Brooks, Peter. *Realist Vision.* New Haven, Conn.: Yale University Press, 2005.

Browning, Gary L. *A "Labyrinth of Linkages" in Tolstoy's "Anna Karenina."* Boston: Academic Studies Press, 2010.

———. "Peasant Dreams in *Anna Karenina.*" *Slavic and East European Journal* 44, no. 1 (2000): 525–36.

Brunson, Molly. *Russian Realisms: Literature and Painting, 1840–1880.* DeKalb: Northern Illinois University Press, 2016.

Buckler, Julie. *Mapping St. Petersburg: Imperial Text and Cityscape.* Princeton, N.J.: Princeton University Press, 2007.

Buck-Morss, Susan. "Envisioning Capital: Political Economy on Display." *Critical Inquiry* 21, no. 2 (Winter 1995): 434–67.

Burds, Jeffrey. *Peasant Dreams and Market Politics: Labor Migration and the Russian Village, 1861–1905.* Pittsburgh: University of Pittsburgh Press, 1998.

Burry, Alexander, and S. Ceilidh Orr. "The Railway and the Elemental Force: Slavophilism, Pan-Slavism, and Apocalyptic Anxieties in *Anna Karenina.*" In Bowers and Kokobobo, *Russian Writers and the Fin de Siècle,* 69–86.

Buryshkin, P. A. *Moskva kupecheskaia.* Moscow: Vysshaia shkola, 1991.

Catteau, Jacques. *Dostoevsky and the Process of Literary Creation.* Translated by Audrey Littlewood. Cambridge: Cambridge University Press, 1989.

Chaadaev, P. Ia. *Polnoe sobranie sochinenii i izbrannye pis'ma.* Moscow: Nauka, 1991.

Chekhov, A. P. *Polnoe sobranie sochinenii i pisem v tridtsati tomakh.* 30 vols. Moscow: Nauka, 1974–83.

Chekhov, Anton. *Anton Chekhov's Selected Short Stories.* Edited by Cathy Popkin. New York: Norton, 2014.

———. *The Complete Short Novels.* Translated by Richard Pevear and Larissa Volokhonsky. New York: Vintage, 2004.

———. *The Plays of Anton Chekhov.* Translated by Paul Schmidt. New York: Harper Perennial, 1999.

Chernyshevskii, N. G. *Polnoe sobranie sochinenii v piatnadtsati tomakh.* 15 vols.

Moscow: Gosudarstvennoe izdatel'stvo "Khudozhestvennaia literatura," 1939–53.

Chernyshevsky, Nikolai. *What Is to Be Done?* Translated by Michael R. Katz. Ithaca, N.Y.: Cornell University Press, 1989.

Chicherin, Boris Nikolaevich. *Sobstvennost' i gosudarstvo*. Edited by A. I. Narezhnyi. Moscow: Rossiiskaia politicheskaiia entsiklopediia, 2010.

Christa, Boris. "Dostoevskii and Money." In *The Cambridge Companion to Dostoevskii*, 93–110.

Christian, David. "A Neglected Reform: The Abolition of Tax Farming in Russia." In *Russia's Great Reforms, 1855–1881*, edited by Ben Eklof, John Bushnell, and Larissa Zakharova, 102–14. Bloomington: Indiana University Press, 1994.

Christian, R. F. "The Passage of Time in *Anna Karenina*." *Slavonic and East European Review* 45, no. 104 (January 1967): 207–10.

Chudakov, Alexander. "The Poetics of Chekhov: The Sphere of Ideas." Translated by Julian Graffy. *New Literary History* 9, no. 2 (1978): 353–80.

Clemens, Valdine. *The Return of the Repressed: Gothic Horror from "The Castle of Otronto" to "Alien."* Albany: State University of New York Press, 1999.

Clowes, Edith W., Samuel D. Kassow, and James L. West, eds. *Between Tsar and People: Educated Society and the Quest for Public Identity in Late Imperial Russia*. Princeton, N.J.: Princeton University Press, 1991.

Comer, William J. "Rogozhin and the 'Castrates': Religious Traditions in Dostoevsky's *The Idiot*." *Slavic and East European Journal* 40, no. 1 (Spring 1996): 85–99.

Cornwell, Neil, ed. *The Gothic-Fantastic in Russian Literature*. Amsterdam: Rodopi, 1999.

Corrigan, Yuri. *Dostoevsky and the Riddle of the Self*. Evanston, Ill.: Northwestern University Press, 2017.

Costlow, Jane T. *Heart-Pine Russia: Walking and Writing the Nineteenth-Century Forest*. Ithaca, N.Y.: Cornell University Press, 2013.

Courtemanche, Eleanor. *The "Invisible Hand" and British Fiction, 1818–1860: Adam Smith, Political Economy, and the Genre of Realism*. New York: Palgrave Macmillan, 2011.

Culler, Jonathan. *Structuralist Poetics*. London: Routledge, 2002.

Dal', Vladimir. *Tolkovyi slovar' zhivogo velikorusskogo iazyka*. 4 vols. Moscow: Izdanie knigoprodavtsa-tipografa M. O. Vol'fa, 1880.

de Certeau, Michel. *The Practice of Everyday Life*. Translated by Steven Rendall. Berkeley: University of California Press, 1984.

Demetz, Peter. "Balzac and the Zoologists: A Concept of Type." In *The Disciplines of Criticism: Essays in Literary Theory, Intepretation, and History*, edited by Peter Demetz, Thomas Greene, and Lowry Nelson Jr., 397–418. New Haven, Conn.: Yale University Press, 1968.

Denning, Michael. *Culture in the Age of Three Worlds*. London: Verso, 2004.

de Vogüé, E.-M. *The Russian Novel*. Translated by H. A. Sawyer. New York: Alfred A. Knopf, 1916.

Dinershtein, E. A. *"Fabrikant" chitatelei A. F. Marks*. Moscow: Kniga, 1986.

Dobroliubov, N. A. "Chto takoe oblomovshchina?" In *Izbrannye stat'i*, edited by V. A. Eremin, 157–59. Moscow: Izdatel'stvo Sovetskaia Rossiia, 1978.

Dodd, Nigel. *The Social Life of Money*. Princeton, N.J.: Princeton University Press, 2014.

Dostoevskii, F. M. *Polnoe sobranie sochienii v tridtsati tomakh*. 30 vols. Leningrad: Nauka, 1972–90.

Dostoevsky, Fyodor. *The Brothers Karamazov*. Translated by Richard Pevear and Larissa Volokhonsky. New York: Farrar, Straus and Giroux, 1990.

———. *Crime and Punishment*. Translated by Richard Pevear and Larissa Volokhonsky. New York: Vintage, 1992.

———. *The Idiot*. Translated by Richard Pevear and Larissa Volokhonsky. New York: Vintage, 2001.

———. *A Writer's Diary*. Vol. 1, *1873–1876*. Translated by Kenneth Lantz. Evanston, Ill.: Northwestern University Press, 1994.

Durkin, Andrew R. "Chekhov and the Journals of His Time." In Martinsen, *Literary Journals in Imperial Russia*, 228–45.

Dwyer, Anne. "Of Hats and Trains: Cultural Traffic in Leskov's and Dostoevskii's Westward Journeys." *Slavic Review* 70, no. 1 (Spring 2011): 67–93.

Eikhenbaum, B. M. *Lev Tolstoi: Semidesiatye gody*. Leningrad: Sovetskii pisatel', 1960.

Elbert, Monika, and Wendy Ryden. Introduction to *Haunting Realities: Naturalist Gothic and American Realism*, edited by Monika Elbert and Wendy Ryden, 1–14. Tuscaloosa: University of Alabama Press, 2017.

Entsiklopedicheskii slovar' Brokgauza i Efrona. 82 vols. Saint Petersburg: Tipo-Litografiia I. A. Efrona, 1890–1907.

Epstein, Mikhail. *The Transformative Humanities: A Manifesto*. Translated and edited by Igor Klyukanov. New York: Bloomsbury, 2012.

Evans, David H. "'That Great Leviathan . . . Which Is but an Artificial Man': *Moby-Dick* and the Lowell Factory System." *ELQ: A Journal of the American Renaissance* 50, no. 4 (2004): 315–50.

Fanger, Donald. *Dostoevsky and Romantic Realism: A Study of Dostoevsky in Relation to Balzac, Dickens, and Gogol*. Evanston, Ill.: Northwestern University Press, 1998.

Fasmer, Maks [Max Vasmer]. *Etimologicheskii slovar' russkogo iazyka*. Translated and edited by O. N. Trubachev. 3rd ed. Saint Petersburg: Azbuka, 1996.

Fedyashin, Anton A. *Liberals under Autocracy: Modernization and Civil Society in Russia, 1866–1904*. Madison: University of Wisconsin Press, 2012.

Fet, A. A. "Zametki o vol'nonaemnom trude." In *Zhizn' Stepanovki, ili Liricheskoe khoziaistvo*, edited by V. A. Kosheleva, 59–123. Moscow: Novoe literaturnoe obozrenie, 2002.

Fisher, Mark. *Capitalist Realism: Is There No Alternative?* Winchester, UK: Zero Books, 2009.

Flath, Carol A. "Delineating the Territory of Čechov's 'A Woman's Kingdom.'" *Russian Literature* 44 (1998): 389–408.

Flerovskii, N. [V. V. Bervi]. *Polozhenie rabochego klassa v Rossii.* Edited by B. M. Breitman. Moscow: Gosudarstvennoe sotsial'no-ekonomicheskoe izdatel'stvo, 1938.

Francis, Mark. *Herbert Spencer and the Invention of Modern Life.* Ithaca, N.Y.: Cornell University Press, 2007.

Frank, Joseph. *Dostoevsky: The Mantle of the Prophet, 1871–1881.* Princeton, N.J.: Princeton University Press, 2003.

———. *Dostoevsky: The Miraculous Years, 1865–1871.* Princeton, N.J.: Princeton University Press, 1995.

———. *Dostoevsky: The Stir of Liberation, 1860–1865.* Princeton, N.J.: Princeton University Press, 1986.

Frazier, Melissa. *Romantic Encounters: Writers, Readers, and the "Library for Reading."* Stanford, Calif.: Stanford University Press, 2007.

Fridlender, G. M. *Realizm Dostoevskogo.* Moscow: Nauka, 1964.

Friedgut, Theodore H. *Iuzovka and Revolution.* Vol. 1, *Life and Work in Russia's Donbass, 1869–1924.* Princeton, N.J.: Princeton University Press, 1989.

Fusso, Susanne. *Editing Turgenev, Dostoevsky, and Tolstoy: Mikhail Katkov and the Great Russian Novel.* DeKalb: Northern Illinois University Press, 2017.

Gastev, Aleksei. *Poeziia rabochego udara.* Petrograd: Izdatel'stvo "Proletkul'ta," 1918.

Gatrell, Peter. *The Tsarist Economy, 1850–1917.* London: B. T. Batsford, 1986.

Genette, Gérard. *Narrative Discourse: An Essay in Method.* Translated by Jane E. Lewin. Ithaca, N.Y.: Cornell University Press, 1980.

Gerschenkron, Alexander. "Economic Backwardness in Historical Perspective." In *Economic Backwardness in Historical Perspective: A Book of Essays,* 5–30. Cambridge, Mass.: Harvard University Press, 1962.

———. "Time Horizon in Russian Literature." *Slavic Review* 34, no. 4 (December 1975): 692–715.

Gershgorn, Dave. "We Don't Understand How AI Make Most Decisions, So Now Algorithms Are Explaining Themselves." *Quartz,* December 20, 2016. https://qz.com/865357/we-dont-understand-how-ai-make-most-decisions-so -now-algorithms-are-explaining-themselves/.

Gertsen, A. I. *Sobranie sochinenii v tridtsati tomakh.* 30 vols. Moscow: Izdatel'stvo Akademii Nauk SSSR, 1954–60.

Glickman, Rose L. "Industrialization and the Factory Worker in Russian Literature." *Canadian Slavic Studies* 4, no. 4 (Winter 1970): 629–52.

Goes, Gudrun. "'Tolles Geld': Geld, Unternehmertum und Kommerz in der russischen Literatur." In *Geld: Interdisziplinäre Sichtweisen,* edited by Susanne Peters, 226–33. Wiesbaden: Springer, 2017.

Gogol, N. V. *Sobranie sochinenii v shesti tomakh*. 6 vols. Edited by A. Slonimskii. Moscow: Khudozhestvennaia literatura, 1953.

Gogol, Nikolai. *Dead Souls*. Translated by Bernard Guilbert Guerney. Revised and edited by Susanne Fusso. New Haven, Conn.: Yale University Press, 1996.

Golovin, K. *Russkii roman i russkoe obshchestvo*. 2nd ed. Saint Petersburg: Izdanie A. F. Marksa, 1904.

Goncharov, I. A. *Polnoe sobranie sochinenii i pisem v dvadtsati tomakh*. 20 vols. Edited by V. A. Tunimanov et al. Saint Petersburg: Nauka, 1997.

Gorlov, Ivan. *Nachala politicheskoi ekonomii*. 2 vols. Saint Petersburg: Tipografiia P. A. Kulisha, 1859–62.

Goscilo, Helena. "Motif-Mesh as Matrix: Body, Sexuality, Adultery, and the Woman Question." In *Approaches to Teaching Tolstoy's "Anna Karenina,"* edited by Liza Knapp and Amy Mandelker, 83–89. New York: Modern Language Association, 2003.

Graeber, David. *Debt: The First 5,000 Years*. New York: Melville House, 2011.

Gregory, Paul R. *Before Command: An Economic History of Russia from Emancipation to the First Five-Year Plan*. Princeton, N.J.: Princeton University Press, 1994.

Grigorovich, D. V. *Rybaki: Povesti*. Moscow: Khudozhestvennaia literatura, 1966.

Grigoryan, Bella. *Noble Subjects: The Russian Novel and the Gentry, 1762–1861*. DeKalb: Northern Illinois University Press, 2018.

Grossman, Joan Delaney. "Rise and Decline of the 'Literary' Journal, 1880–1917." In Martinsen, *Literary Journals in Imperial Russia*, 171–96.

Guffey, Elizabeth, and Kate C. Lemay. "Retrofuturism and Steampunk." In *The Oxford Handbook of Science Fiction*, edited by Rob Latham, 434–45. Oxford: Oxford University Press, 2014.

Gukovskii, G. A. *Pushkin i problemy realisticheskogo stilia*. Moscow: Goslitizdat, 1957.

Guski, Andreas. "'Geld ist geprägte Freiheit': Paradoxien des Geldes bei Dostoevskij (II)." *Dostoevsky Studies*, n.s., 20 (2016): 103–65.

———, and Ulrich Schmid, eds. *Literatur und Kommerz im Russland des 19. Jahrhunderts: Institutionen, Akteure, Symbole*. Zurich: Pano Verlag, 2004.

Gustafson, Richard F. *Leo Tolstoy: Resident and Stranger: A Study in Fiction and Theology*. Princeton, N.J.: Princeton University Press, 1986.

Haywood, Richard Mowbray. *Russia Enters the Railway Age, 1842–1855*. New York: Columbia University Press, 1998.

Hicks, Jeremy. *Mikhail Zoshchenko and the Poetics of Skaz*. Nottingham, Eng.: Astra Press, 2000.

Hilton, Marjorie L. *Selling to the Masses: Retailing in Russia, 1880–1930*. Pittsburgh: University of Pittsburgh Press, 2012.

Bibliography

Hirschman, Albert O. *The Passions and the Interests: Political Arguments for Capitalism before Its Triumph*. Princeton, N.J.: Princeton University Press, 1977.

Hobsbawm, Eric. *The Age of Capital, 1848–1875*. New York: Vintage, 1996.

———. *The Age of Revolution: Europe, 1789–1848*. London: Abacus, 1977.

Hoch, Steven L. "The Banking Crisis, Peasant Reform, and Economic Development in Russia, 1857–1861." *American Historical Review* 96, no. 3 (June 1991): 795–820.

Hodgson, Geoffrey M. "Albert Schäffle's Critique of Socialism." In *Economic Theory and Economic Thought: Essays in Honour of Ian Steedman*, edited by John Vinzt et al., 296–315. London: Routledge, 2010.

Holland, Kate. "The Legend of the *Ladonka* and the Trial of the Novel." In Jackson, *A New Word on "The Brothers Karamazov,"* 192–99.

———. *The Novel in the Age of Disintegration: Dostoevsky and the Problem of Genre in the 1870s*. Evanston, Ill.: Northwestern University Press, 2003.

Hollander, Robert. "The Apocalyptic Framework in Dostoevsky's *The Idiot*." *Mosaic* 7, no. 2 (January 1974): 123–49.

Hollier, Denis. "The Use-Value of the Impossible." Translated by Liesl Ollman. *October* 60 (Spring 1992): 3–24.

Holmgren, Beth. *Rewriting Capitalism: Literature and the Market in Late Tsarist Russia and the Kingdom of Poland*. Pittsburgh: Pittsburgh University Press, 1998.

Holquist, Michael. *Dostoevsky and the Novel*. Princeton, N.J.: Princeton University Press, 1978.

———. "The Supernatural as Social Force in *Anna Karenina*." In *The Supernatural in Slavic and Baltic Literature: Essays in Honor of Victor Terras*, edited by Amy Mandelker and Roberta Reeder, 176–90. Columbus, Ohio: Slavica, 1988.

Hruska, Anne. "Ghosts in the Garden: Anne Radcliffe and Tolstoy's *Childhood, Boyhood, Youth*." *Tolstoy Studies Journal*, no. 9 (1997): 1–10.

———. "Love and Slavery: Serfdom, Emancipation, and Family in Tolstoy's Fiction." *Russian Review* 66 (October 2007): 627–46.

Ivanits, Linda J. *Dostoevsky and the Russian People*. Cambridge: Cambridge University Press, 2008.

———. "Three Instances of the Peasant Occult in Russian Literature: Intelligentsia Encounters *Narod*." In *The Occult in Russian Literature and Culture*, edited by Bernice Glatzer Rosenthal, 59–74. Ithaca, N.Y.: Cornell University Press, 1997.

Ivanov, Viacheslav. *Dostoevskii: Tragediia. Mif. Mistika*. In *Sobranie sochinenii*. Vol. 4. Edited by D. V. Ivanov et al., 483–588. Brussels: Foyer Oriental Chrétien, 1987.

Jackson, Robert Louis. "Alyosha's Speech at the Stone: 'The Whole Picture.'" In Jackson, *A New Word on "The Brothers Karamazov,"* 234–53.

————, ed. *A New Word on "The Brothers Karamazov."* Evanston, Ill.: Northwestern University Press, 2004.

————. "Chekhov's 'A Woman's Kingdom': A Drama of Character and Fate." *Russian Language Journal / Russkii iazyk* 39, nos. 132/134 (1985): 1–11.

————. *Dostoevsky's Quest for Form: A Study of His Philosophy of Art.* 2nd ed. Bloomington, Ind.: Physsard, 1978.

————. "Text and Subtext in the Opening and Closing Lines of 'The Death of Ivan Ilych,' or, Phonic Orchestration in the Semantic Development of the Story." *Tolstoy Studies Journal*, no. 9 (1997): 11–24.

Jameson, Fredric. *The Antinomies of Realism.* London: Verso, 2013.

———— "Cognitive Mapping." In *Marxism and the Interpretation of Culture*, edited by Cary Nelson and Lawrence Grossberg, 347–57. Urbana: University of Illinois Press, 1988.

————. *The Political Unconscious: Narrative as a Socially Symbolic Act.* Ithaca, N.Y.: Cornell University Press, 1981.

————. *Postmodernism, or, The Cultural Logic of Late Capitalism.* Durham, N.C.: Duke University Press, 1990.

Jessop, Bob. "Cultural Political Economy and Critical Policy Studies." *Critical Policy Studies* 3, nos. 3–4 (October–December 2009): 336–56.

Johae, Antony. "Towards an Iconography of *Crime and Punishment.*" In *Dostoevsky and the Christian Tradition*, edited by George Pattison and Diane Oenning Thompson, 173–88. Cambridge: Cambridge University Press, 2001.

Juharyan, Victoria. "Tolstoi's Own Master and Slave Dialectic: 'Khoziain i rabotnik' as a Rewriting of a Hegelian Narrative." *Slavic and Eastern European Journal* 61, no. 1 (Spring 2017): 29–48.

Kagarlitsky, Boris. *Empire of the Periphery: Russia and the World System.* London: Pluto Press, 2008.

Kahan, Arcadius. *Russian Economic History: The Nineteenth Century.* Chicago: University of Chicago Press, 1989.

Karasev, P. S. "Obshchii obzor gazetnoi periodiki." In *Ocherki po istorii russkoi zhurnalistiki i kritiki*, vol. 2, edited by V. G. Berezina, N. P. Emel'ianov, N. I. Sokolov, and N. I. Totubalin, 449–62. Leningrad: Izdatel'stvo Leningradskogo universiteta, 1965.

Karpi, Guido [Guido Carpi]. "'Den'gi do zarezu nuzhny': Temy deneg i agressi v 'Brat'iakh Karamazovykh' (opyt statisticheskogo analiza)." *Philologica* 9, nos. 21/23 (2012): 73–103.

————. *Dostoevskii-ekonomist: Ocherki po sotsiologii literatury.* Moscow: Falanster, 2012.

Kasatkina, Tat'iana. "Rol' khudozvestvennoi detali i osobennosti funktsionirovaniia slova v romane F. M. Dostoevskogo 'Idiot.'" In *Roman F. M. Dostoevskogo "Idiot": Sovremennoe sosotianie izucheniia*, edited by T. A. Kasatkina, 60–99. Moscow: Nasledie, 2001.

Kataev, V. B. "Boborykin i Chekhov (k istorii poniatiia 'intelligentsii' v russkoi literature)." In *Chekhov plius* . . . , 133–56. Moscow: Iazyki slavianskoi kul'tury, 2004.

———. "Chekhov i ego literaturnoe okruzhenie (80-e gody XIX veka)." In *Sputniki Chekhova*, edited by V. B. Kataev, 5–47. Moscow: Izdatel'stvo Moskovskogo universiteta, 1982.

———. *Proza Chekhova: Problemy interpretatsii*. Moscow: Izdatel'stvo Moskovskogo universiteta, 1979.

[Katkov, Mikhail]. "Chto sluchilos' po smerti Anny Kareninoi?" *Russkii vestnik*, no. 7 (July 1877): 448–62.

Katz, Michael R. *Dreams and the Unconscious in Nineteenth-Century Russian Fiction*. Hanover, N.H.: University Press of New England, 1984.

Kern, Stephen. *The Culture of Time and Space, 1880–1918*. Cambridge, Mass.: Harvard University Press, 2003.

Kingston-Mann, Esther. *In Search of the True West: Culture, Economics, and Problems of Russian Development*. Princeton, N.J.: Princeton University Press, 1999.

Kliger, Ilya. *The Narrative Shape of Truth: Veridiction in Modern European Literature*. University Park: Pennsylvania State University Press, 2011.

———. "Shapes of History and the Enigmatic Hero in Dostoevsky: The Case of *Crime and Punishment*." *Comparative Literature* 62, no. 3 (2010): 228–45.

Klioutchkine, Konstantine. "Modern Print Culture." In *Dostoevsky in Context*, edited by Deborah A. Martinsen and Olga Maiorova, 221–28. Cambridge: Cambridge University Press, 2015.

———. "The Rise of *Crime and Punishment* from the Air of the Media." *Slavic Review* 61, no. 1 (Spring 2002): 88–108.

Kliuchkin, Konstantin [Konstantine Klioutchkine]. "Sentimental'naia kommertsiia: 'Pis'ma russkogo puteshestvennika' N. M. Karamzina." *Novoe literaturnoe obozrenie* 25 (1997): 84–98.

Knapp, Liza. *"Anna Karenina" and Others: Tolstoy's Labyrinth of Plots*. Madison: University of Wisconsin Press, 2016.

Knight, Will. "The Dark Secret at the Heart of AI." *MIT Technology Review*, April 11, 2017. https://www.technologyreview.com/s/604087/the-dark-secret -at-the-heart-of-ai/.

Kocka, Jürgen. *Capitalism: A Short History*. Translated by Jeremiah Riemer. Princeton, N.J.: Princeton University Press, 2016.

Kokobobo, Ani. *Russian Grotesque Realism: The Great Reforms and the Gentry Decline*. Columbus: Ohio State University Press, 2018.

Kolyshko, I. *Ocherki sovremennoi Rossii*. Saint Petersburg: Tipografiia tovarishchestva "Obshchestvennaia pol'za," 1887.

Kotsonis, Yanni. *States of Obligation: Taxes and Citizenship in the Russian Empire and Early Soviet Republic*. Toronto: University of Toronto Press, 2014.

Krugman, Paul. "Innovating Our Way to Financial Crisis." *New York Times*, December 3, 2007. http://www.nytimes.com/2007/12/03/opinion/03krugman.html.

Kuleshov, V. I. "O russkom naturalizme i o P. D. Boborykine." In *V poiskakh tochnosti i istiny*, 170–201. Moscow: Sovremennik, 1986.

Kupensky, Nicholas. "The Soviet Industrial Sublime: The Awe and Fear of Dneprostroi, 1927–1932." PhD diss., Yale University, 2017.

Kuprin, A. I. *Sobranie sochinenii v deviati tomakh.* 9 vols. Edited by E. Rotshtein and P. Viacheslavov. Moscow: Pravda, 1964.

Lantz, Kenneth. *The Dostoevsky Encyclopedia.* Westport, Conn.: Greenwood, 2004.

Leatherbarrow, W. J., ed. *The Cambridge Companion to Dostoevskii.* Cambridge: Cambridge University Press, 2006.

Lenhoff, Gail L., and Janet L. B. Martin. "The Commercial and Cultural Context of Afanasij Nikitin's Journey beyond the Three Seas." *Jahrbücher für Geschichte Osteuropas*, n.s., 37, no. 3 (1989): 321–44.

Lesjak, Carolyn. *Working Fictions: A Genealogy of the Victorian Novel.* Durham, N.C.: Duke University Press, 2006.

Leskov, N. S. *Sobranie sochinenii v odinadtsati tomakh.* 11 vols. Edited by B. G. Bazanov et al. Moscow: Khudozhestvennaia literatura, 1956–58.

Leskov, Nikolai. *The Satirical Stories of Nikolai Leskov.* Translated and edited by William B. Edgerton. New York: Pegasus, 1969.

Lessing, Doris. "Unwritten Novels." *London Review of Books* 12, no. 1 (January 11, 1990). https://www.lrb.co.uk/v12/n01/doris-lessing/unwritten-novels.

Levin, Harry. *The Gates of Horn: A Study of Five French Realists.* New York: Oxford University Press, 1963.

Lincoln, W. Bruce. *The Great Reforms: Autocracy, Bureaucracy, and the Politics of Change in Imperial Russia.* DeKalb: Northern Illinois University Press, 1990.

———. *In the Vanguard of Reform: Russia's Enlightened Bureaucrats, 1825–1861.* DeKalb: Northern Illinois University Press, 1982.

Linin, A. M. *K istorii burzhuaznogo stilia v russkoi literature (tvorchestvo P. D. Boborykina).* Rostov-on-Don, 1935.

Lizunov, Pavel V. "Russian Society and the Stock Exchange in the Late Nineteenth and Early Twentieth Centuries." *Russian Studies in History* 54, no. 2 (2015): 106–42.

Lotman, Iu. M. "Theme and Plot: The Theme of Cards and the Card Game in Russian Literature of the Nineteenth Century." Translated by C. R. Pike. *PTL* 3, no. 3 (October 1978): 455–92.

Lotman, L. M. *Realizm russkoi literatury 60-kh godov XIX veka (istoki i esteticheskoe svoeobrazie).* Leningrad: Nauka, 1964.

Lounsbery, Anne. "Dostoevskii's Geography: Centers, Peripheries, and Networks in *Demons.*" *Slavic Review* 66, no. 2 (Summer 2007): 211–29.

———. *Life Is Elsewhere: Symbolic Geography in the Russian Provinices, 1800–1917.* DeKalb: Northern Illinois University Press, 2019 .

———. "On Cultivating One's Own Garden with Other People's Labor: Serfdom in 'A Landowner's Morning.'" In *Before They Were Titans: Essays on the Early Works of Dostoevsky and Tolstoy*. Edited by Elizabeth Cheresh Allen, 267–98. Boston: Academic Studies Press, 2015.

———. "Provinces, Regions, Circles, Grids: How Literature Has Shaped Russian Geographical Identity." In *Russia's Regional Identities: The Power of the Provinces*, edited by Edith W. Clowes, Gisela Erbslöh, and Ani Kokobobo, 44–68. London: Routledge, 2018.

———. *Thin Culture, High Art: Gogol, Hawthorne, and Authorship in Nineteenth-Century Russia and America*. Cambridge, Mass.: Harvard University Press, 2007.

———. "The World on the Back of a Fish: Mobility, Immobility, and Economics in *Oblomov*." *Russian Review* 70 (January 2011): 43–64.

Lukács, Georg. *Balzac und der französische Realismus*. East Berlin: Aufbau-Verlag, 1952.

———. *The Theory of the Novel: A Historico-Philosophical Essay on the Forms of Great Epic Literature*. Translated by Anna Bostock. Cambridge, Mass.: MIT Press, 1971.

MacNair, John. "'Zolaizm' in Russia." *Modern Language Review* 95, no. 2 (April 2000): 450–62.

Magda, Mina. "Anna's Things: Narrative and Materiality in *Anna Karenina*." Unpublished manuscript, last modified April 2, 2019.

Makeev, Mikhail. *Nekrasov: Poet i predprinimatel' (ocherki o vzaimodeistvii literatury i ekonomiki)*. Moscow: MAKS Press, 2008.

Mamin-Sibiriak, D. N. *Sobranie sochinenii v vos'mi tomakh*. 8 vols. Moscow: Khudozhestvennaia literatura, 1954.

Mandelker, Amy. *Framing "Anna Karenina": Tolstoy, the Woman Question and the Victorian Novel*. Columbus: Ohio State University Press, 1993.

Marks, K. [Karl Marx]. *Kapital: Kritika politicheskoi ekonomii. Tom pervyi*. No translator. Saint Petersburg: Izdanie N. P. Poliakova, 1872.

Marrese, Michelle Lamarche. *A Woman's Kingdom: Noblewomen and the Control of Property in Russia, 1700–1861*. Ithaca, N.Y.: Cornell University Press, 2002.

Martinsen, Deborah A., ed. *Literary Journals in Imperial Russia*. Cambridge: Cambridge University Press, 1997.

Marx, Karl. *Capital: A Critique of Political Economy*. Vol. 1. Translated by Ben Fowkes. London: Penguin, 1976.

———. *Marx/Engels Gesamtausgabe*. Part 2, vol. 5, *Das Kapital: Kritik der Politischen Ökonomie. Erster Band. Hamburg 1867*. Berlin: Dietz Verlag, 1983.

———. *Selected Writings*. Edited by Lawrence H. Simon. Indianapolis: Hackett, 1994.

Marx, Leo. *The Machine in the Garden: Technology and the Pastoral Ideal in America*. New York: Oxford University Press, 1964.

Matzner-Gore, Greta. "Dmitry Grigorovich and the Limits of Empiricism." *Russian Review* 77 (July 2018): 359–77.

———. "Kicking Maksimov Out of the Carriage: Minor Characters, Exclusion, and *The Brothers Karamazov*." *Slavic and East European Journal* 58, no. 3 (2014): 419–36.

May, Charles E. "Chekhov and the Modern Short Story." In *The New Short Story Theories*, edited by Charles E. May, 199–217. Athens: Ohio University Press, 1994.

May, Rachel. *The Translator in the Text: On Reading Russian Literature in English*. Evanston, Ill.: Northwestern University Press, 1994.

McCauley, Karen A. "Production Literature and the Industrial Imagination." *Slavic and East European Journal* 42, no. 3 (Autumn 1998): 444–66.

McCloskey, Deirdre N. *The Rhetoric of Economics*. 2nd ed. Madison: University of Wisconsin Press, 1998.

McNamara, Kevin R. *Urban Verbs: Arts and Discourses of American Cities*. Stanford, Calif.: Stanford University Press, 1996.

McReynolds, Susan. *Redemption and the Merchant God: Dostoevsky's Economy of Salvation and Antisemitism*. Evanston, Ill.: Northwestern University Press, 2008.

———. "'You Can Buy the Whole World': The Problem of Redemption in *The Brothers Karamazov*." *Slavic and East European Journal* 52, no. 1 (Spring 2008): 87–111.

Meerson, Olga. *Dostoevsky's Taboos*. Dresden: Dresden University Press, 1998.

Meijer, Jan M. "A Note on Time in *Brat'ja Karamazovy*." In J. van der Eng and J. M. Meijer, *"The Brothers Karamazov" by F. M. Dostoevskij*, 47–62. The Hague: Mouton, 1971.

Melville, Herman. "The Paradise of Bachelors and the Tartarus of Maids." In *Pierre, or, The Ambiguities; Israel Potter, His Fifty Years of Exile; The Piazza Tales, The Confidence-Man, His Masquerade; Uncollected Prose, Billy Budd, Sailor (An Inside Narrative)*, edited by Harrison Hayford, 1257–79. New York: Library of America, 1984.

Meyer, Priscilla. *How the Russians Read the French: Lermontov, Dostoevsky, Tolstoy*. Madison: University of Wisconsin Press, 2008.

Mikhailovskii, N. K. *Literaturnaia kritika i vospominaniia*. Moscow: Iskusstvo, 1995.

———. *Literaturno-kriticheskie stat'i*. Edited by G. A. Bialyi. Moscow: Khudozhestvennaia literatura, 1957.

———. *Poslednie sochineniia*. 2 vols. Saint Petersburg: Tipografiia N. N. Kablukova, 1905.

———. *Sochineniia*. 6 vols. 2nd ed. Saint Petersburg: Tipografiia I. N. Skorokhodova, 1879–88.

Mikhel'son, [A. D.]. *Ob"iasnitel'nyi slovar' inostrannykh slov voshedshikh v upotreblenie v russkii iazyk, s ob"iasneniem ikh kornei.* 9th ed. Moscow: "Russkaia tipografiia" A. O. Liutetskogo, 1883.

Miller, Robin Feuer. *"The Brothers Karamazov": Worlds of the Novel.* New Haven, Conn.: Yale University Press, 2008.

———. *Dostoevsky and "The Idiot": Author, Narrator, and Reader.* Cambridge, Mass.: Harvard University Press, 1981.

———. *Dostoevsky's Unfinished Journey.* New Haven, Conn.: Yale University Press, 2007.

[Minaev, D. D.]. "Nota Bene." *Iskra,* no. 18 (May 1868): 220–22.

Mironov, Boris. *The Standard of Living and Revolutions in Russia, 1700–1917.* Edited by Gregory L. Freeze. New York: Routledge, 2012.

Mirsky, Prince D. S. *Contemporary Russian Literature, 1881–1925.* New York: Alfred A. Knopf, 1926.

Mitchell, Timothy. "Rethinking Economy." *Geoforum* 39 (2008): 1116–21.

Moon, David. *The Abolition of Serfdom in Russia, 1762–1907.* London: Routledge, 2002.

Moretti, Franco. *The Bourgeois: Between History and Literature.* London: Verso, 2014.

———. *The Way of the World: The Bildungsroman in European Culture.* Translated by Albert Sbragia. New ed. London: Verso, 2000.

Morson, Gary Saul. *"Anna Karenina" in Our Time: Seeing More Wisely.* New Haven, Conn.: Yale University Press, 2007.

———, and Morton Schapiro. *Cents and Sensibility: What Economics Can Learn from the Humanities.* Princeton, N.J.: Princeton University Press, 2017.

Moser, Charles A. *"The Brothers Karamazov* as a Novel of the 1860s." *Dostoevsky Studies* 7 (1986): 73–80.

———. *Pisemsky: A Provincial Realist.* Cambridge, Mass.: Harvard University Press, 1969.

Moshenskii, S. Z. *Rynok tsennykh bumag Rossiiskoi imperii.* Moscow: Ekonomika, 2014.

Murav, Harriet. "From *Skandalon* to Scandal: Ivan's Rebellion Reconsidered." *Slavic Review* 63, no. 4 (Winter 2004): 756–70.

Nabokov, Vladimir. *Lectures on Russian Literature.* Edited by Fredson Bowers. Orlando, Fla.: Harcourt, 1981.

Nechaeva, V. S. *Zhurnal M. M. i F. M. Dostoevskikh "Epocha," 1864–1865.* Moscow: Nauka, 1975.

Nefedov, F. D. "Nashi fabriki i zavody." In *Izbrannye proizvedeniia: Povesti, rasskazy, legendy,* 3–43. Ivanovo: Ivanovskoe knizhnoe izdatel'stvo, 1959.

Nekrasov, N. A. *Polnoe sobranie sochinenii i pisem v piatnadtsati tomakh.* 15 vols. Leningrad: Nauka, 1981–2000.

Neuhäuser, Rudolf. *F. M. Dostojevskij: Die großen Romane und Erzählungen: Interpretationen und Analysen*. Vienna: Böhlau Verlag, 1993.

Newlin, Thomas. "Peasant Dreams, Peasant Nightmares: On Tolstoy and Cross-Dressing." *Russian Review* 78 (October 2019): 595–618.

———. *The Voice in the Garden: Andrei Bolotov and the Anxieties of Russian Pastoral, 1738–1833*. Evanston, Ill.: Northwestern University Press, 2001.

Nikolaev, D. D. "'Literaturnye portrety bezvremen'ia': Ot N. K. Mikhailovskogo k A. A. Izmailovu." In *Bezvremen'e kak siuzhet: Stat'i i materialy*, edited by S. A. Vasil'eva and A. Iu. Sorochan, 30–43. Tver': Izdatel'stvo M. Batasovoi, 2017.

O'Driscoll, Seamas. "Invisible Forces: Capitalism and the Russian Literary Imagination (1855–1881)." PhD diss., Harvard University, 2005.

Offord, Dereck. "The Contribution of V. V. Bervi-Flerovsky to Russian Populism." *Slavonic and East European Review* 66, no. 2 (April 1988): 236–51.

Ogle, Vanessa. *The Global Transformation of Time, 1870–1950*. Cambridge, Mass.: Harvard University Press, 2015.

Ollivier, Sophie. "Argent et révolution dans Les Démons." *Dostoevsky Studies* 5 (1984): 101–15.

Onion, Rebecca. "Reclaiming the Machine: An Introductory Look at Steampunk in Everyday Practice." *Neo-Victorian Studies* 1, no. 1 (Autumn 2008): 138–63.

Orwell, George. "Charles Dickens." In *All Art Is Propaganda: Critical Essays*, compiled by George Packer, 1–62. New York: Mariner Books, 2009.

Paine, Jonathan. *Selling the Story: Transaction and Narrative Value in Balzac, Dostoevsky, and Zola*. Cambridge, Mass.: Harvard University Press, 2019.

Palat, Madhavan K. "Rabochii." *Jahrbücher für Geschichte Osteuropas*, n.s., 50, no. 3 (2002): 345–74.

Paperno, Irina. *Who, What Am I? Tolstoy Struggles to Narrate the Self*. Ithaca, N.Y.: Cornell University Press, 2014.

Pavlenko, Alexei. "Peasant as the Political Unconscious of *Anna Karenina*: Vengeance, Its Forms and Roots." *Tolstoy Studies Journal*, no. 26 (2014): 19–28.

Pavlov, F. *Za desiat' let praktiki (otryvki vospominanii, vpechatlenii i nabliudenii iz fabrichnoi zhizni)*. Moscow: Tipo-litografiia V. Rikhter, 1901.

Peace, Richard. *Dostoyevsky: An Examination of the Major Novels*. Cambridge: Cambridge University Press, 1971.

———. "From Pantheon to Pandemonium." In Cornwell, *The Gothic-Fantastic in Russian Literature*, 23–36.

Pickford, Henry W. *Thinking with Tolstoy and Wittgenstein: Expression, Emotion, and Art*. Evanston, Ill.: Northwestern University Press, 2016.

Piretto, Gian Piero. "Staraia Russa and Petersburg: Provincial Realities and Metropolitan Reminiscences in *The Brothers Karamazov*." *Dostoevsky Studies* 7 (1986): 81–86.

Pisarev, I. D. *Polnoe sobranie sochinenii i pisem.* Edited by F. F. Kuznetsov et al. Moscow: Nauka, 2000–2007.

Polanyi, Karl. *The Great Transformation: The Political and Economic Origins of Our Time.* Boston: Beacon, 2001.

Polonskii, Ia. P. *Stikhotvoreniia.* Edited by B. M. Eikhenbaum. 3rd ed. Leningrad: Sovetskii pisatel', 1957.

Polotskaia, E. A. "'Tri goda': Ot romana k povesti." In *V tvorcheskoi laboratorii Chekhova*, edited by L. D. Opul'skaia, Z. S. Papernyi, and S. E. Shatalov, 13–34. Moscow: Nauka, 1974.

Polunov, Alexander. *Russia in the Nineteenth Century: Autocracy, Reform, and Social Change, 1814–1914.* Translated by Marshall S. Shatz, edited by Thomas C. Owen and Larissa G. Zakharova. Armonk, N.Y.: M. E. Sharpe, 2005.

Poovey, Mary. *Genres of the Credit Economy: Mediating Value in Eighteenth- and Nineteenth-Century Britain.* Chicago: University of Chicago Press, 2008.

Popkin, Cathy. *The Pragmatics of Insignificance: Chekhov, Zoshchenko, Gogol.* Stanford, Calif.: Stanford University Press, 1993.

Porter, Jillian. "Dostoevsky's Narrative Economy: Rainbow Bills in *The Brothers Karamazov.*" *Dostoevsky Studies* 22 (2018): 73–88.

——. *Economies of Feeling: Russian Literature under Nicholas I.* Evanston, Ill.: Northwestern University Press, 2017.

Postoutenko, Kirill. "Wandering as Circulation: Dostoevsky and Marx on the 'Jewish Question.'" In *The Economy in Jewish History: New Perspectives on the Interrelationship between Ethnicity and Economic Life*, edited by Gideon Reuveni and Sarah Wobick-Segev, 43–61. New York: Berghahn Books, 2011.

Pravilova, Ekaterina. *A Public Empire: Property and the Quest for the Common Good in Imperial Russia.* Princeton, N.J.: Princeton University Press, 2014.

Pursglove, Michael. "Does Russian Gothic Verse Exist? The Case of Vasilii Zhukovskii." In Cornwell, *The Gothic-Fantastic in Russian Literature*, 83–102.

Pushkin, A. S. *Sobranie sochinenii v desiati tomakh.* 10 vols. Moscow: Khudozhestvennaia literatura, 1959–62.

Reitblat, A. *Ot Bovy k Bal'montu: Ocherki po istorii chteniia v Rossii vo vtoroi polovine XIX veka.* Moscow: MPI, 1991.

Remizov, A. M. *Sobranie sochinenii.* Edited by A. M. Gracheva et al. Moscow: Russkaia kniga, 2000–2002.

Reshetnikov, F. M. *Izbrannye proizvedeniia v dvukh tomakh.* 2 vols. Moscow: Khudozhestvennaia literatura, 1956.

——. *Iz literaturnogo naslediia F. M. Reshetnikova.* Edited by I. I. Veksler. Leningrad: Akademiia nauk SSSR, 1932.

Resis, Albert. "*Das Kapital* Comes to Russia." *Slavic Review* 29, no. 2 (June 1970): 174–204.

Rieber, Alfred J. *Merchants and Entrepreneurs in Late Imperial Russia.* Chapel Hill: University of North Carolina Press, 1982.

Robbins, Richard G., Jr. *Famine in Russia, 1891–92: The Imperial Government Responds to a Crisis.* New York: Columbia University Press, 1975.

Rosenshield, Gary. *Challenging the Bard: Dostoevsky and Pushkin: A Study of Literary Relationship.* Madison: University of Wisconsin Press, 2013.

Rosenthal, Bernice Glatzer. *Dmitri Sergeevich Merezhkovsky and the Silver Age: The Development of a Revolutionary Mentality.* The Hague: Martinus Nijhoff, 1975.

———. "The Search for a Russian Orthodox Work Ethic." In Clowes, Kassow, and West, *Between Tsar and People,* 57–74.

Ruttenberg, Nancy. *Dostoevsky's Democracy.* Princeton, N.J.: Princeton University Press, 2008.

Saltykov-Shchedrin, M. E. *Sobranie sochinenii v dvadtsati tomakh.* 20 vols. Moscow: Khudozhestvennaia literatura, 1965–77.

Sato, Yusuke, and V. V. Sorokina. "'Malen'kii muzhik s vz"eroshennoi borodoi': Ob odnom simvolicheskom obraze v 'Anne Kareninoi.'" *Philologica* 5, nos. 11/13 (1998): 139–54.

Scarry, Elaine. *Resisting Representation.* New York: Oxford University Press, 1994.

Schivelbusch, Wolfgang. *The Railway Journey: The Industrialization of Time and Space in the Nineteenth Century.* Berkeley: University of California Press, 2014.

Serafimovich, A. S. *Sobranie sochinenii v chetyrekh tomakh.* 4 vols. Moscow: Izdatel'stvo "Pravda," 1980.

Serebrov, I., ed. *Sbornik proletarskikh pisatelei.* Saint Petersburg: Izdatel'stvo "Priboi," 1914.

Shaikevich, A. Ia. "Prostranstvo semanticheskikh slovarei." In *Iazyk kak materiia smysla: Sbornik statei v chest' akademika N. Iu. Shvedovoi,* 695–707. Moscow: Azbukovnik, 2007.

———. "'Killing Realism': Insight and Meaning in Anton Chekhov." *Slavic and East European Journal* 54, no. 2 (Summer 2010): 297–316.

Sheffle, A. [Albert Schäffle]. *Kapitalizm i sotsializm: Preimushchestvenno v primenenii k razlichnym vidam imushchestva i komercheskikh sdelok.* Saint Petersburg: V tipografii M. Khana, 1871.

Shell, Marc. *The Economy of Literature.* Baltimore: Johns Hopkins University Press, 1978.

Shklovskii, Viktor. *Za i protiv: Zametki o Dostoevskom.* Moscow: Sovetskii pisatel', 1957.

Shonkwiler, Alison, and Leigh Claire La Berge. "Introduction: A Theory of Capitalist Realism." In *Reading Capitalist Realism,* edited by Alison Shonkwiler and Leigh Claire La Berge, 1–25. Iowa City: University Press of Iowa, 2014.

Shtakhenshneider, E. A. *Dnevnik i zapiski, 1854–1886.* Newtonville, Mass.: Oriental Research Partners, 1980.

Singh, Devin. *Divine Currency: The Theological Power of Money in the West.* Stanford, Calif.: Stanford University Press, 2018.

Skavronskii, N. [Aleksandr Ushakov]. *Ocherki Moskvy*. 3 vols. Moscow: V tipografii Bakhmeteva, 1862–68.

Smith, Adam. *An Inquiry into the Nature and Causes of the Wealth of Nations*. Edited by Edwin Cannan. Chicago: University of Chicago Press, 1979.

Sokolov, N. V. "Torgovlia i kredit bez deneg." In *Ekonomicheskie vorposy i zhurnal'noe delo*. Saint Petersburg: V pechati V. Golovina, 1866.

Spulber, Nicolas. *Russia's Economic Transitions: From Late Tsarism to the New Millennium*. Cambridge: Cambridge University Press, 2003.

Steiner, George. *Tolstoy or Dostoevsky: An Essay in the Old Criticism*. New Haven, Conn.: Yale University Press, 1996.

Stenbock-Fermor, Elisabeth. *The Architecture of "Anna Karenina": A History of Its Writing, Structure, and Message*. Lisse, Netherlands: Peter de Ridder Press, 1975.

Stendhal. *The Red and the Black: A Chronicle of the Nineteenth Century*. Edited and translated by Catherine Slater. Oxford: Oxford University Press, 1991.

Tapp, Alyson. "Moving Stories: (E)motion and Narrative in *Anna Karenina*." *Russian Literature* 61, no. 3 (2007): 341–61.

Tęgoborski, M. L. de. *Commentaries on the Productive Forces of Russia*. 2 vols. London: Longman, Brown, Green, and Longmans, 1855.

———. *Études sur les forces productives de la Russie*. Paris: Joules Renouard et cie., 1852–55.

Terras, Victor. *Belinskij and Russian Literary Criticism: The Heritage of Organic Aesthetics*. Madison: University of Wisconsin Press, 1974.

Todd, William Mills, III. "*The Brothers Karamazov* and the Poetics of Serial Publication." *Dostoevsky Studies* 7 (1986): 87–97.

———. "Dostoevskii as a Professional Writer." In Leatherbarrow, *The Cambridge Companion to Dostoevskii*, 66–92.

———. *Fiction and Society in the Age of Pushkin*. Cambridge, Mass.: Harvard University Press, 1986.

———. "The Ruse of the Russian Novel." In *The Novel*, vol. 1, *History, Geography, Culture*, edited by Franco Moretti, 402–23. Princeton, N.J.: Princeton University Press, 2006.

Tolstaia, Tat'iana. "Kuptsy i khudozhniki." In *Izium: Izbrannoe*, 117–32. Moscow: Podkova, 2002.

Tolstoi, L. N. *Anna Karenina*. Edited by V. A. Zhdanov and E. E. Zaidenshnur. Moscow: Nauka, 1970.

———. *Perepiska s russkimi pisateliami*. 2 vols. Edited by S. A. Rozanova. 2nd ed. Moscow: Khudozhestvennaia literatura, 1978.

———. *Polnoe sobranie sochinenii*. 90 vols. Moscow: Khudozhestvennaia literatura, 1928–58.

———. *Sobranie sochinenii v 22 tomakh*. 22 vols. Moscow: "Khudozhestvennaia literatura," 1978–85.

————. *Anna Karenina*. Translated by Richard Pevear and Larissa Volokhonsky. London: Penguin, 2000.

Tolstoy, Leo, and Ben H. Winters. *Android Karenina*. Translated by Constance Garnett. Philadelphia: Quirk Books, 2010.

Tooze, J. Adam. "Imagining National Economies: National and International Economic Statistics, 1900–1950." In *Imagining Nations*, edited by Geoffrey Cubitt, 212–28. Manchester: Manchester University Press, 1998.

Tugan-Baranovsky, Mikhail. *The Russian Factory in the 19th Century*. Translated by Arthur Levin and Claora C. Levin, supervised by Gregory Grossman. Homewood, Ill.: Richard D. Irwin, 1970.

Turgenev, I. S. *Perepiska I. S. Turgeneva v dvukh tomakh*. 2 vols. Edited by V. N. Baskakova et al. Moscow: Khudozhestvennaia literatura, 1986.

————. *Polnoe sobranie sochinenii i pisem*. 30 vols. 2nd ed. Moscow: Nauka, 1978–.

Turgenev, Ivan. *Virgin Soil*. Translated by Michael Pursglove. Richmond, Eng.: Alma Classics, 2015.

Tvardovskaia, Valentina. "Postreform Russia's Social Inventory in *The Brothers Karamazov*." *Russian Studies in History* 47, no. 1 (2008): 51–71.

Ukazatel' russkogo otdela filadel'fiiskoi mezhdunarodnoi vystavki 1876 goda / Catalogue of the Russian Section International Exhibition of 1876 at Philadelphia. Saint Petersburg: V tipografii "Obshchestvennaia pol'za," 1876.

Ukhov, Andrey D. "Financial Innovation and Russian Government Debt before 1918." Yale-ICF Working Paper No. 03-20, May 5, 2003. https://scholarship.sha.cornell.edu/cgi/viewcontent.cgi?article=1006&context=workingpapers.

[Ushakov, A. S.]. *Nashe kupechestvo i torgovlia: S ser'eznoi i karikaturnoi storony. Sbornik, izdannyi pod redaktsieiu russkogo kuptsa*. 3 vols. Moscow: V tipografii Gracheva i comp., 1865.

V. V. [V. P. Vorontsov]. *Sud'by kapitalizma v Rossii*. Saint Petersburg: Tipografiia M. M. Stasiulevicha, 1882.

V—n. "Novye knigi." *Delo*, no. 4 (April 1878).

Valentino, Russell Scott. "What's a Person Worth? Character and Commerce in Dostoevsky's *Double*." In *American Contributions to the 13th International Congress of Slavists: Ljubljana, August 2003*, vol. 2: *Literature*, edited by Robert A. Maguire and Alan Timberlake, 203–12. Bloomington, Ind.: Slavica, 2003.

————. *The Woman in the Window: Commerce, Consensual Fantasy, and the Quest for Masculine Virtue in the Russian Novel*. Columbus: Ohio State University Press, 2014.

Vatsuro, Vadim. *Goticheskii roman v Rossii*. Moscow: Novoe literaturnoe obozrenie, 2002.

Vdovin, Aleksei. "'Nevedomyi mir': Russkaia i evropeiskaia estetika i problema reprezentatsii krest'ian v literature serediny XIX veka." *Novoe literaturnoe*

obozrenie, no. 141 (2016). https://www.nlobooks.ru/magazines/novoe
_literaturnoe_obozrenie/141_nlo_5_2016/article/12185/.

Vengerov, S. A. *Ocherki po istroii russkoi literatury*. Saint Petersburg: Tipografiia t-va "Obshchestvennaia pol'za," 1907.

Vetlovskaia, V. E. *Roman F. M. Dostoevskogo "Brat'ia Karamazovy."* Saint
Petersburg: Pushkinskii Dom, 2007.

Vitte, S. [Witte, Sergei]. "Manufakturnoe krepostnichestvo." *Rus'* 3 (1885): 18–19.

Volgin, Igor'. *Poslednii god Dostoevskogo: Istoricheskie zapiski*. 4th ed. Moscow:
AST, 2010.

Von Laue, T. H. "A Secret Memorandum of Sergei Witte on the Industrialization of Imperial Russia." *Journal of Modern History* 26, no. 1 (March 1954):
60–74.

Wachtel, Andrew. "Rereading 'The Queen of Spades.'" *Pushkin Review* 3 (2000):
13–21.

Walicki, Andrzej. *The Controversy over Capitalism: Studies in the Social Philosophy of the Russian Populists*. New York: Oxford University Press, 1969.

Wasiolek, Edward. "Design in the Russian Novel." In *The Russian Novel from
Pushkin to Pasternak*, edited by John Garrard, 51–63. New Haven, Conn.:
Yale University Press, 1983.

———. *Dostoevsky: The Major Fiction*. Cambridge, Mass.: MIT Press, 1964.

———. *Tolstoy's Major Fiction*. Chicago: University of Chicago Press, 1978.

Watt, Ian. *The Rise of the Novel: Studies in Defoe, Richardson, and Fielding*.
Berkeley: University of California Press, 1971.

Weiner, Adam. *How Bad Writing Destroyed the World: Ayn Rand and the Literary Origins of the Financial Crisis*. New York: Bloomsbury Academic, 2016.

Weir, Justin. *Leo Tolstoy and the Alibi of Narrative*. New Haven, Conn.: Yale
University Press, 2011.

Wellek, René. "The Concept of Realism in Literary Scholarship." In *Concepts
of Criticism*, edited by Stephen G. Nichols Jr., 222–55. New Haven, Conn.:
Yale University Press, 1963.

White, James D. *Marx and Russia: The Fate of a Doctrine*. London: Bloomsbury
Academic, 2019.

Williams, Raymond. "Base and Superstructure in Marxist Cultural Theory." *New
Left Review* 82 (November–December 1973): 3–16.

———. *Culture and Society, 1780–1950*. Garden City, N.Y.: Anchor Books,
1960.

———. *Keywords: A Vocabulary of Culture and Society*. Rev. ed. New York: Oxford University Press, 1983.

———. "The Welsh Industrial Novel." In *Culture and Materialism: Selected
Essays*, 213–29. London: Verso, 2005.

Williams, Rowan. *Dostoevsky: Language, Faith, and Fiction*. Waco, Tex.: Baylor
University Press, 2011.

Wirtschafter, Elise Kimerling. *From Serf to Russian Soldier*. Princeton, N.J.: Princeton University Press, 1990.

———. *Structures of Society: Imperial Russia's "People of Various Ranks."* DeKalb: Northern Illinois University Press, 1994.

Wolff, Larry. *Inventing Eastern Europe: The Map of Civilization on the Mind of the Enlightenment*. Stanford, Calif.: Stanford University Press, 1994.

Woloch, Alex. *The One vs. the Many: Minor Characters and the Space of the Protagonist in the Novel*. Princeton, N.J.: Princeton University Press, 2003.

Woodmansee, Martha, and Mark Osteen. *The New Economic Criticism: Studies at the Intersection of Literature and Economics*. New York: Routledge, 1999.

Woolf, Virginia. "The Russian Point of View." In *The Common Reader*, 243–56. New York: Harcourt, Brace, 1925.

Wortman, Richard. *The Crisis of Russian Populism*. London: Cambridge University Press, 1967.

Young, Sarah J. *Dostoevsky's "The Idiot" and the Ethical Foundations of Narrative: Reading, Narrating, Scripting*. London: Anthem Press, 2004.

———. "Holbein's *Christ in the Tomb* in the Structure of *The Idiot*." *Russian Studies in Literature* 44, no. 1 (Winter 2007–8): 90–102.

Zelinskii, V. *Kriticheskii komentarii k sochineniiam F. M. Dostoevskogo: Sbornik kriticheskikh statei*. Vol. 3. 3rd ed. Moscow: Tipografiia I. A. Balandina, Volkhonka, 1901.

———. *Kriticheskii komentarii k sochineniiam F. M. Dostoevskogo: Sbornik kriticheskikh statei*. Vol. 4. 3rd ed. Moscow: Tipo-lit. V. Rikhter, 1906.

Zelnik, Reginald E. *Labor and Society in Tsarist Russia: The Factory Workers of St. Petersburg, 1855–1870*. Stanford, Calif.: Stanford University Press, 1971.

Ziber, N. "Ekonomicheskaia teoriia Marksa." *Slovo*, no. 1 (January 1878): 174–204.

Zink, Andrea. "Nikolai Leskov's National Economies: An Investigation of Work and Commerce." *Zeitschrift für Slawistik* 62, no. 2 (2017): 199–225.

Zola, Émile. *Germinal*. Translated by Peter Collier. Oxford: Oxford University Press, 2008.

Index

Index

merchants: conflict with capitalists, 28–29, 103, 104, 117, 118–19, 173–74; contrasted with capitalists, 25–26, 28, 58, 103, 105, 106, 112, 116, 125, 132, 139, 159; guilds, 26, 112, 196–97n38; hoarding, 109–10, 132; as misers, 105, 108, 110; Moscow, 14, 58, 109, 111, 171, 196n32; rise of, 14, 21, 57, 58, 102, 106, 195n15, 196n32; tales of, 18; Ushakov on, 105–6; Volga, 30, 196n31; wealth of, 26, 58, 102–3, 105–6, 113, 116, 132
"Merchants and Artists" (Tolstaia), 121, 133
Merezhkovsky, Dmitry, 149
meshchanin, 136
Mikhailovsky, Nikolai, 15, 50, 51, 152–53
Mikhel'son, A. D., 9–10
millionaires, 136, 159, 171
mills, 27, 43, 56, 62, 86; calico, 40–41, 45, 46; paper, 44–45, 48, 56; steel, 64–65, 69, 162–63, 164
Minaev, D. D., 102
mining, 38, 52, 123, 146, 147, 186n26
misers, 18, 22, 23, 109–10, 133, 196n30; merchants as, 105, 108, 110; as opposite of capitalists, 23, 109
modernity: Tolstoy's resistance to, 28, 69, 73, 74, 77, 88, 96, 168; train as icon of, 73, 84, 168
Molokh (Kuprin), 38, 64–65, 147, 174
money: *assignatsiia*, 107, 121, 195n25; circulation of, 24, 109–10, 118, 130; fungibility of, 117, 129, 138–39, 185n21; illiquid, 106, 125; invisibility of, 28–29, 108, 117, 119, 125; *kreditnyi bilet*, 107; material quality of, 107, 108, 113, 115, 128; sums of, 103, 107, 109, 111, 113, 115–16, 126, 127, 132, 134–38, 156; theology and, 29, 133, 140–42, 144. *See also under Brothers Karamazov, The*; Dostoevsky, Fyodor; *Idiot, The*
Money (Zola), 147, 174
moneylenders, 1, 104–4, 106, 110
Moscow, 5, 185n21; Boborykin's novels on, 14, 26, 57–59; business life, 23, 58; Chekhov's planned novel on, 166; merchant quarter, 58, 109, 171; merchants, 14, 58, 109, 111, 171, 196n32; Old Believers' cemetery, 109; peasant migrants in, 5, 146; Petrovka Street, 138; railway

connecting Saint Petersburg and, 16, 75, 78, 91; Rogozhskoe, 109
Mother (Gorky), 174, 188n91
Mountain Pass, The (Boborykin), 147
"Mr. Prokharchin" (Dostoevsky), 23, 133, 196n30
muzhiki. See under Anna Karenina; *rabochii*; workers

Nabokov, Vladimir, 75, 76, 90, 91
Nana (Zola), 77
narodniki, 14, 40, 54, 149, 187n69
narration. *See* description versus narration; *skaz*
Natural School, 39, 47, 149
Nefedov, F. D., 86
Nekrasov, Nikolai, 14, 32; "The Railroad," 83, 87
Nemirovich-Danchenko, Vladimir, 30, 147
"New America, The" (Blok), 145, 175–76
New Economic Criticism, 18
Nicholas II, 10
nobility: decline of, 21–22, 26, 58, 104, 112, 114, 116, 124, 125, 129, 146, 168, 173; forest question and, 123–24; impoverishment of, 102, 105, 112, 127; wealth fluctuations of, 20, 114. *See also* landowners; *pomeshchiki*
Not a Hero (Potapenko), 149
Notes from the House of the Dead (Dostoevsky), 200n54
Notes of a Hunter (Turgenev), 44, 45, 48
Notes of the Fatherland, 14, 15, 32, 49, 50, 148
novel: of Boborykin, 14, 26, 57–59, 147, 155; of Dostoevsky, 3, 17, 28, 29, 100, 148, 155, 158, 195n18; factory labor in, 35–38; industrial, 37, 158; of Melnikov-Pechersky, 30, 106; postreform, 17, 21–22, 23, 27, 30; production, 65, 175; of Tolstoy, 29, 148, 155, 158. *See also Anna Karenina*; *Brothers Karamazov, The*; *Crime and Punishment*; *Dead Souls*; *Fishermen, The*; *Gambler, The*; *Idiot, The*; *Kitai-Gorod*; *Oblomov*; *Privalov's Millions*; *Virgin Soul*; *Where Is It Better?*
novel, realist: *Anna Karenina*'s relationship to, 81, 84, 90, 98; characteristics, 35, 54, 76, 81, 84, 98, 100, 104, 176, 199n40; *skaz* as alternative to, 188n86

Index